VALUATION FOR M&A

Wiley M&A Library

Buying and Selling Businesses: Including Forms, Formulas, and Industry Secrets by William W. Bumstead

Cost of Capital: Estimation and Applications by Shannon Pratt

Joint Ventures: Business Strategies for Accountants, Second Edition by Joseph M. Morris

Mergers and Acquisitions: Business Strategies for Accountants, Second Edition by Joseph M. Morris

Mergers, Acquisitions, and Corporate Restructurings, Third Edition by Patrick A. Gaughan

Nonprofit Mergers and Alliances: A Strategic Planning Guide by Thomas A. McLaughlin

PartnerShift, Second Edition by Ed Rigsbee

Winning at Mergers and Acquisitions: The Guide to Market-Focused Planning and Integration by Mark N. Clemente and David S. Greenspan

VALUATION FOR M&A

Building Value in
Private Companies

Frank C. Evans

David M. Bishop

John Wiley & Sons, Inc.

New York • Chichester • Weinheim • Brisbane • Singapore • Toronto

This publication is designed to provide accurate and authoritative information in
regard to the subject matter covered. It is sold with the understanding that the
publisher is not engaged in rendering legal, accounting, or other professional
services. If legal advice or other expert assistance is required, the services of a
competent professional person should be sought.

Library of Congress Cataloging-in-Publication Data:
Evans, Frank C.
   Valuation for M&A : building value in private companies / Frank C. Evans,
   David M. Bishop.
      p. cm. – (Wiley M&A library)
   Includes index.
   ISBN 0-471-41101-9 (cloth : alk. paper)
      1. Corporations–Valuation. 2. Consolidation and merger of corporations. I.
   Title: Valuation for M&A. II. Title: Valuation for M and A. III. Bishop, David
   M., 1940- IV. Title. V. Series.

   HG4028. V3 E93 2001
   658.15–dc21   2001035231

Printed in the United States of America.
10 9 8 7 6

Preface

The mystery surrounding a company's value often causes executives to make bad investment and operational decisions. But these poor choices can be avoided. Accurate valuations are possible and M&A deals can succeed for both buyers and sellers. The keys to success are in the pages that follow.

Through providing valuation advisory services to hundreds of companies and thousands of corporate executives, we have developed the tools to accurately measure and successfully build value in companies. By employing these techniques, owners and managers can determine their company's value, what drives it, and how to enhance that value both in M&A and through daily operations.

In M&A, sellers, buyers, and even their advisors struggle over the value of a business. Often, they are frustrated by what they see as the other side's unrealistic expectations. The following uncertainties abound:

- Do profits, usually computed as EBIT or EBITDA, represent the company's true return to shareholders?
- Is the forecasted performance realistic?
- What is an appropriate rate of return or multiple, considering the investment's risk?
- Should the transaction be structured as an asset or stock deal?
- Has the seller properly prepared and packaged the company to get the best price?
- What personal issues are of critical importance to the seller?
- Has the buyer found the best target and accurately quantified potential synergies?
- Does the deal make sense at the quoted price?

Greater fundamental mystery exists in private companies—those not traded on a public stock market, including thinly traded public companies or divisions of large corporations. Most owners and managers operate these companies year after year without ever knowing the answers to these basic questions:

- What is the company worth?
- How much more would a strategic buyer pay to acquire it?
- What factors most affect the company's stock value?
- What is the owners' real return on investment and rate of return?
- Does that return justify the risk?
- Are owners better off selling, and if so, how and when?

This book provides the tools to answer these and related questions. It is written for investors and managers of companies who lack the guidance of a stock price set by a free and active market. Our solutions to valuation and return on investment questions create accountability and discipline in the M&A process. Our techniques incorporate value enhancement into a private company's annual strategic planning to provide direction to shareholders in their investment decisions. In short, our book is a roadmap to building value in both operating a company and selling or buying one.

Many investors have heard about building value in a public company where the stock price provides the market's reaction to the company's performance. It is much more difficult to develop a successful strategy and measure performance accurately when no stock price exists. Difficult, but not impossible.

We invite our readers to employ these techniques to achieve accurate M&A valuations and to build value in daily operations. Trade the mystery for this roadmap to wealth.

Frank C. Evans
David M. Bishop
June 2001

Contents

The authors wish to thank those who provided valuable assistance to the writing of this book. In addition to Maggie Horne, Cori Surano, Chuck Laverty, and Nancy Bernard at Smith Evans Strimbu Valuation Advisory Services, the talented professionals at John Wiley & Sons, and those individuals acknowledged at the end of certain chapters, our sincere appreciation and thanks go to:

Harry Evans, who offered faith and encouragement, as well as wickedly sharp red pen editorial review.

Frank Evans

Jeanne Bishop, whose talents and support have enriched both this book and my life.

David Bishop

1

Winning through Merger and Acquisition

Buyers and sellers can create a lot of value through merger and acquisition (M&A). Both can win from a transaction. That is the beauty of dealmaking. And that is much of the allure that has driven the tremendous volume of M&A activity in the United States during the 1990s; in recent years this trend has extended worldwide.[1]

This book focuses on business value—what creates it, how to measure it, how to build it, and how to maximize it in merger and acquisition. These concepts are equally important to buyers and sellers because both can and should benefit from a deal. But different results frequently occur. Sellers may sell under adverse conditions or accept too low a price due to lack of preparation or knowledge. And every buyer runs the risk of purchasing the wrong business or paying too much. That is why understanding value—and what drives it—is critical in merger and acquisition.

Wise shareholders and managers do not, however, confine their focus on value to only M&A. Value creation drives their strategic planning and, in the process, creates focus and direction for their company. Their M&A strategy supports and complements their broader goal of building shareholder value and they buy and sell only when the deal creates value for them.

---

[1] Chapter 5 presents a very necessary second view of the potential results of M&A.

This brings us back to the purpose of this book. It explains how to create, measure, and maximize value in merger and acquisition in the context of the broader business goal of building value. Senior managers in most public companies focus on value every day because it is reflected in the movement of their stock price—the daily scorecard of their performance relative to other investment choices. Private companies, however, lack this market feedback and direction. Their shareholders and executives seldom understand what their company is worth or clearly see what drives its value. For this reason, many private companies—and business segments of public companies as well—lack direction and underperform.

Managing the value of a private company, or a division of a public corporation, is particularly difficult because that value is harder to compute and justify. Yet most business activity—and value creation or destruction—occurs at this operational level.

Being able to accurately measure and manage the value of smaller businesses or business segments is critical in the value creation process. And this skill will pay off in M&A as well because most transactions involve smaller entities. Although we read and hear about the big deals that involve large corporations with known stock prices, the median M&A transaction size in the United States in recent years has been about $25 to $40 million. Smaller deals involving closely held companies or segments of public companies are the scene for most M&A activity.

Therefore, every value-minded shareholder and executive must strive to maximize value at this smaller-entity level where daily stock prices do not exist. The concepts and techniques that follow explain how to measure and manage value on a daily basis and particularly in M&A. The discussion begins with an understanding of what value is.

CRITICAL VALUES SHAREHOLDERS OVERLOOK

When buyers see a potential target, their analysis frequently begins by identifying and quantifying the synergies they could achieve through the acquisition. They prepare a model that forecasts the target's potential revenues if they owned it, the adjusted expense levels under their management, and the resulting income or cash flow that they anticipate. They then discount these future returns by their company's cost of capital to determine the target's value to them. Armed with this estimate of value, they begin negotiations aimed at a deal that is intended to create value.

If the target is not a public company with a known stock price, frequently no one even asks what the target is worth to its present owners. However, the value the business creates for the present owners is all that they really have to sell. Most, and sometimes all, of the potential synergies in the deal are created by the buyer, rather than the seller, so the buyer should not have to pay the seller for the value the buyer creates. But in the scenario just described, the buyer is likely to do so because his or her company does not know what the target is worth as a stand-alone business. Consequently, the buyer also does not know what the synergies created by his or her company through the acquisition are worth, or what the company's initial offer should be.

Sellers are frequently as uninformed or misinformed as buyers. Many times the owners of the target do not know if they should sell, how to find potential buyers, which buyers can afford to pay the most to acquire them, what they could do to maximize their sale value, or how to go about the sale process. After all, many sellers are involved in only one such transaction in their career. They seldom know what their company is currently worth as a stand-alone business, what value drivers or risk drivers most influence its value, or how much more, if any, it would be worth to a strategic buyer. Typically none of their team of traditional advisors—their controller, outside accountant, banker, or attorney—is an expert in business valuation. Few of these professionals understand what drives business value or the subtle distinction between the value of a company as a stand-alone business versus what it could be worth in the hands of a strategic buyer.

The seller could seek advice from an intermediary, most commonly an investment banker or business broker. But these advisors typically are paid a commission—if and only if they achieve a sale. Perhaps current owners could achieve a higher return by improving the business to position it to achieve a greater value before selling. This advice is seldom popular with intermediaries because it postpones or eliminates their commission.

With sound advice so hard to find, sellers frequently postpone sale considerations. Delay is often the easier emotional choice for many entrepreneurs who identify personally with their company. But with delay, opportunities are frequently lost. External factors, including economic, industry, and competitive conditions that may dramatically affect value, can change quickly. Consolidation trends, technological innovations, or regulatory and tax reforms also can expand or contract M&A opportunities and value.

Procrastination also can hamper estate planning and tax strategies because delays reduce options. And the bad consequences are particularly acute when value is rapidly increasing.

Thus, buyers and sellers have very strong incentives to understand value, manage what drives it, and track it to their mutual benefit.

STAND-ALONE FAIR MARKET VALUE

With a proper focus on maximizing shareholder value, buyers and sellers begin by computing the target company's stand-alone fair market value, the worth of what the sellers currently own. This value reflects the company's size, access to capital, depth and breadth of products and services, quality of management, market share and customer base, levels of liquidity and financial leverage, and overall profitability and cash flow as a stand-alone business.

With these characteristics in mind, *fair market value* is defined by Revenue Ruling 59–60 of the Internal Revenue Service as ". . . the amount at which the property would change hands between a willing buyer and a willing seller when the former is not under compulsion to buy and the latter is not under any compulsion to sell, both parties having reasonable knowledge of the relevant facts."

Fair market value includes the following assumptions:

- Buyers and sellers are hypothetical, typical of the market, and acting in their own self-interest.
- The hypothetical buyer is prudent but without synergistic benefit.

- The business will continue as a going concern and not be liquidated.
- The hypothetical sale will be for cash.
- The parties are able as well as willing.

The buyer under fair market value is considered to be a "financial" and not a "strategic" buyer. The buyer contributes only capital and management of equivalent competence to that of the current management. This excludes the buyer who, because of other business activities, brings some "value-added" benefits to the company that will enhance the company being valued and/or the buyer's other business activities, for example, being acquired by other companies in the same or a similar industry. Also excluded is the buyer who is already a shareholder, creditor, or related or controlled entity who might be willing to acquire the interest at an artificially high or low price due to considerations not typical of the motivation of the arm's-length financial buyer.

The seller in the fair market value process is also hypothetical and possesses knowledge of the relevant facts, including the influences on value exerted by the market, the company's risk and value drivers, and the degree of control and lack of marketability of that specific interest in the business.

Investment value is the value to a particular buyer based on that buyer's circumstances and investment requirements. This value includes the synergies or other advantages the strategic buyer anticipates will be created through the acquisition.

Fair market value should represent the minimum price that a financially motivated seller would accept because the seller, as the owner of the business, currently enjoys the benefits this value provides. The controlling shareholder in a privately held company frequently possesses substantial liquidity because he or she can harvest the cash flow the company generates or sell the company. The lack-of-control or minority shareholder generally possesses far less liquidity. As a result, the value of a lack-of-control interest is usually substantially less than that interest's proportionate ownership in the value of the business on a control basis.

Prospective buyers who have computed stand-alone fair market value should also recognize that this is the base value from which their negotiating position should begin. The maximum value the buyer expects to create from the deal is the excess of investment value over fair market value. So any premium the buyer pays above fair market value reduces the buyer's potential gain because the seller receives this portion of the value created.

Sellers frequently are motivated by nonfinancial considerations, such as their desire to pass ownership of the company on to their children, or, if they work in the company, to retire or do something else. When these nonfinancial considerations exist, it is particularly important for shareholders to understand the financial effect of decisions made for personal reasons. Opportunistic buyers can take advantage of sellers, particularly those who are in adverse personal circumstances. Once again, this fact stresses the need for a continual focus on value and implementation of a strategic planning process that routinely considers sale of the company as a viable option to maximize shareholder value. This process accommodates shareholders' nonfinancial goals and provides the time and structure to achieve them and manage value as well.

INVESTMENT VALUE TO STRATEGIC BUYERS

The investment value of a target is its value to a specific strategic buyer, recognizing that buyer's attributes and the synergies and other integrative benefits that can be achieved through the acquisition. Also known as strategic value, the target's investment value is probably different to each potential buyer because of the different synergies that each can create through the acquisition. For example, one buyer may have a distribution system, product line, or sales territory in which the target would fit better than with any other potential buyer. Generally this is the company to which the target is worth the most. Well-informed buyers and sellers determine these strategic advantages in advance and negotiate with this knowledge.

The difference between fair market value and investment value is portrayed in Exhibit 1-1, which shows an investment value for two potential buyers. The increase in investment value over the company's fair market value is most commonly referred to as a control premium, but this term is somewhat misleading. Although the typical buyer does acquire control of the target through the

Exhibit 1-1   Fair Market Value versus Investment Value

Investment Value – 2	_____
Investment Value – 1	_____
Acquisition Premium	
Fair Market Value	_____

acquisition, the premium paid is generally to achieve the synergies that the combination will create. Thus, this premium is more accurately referred to as an acquisition premium because the primary force driving it is synergies, rather than control, which is only the authority necessary to activate the synergy.

The obvious questions this discussion generates are:

- Why should a buyer pay more than fair market value?
- If the buyer must pay an acquisition premium to make the acquisition, how much above fair market value should the buyer pay (i.e., how large should the acquisition premium be, either as a dollar amount or as a percentage of fair market value)?

Chapter 4 summarizes statistics that indicate that the mean and median acquisition premiums for purchases of public companies in the United States have been about 40% and 30%, respectively, over the last 10 years. These figures are not presented as a guideline or as a target. Premiums paid are based on competitive factors, consolidation trends, economies of scale, and buyer and seller motivations; facts that again emphasize the need to thoroughly understand value and industry trends before negotiations begin. For example, a company with a fair market value of $10 million has a much stronger bargaining position if its maximum investment value is $20 million than if it is only $12 million. To negotiate the best possible price, however, the seller should attempt to determine what its maximum investment value is, which potential buyer may have the capacity to pay the most in an acquisition, and what alternatives each buyer has, and then negotiate accordingly.

Generally speaking, buyers should begin their negotiations based on fair market value. Before they enter the negotiation process, where emotional factors and the desire to "do the deal" take over, buyers should establish their walk-away price. This is the maximum amount above fair market value that they are willing to pay to make the acquisition. Establishing the maximum price in advance encourages buyers to focus on value rather than on "winning" the deal. Naturally, the farther the price moves above fair market value toward that buyer's investment value, the less attractive the deal becomes. Value-oriented buyers recognize that acquisitions at a price close to their investment value require them to fully achieve almost all forecasted synergies—on time—to achieve the forecasted value. And the closer the acquisition price gets to their investment value, the less value the acquisition can create for the buyer's shareholders and the smaller the buyer's potential margin of error. When a seller demands too high a price, the buyer's better option is often to decline that deal and look for one with a better potential to create value.

This fact illustrates a fundamental but essential lesson in making any investment: *Identify the distinction between a good company and a good investment.* While a good company may possess many strengths, it will prove to be a bad investment if the price paid for it is too high. Conversely, a company with weaknesses may offer a good investment opportunity if the price is adequately low relative to the forecasted returns, particularly to the strategic buyer who possesses the strengths to compensate for the target's weaknesses.

"WIN-WIN" BENEFITS OF MERGER AND ACQUISITION

To illustrate the "win-win" benefits of M&A to buyers and sellers, the following discussion summarizes the valuation of Cardinal Publishing Company, which is presented in detail in Chapter 16. Many of the technical steps in this illustration are explained only briefly. Each step is described in detail in the chapters that follow. Various technical issues will be introduced in italicized print with a reference to the chapter that explains how to handle these matters.

Cardinal was founded about 10 years ago by Lou Bertin, who had enjoyed a successful career in advertising. Bertin believed that many people shared his love for the outdoors and simple country living and that they would subscribe to journals dedicated to this topic. Armed with his entrepreneurial spirit, substantial expertise in direct-mail advertising, $1.7 million of his and two 10% minority investors' equity cash, and a well-conceived business plan, he founded Cardinal. Following a folksy tone and style, combined with excellent photography, minimal advertising, attractive subscription rates, and creative direct mail promotions, Cardinal grew rapidly from concept to several specialized, profitable journals.

As with most emerging companies, however, several major risks and constraints weighed heavily on Bertin. He is looking to retire or at least reduce his hours. And although Cardinal is successful, Bertin has seen his personal wealth increasingly tied to the fate of the company at a time in his life when he knows diversification is the much wiser investment strategy. *Should Bertin's 80% equity interest in Cardinal be valued or some other investment? Would the valuation process or computation be different if he owned a 100% interest and there were no minority shareholders, or if all of the stock were owned by minority shareholders?* (See Chapter 12).

Sales for Cardinal's latest year top $75 million, and earnings before interest and taxes (EBIT) adjusted to reflect ongoing operations will be about $7.5 million. *Is EBIT the best measure of return for Cardinal? Would it be more accurate to use revenue or net income before or after taxes or cash flow?* (See Chapter 6). Cardinal is heavily leveraged. To move toward long-term stability, significant additional capital spending is required. *Does the financial leverage affect value, and if so, how?* (See Chapter 9). *Does the anticipated capital spending affect value and how do we account for it?* (See Chapter 6).

The company's product line is narrow by industry standards, although it has developed a loyal and rapidly growing base of affluent readers. Because of Cardinal's specialty nature, the company has a weak distribution system—completely reliant on general distributors—which complicated Bertin's efforts to add new products and attract more advertising. *How can the valuation reflect these various risk drivers and value drivers? What if the buyer can eliminate some of these weaknesses?* (See Chapters 3 and 8). Bertin's staff is comprised primarily of family members and outdoor enthusiasts, and Bertin himself has lost the enthusiasm for the strategic planning the company would need to continue its historical growth performance. *Should an adjustment be made if some of these individuals do not materially contribute to the success of the company? Should an adjustment be made if anyone is paid above or below market compensation?* (See Chapter 6).

Bertin has been routinely approached by business brokers and contacts within the publishing industry about a sale of the company, and he is especially concerned that in the last two years, several major publishers have launched new products aimed at his market. Although the new publications lack Cardinal's quality and creativity, they carry much better advertising and are available on newsstands and promoted through tear-out inserts in several national publications. This new competition has led Bertin to postpone planned price increases, and although he continues to look for additional advertising, he cannot attract the companies he seeks most. *Can these competitive issues be identified by reviewing Cardinal's financial statements? What additional research, if any, is required? How are these competitive factors reflected in the valuation?* (See Chapters 3 and 8).

Computation of Cardinal's Stand-Alone, Fair Market Value

As a small- to middle-market-size company, Cardinal carries many risks, including limited capital, high financial leverage, a narrow product line, poor distribution system, and very limited management. When combined with the company's loyal customer base, rapid sales growth, high product quality, and average profitability, these factors generate Cardinal's weighted average cost of capital rate of 18%, which reflects its risk profile and growth prospects. *Is a weighted average cost of capital the same as a discount rate? Is this the same as a capitalization rate?* (See Chapters 7 and 9). When the company's normalized net income to invested capital of $4.8 million for this year is divided by a 14% weighted average cost of capital (WACC) capitalization rate, the fair market value on a stand-alone basis of the enterprise is determined to be $36 million. *Is this the value of equity?* (See Chapter 6). *Why is only 1 year of earnings used to compute value? How does this reflect future year growth?* (See Chapter 7).

Investment Value to Strategic Buyer

The larger public company that wants to quickly acquire a presence in this new "country" market recognizes Cardinal's strengths and weaknesses. Because the larger buyer frequently can eliminate many or all of Cardinal's limitations, it can increase Cardinal's sales growth and profits much more rapidly. Cardinal is also much less risky as a segment of the large company that possesses a broad array of market strengths. *How are these changes in risk reflected in the valuation? Who gets this value?* (See Chapter 3).

When owned by the strategic buyer, Cardinal's stand-alone EBIT could be increased over the next several years through more efficient operations and access to a broader market and an extensive distribution system. In the terminal period following the forecast, Cardinal's growth should be similar to that of the publishing industry. *How should the forecast and the years thereafter be used in computing value?* (See Chapter 7).

While Cardinal has a WACC capitalization rate of 18%, Omni Publications, the buyer, a large, well-known public company, has a WACC discount rate of about 12%. *How are cap rates and discount rates different, and when should each be used?* (See Chapters 7, 8 and 9). Because Cardinal operates in a new market for this buyer, has limited management, and increasing competition, the buyer adjusted its discount rate for the added risk of Cardinal. *Should the buyer use its own discount rate to compute the investment value of Cardinal? If not, how should it be adjusted? How should this rate be affected by Cardinal's high financial leverage?* (See Chapter 9). The multiple period discounting of Cardinal's forecasted net cash flow to invested capital adjusted for synergies determined that Cardinal's invested capital is worth $50 million to one strategic buyer. *What is net cash flow to invested capital, how is it computed, and how many years should be discretely forecasted?* (See Chapter 6). *How does this discounting process reflect the potential adjustments to the return and the rate of return for the risk drivers and value drivers that have been considered?* (See Chapters 7 and 8). The $15 million excess of the $50 million investment value of invested capital over Cardinal's $35 million fair market value means this buyer could pay up to $15 million over stand-alone fair market value to acquire Cardinal. *What should be the minimum value considered by both the buyer and the seller to start the negotiations? How much above $35 million should this buyer be willing to* *pay to acquire Cardinal? Should this decision be influenced by competitors also bidding to acquire Cardinal? If the buyer pays $50 million to acquire Cardinal, is the buyer better off? How?* (See Chapters 1, 4, and 5).

Cardinal's balance sheet shows assets of almost $44 million and equity of $15 million. *How do these affect its value?* (See Chapters 11 and 12). Public companies in Cardinal's industry are selling at EBIT multiples ranging from 3 to 18, with a mean of 8. *Should these be considered, and how? Do the EBIT multiples generate equity value?* (See Chapter 10). Another public publishing company recently sold for a 72% premium over its market value. *Should this transaction be considered in determining value.* (See Chapter 10).

Since Cardinal is not a public company, should there be a discount for lack of marketability? Since Cardinal has minority owners, is a control premium or lack-of-control discount needed? (See Chapter 13).

Can a buyer employ strategies to reduce risk in an acquisition? (See Chapters 4 and 16). *How can buyers most effectively evaluate synergies?* (See Chapter 5).

Can sellers employ a strategy to build value? Can they effectively plan in advance for a sale? (See Chapters 2 and 4).

Buyers and sellers clearly have opportunities to gain through merger and acquisition. In order to create value, however, they must be able to measure and manage it. This process begins with the ability to identify and quantify those factors that create value. Most often, this must be done in a privately held company or a division of a public corporation where stock prices do not exist. The following chapters explain how to build operating value in a private company and how to create, measure, and manage value in merger and acquisition.

2

Building Value in a Nonpublicly Traded Entity

So much has been written about "value" and "creating value" that these concepts have acquired many meanings. Buyers and sellers must recognize how strategies affect value to achieve maximum benefit from purchase or sale decisions, as well as in daily operations where no immediate sale is anticipated. To manage value creation effectively in closely held companies, segments of public companies, and thinly traded public companies, first that value must be measured. Doing so requires precision in the definition and measurement of "return," "investment," and "rate of return" to accurately compute value and return on investment. Yet each of these metrics is almost always measured and reported incorrectly for nonpublic entities. As a result, their true economic performance and any resulting value creation or destruction is unknown, and investors seldom ever even know that they are misinformed. The correct way of determining these metrics begins with understanding valuation and return on investment fundamentals.

VALUE AND VALUE CREATION

"Value" is an expression of the worth of something. It can be measured in different ways. For example, a family heirloom may have great sentimental value but little financial value. This discussion focuses on financial value but recognizes that nonfinancial or personal issues frequently influence investment decisions in nonpublic entities. When investors make decisions for personal reasons, the impact should be quantified so that they understand the financial consequences of their actions.

To realize the financial benefit of an investment, the owner must be able to obtain its return either through ownership or exchange. To measure value and return on investment for comparative purposes, we recognize market conditions and monetary units that enable investor transferability and liquidity.

Valuation and return on investment fundamentals include the following key metrics:

- *Return* is the anticipated future net cash flow from an investment, which is described in Chapter 6. Measures of income are only estimates of economic performance that usually are based on accrual methods of accounting rather than actual cash returns to capital providers. Historical measures of income or cash flow may provide insight about a company's track record, but they are otherwise irrelevant to any current investment decision. Investors should focus exclusively on future net cash flows because that is the only financial benefit to investors.

- *Investment* is computed as the present value of the anticipated future net cash flows described above, discounted at a rate of return that reflects their level of risk. While fair market value most frequently reflects worth to a financial buyer, investment value to a strategic buyer is usually higher, and wise investors should know both amounts. Alternative measures of the value of an investment, such as book value or actual amounts invested in prior periods, are irrelevant. Only the current value can affect the investor's present wealth, through the decision to either hold or sell the investment.

- *Risk* measures the uncertainty that the anticipated future net cash flows will be received. Without consideration of risk, every dollar of future return, no matter how speculative, would be equally attractive. Thus, risk is the essential variable used to quantify the fair market value and investment value of future cash flows. Quantifying the risk or required rate of return for a nonpublic entity requires substantial insight and knowledge. It can, however, be accurately measured, as Chapters 7 to 9 explain.

PUBLIC COMPANY VALUE CREATION MODEL

The path to understanding value creation in nonpublicly traded entities begins with an understanding of the public company model. It estimates future net cash flow returns and provides a value through a stock price that reflects investor perception of the company's relative level of risk.

Value creation and return on investment are reasonably clear for investments in common stock of public corporations. Investors anticipate future cash returns (net cash flows) that they receive in dividend payments and appreciation when the stock is sold. Stock appreciation is a function of the anticipated cash return in the next period and the subsequent expected growth in that return. Thus, the value of common stock in a public company ultimately can be reduced to dividend cash receipts and the anticipated growth in those cash receipts, which is reflected in stock appreciation.

This theory of common stock valuation based on anticipated cash receipts is widely accepted, yet many investment decisions are made based on irrelevant investment or price data. With current stock price information available for public securities, some investors focus on the amount they originally invested in the security while other investors focus on its current value. The latter is the right choice. In accounting language, their original investment is a "sunk cost." It is irrelevant to their current decision because it is not a future return, and it cannot be changed by any choices that investors can make. The current value of the security *is* relevant because it represents the investors' current choice versus alternative investments. Investors should focus on this value because the decision to hold the stock is a decision not to invest that current value in some other way.

With the return correctly identified as net cash flow and the focus on current rather than historic value, risk is quantified. Varying levels of risk are reflected in the relationship between the stock price and its expected return. Higher-risk investments must produce higher rates of return, as investors select from the universe of potential risk versus return choices to achieve their investment goals. With daily stock market prices and periodic company performance measures conveniently available, investors focusing on publicly traded stocks study the current stock values and future cash flows.

This is where past earnings measures enter the analysis. The commonly quoted price-to-earnings (P/E) multiple compares the current stock price to a prior period's earnings, but increasingly investors recognize that future circumstances may differ from the past. This is most evident in how the media currently reports on earnings disclosures. A public company's announced earnings are routinely compared against the market's expectations, which emphasizes the dependence of value on the future, while historical data is used primarily to assess the reliability of forecasts.

Historical data about rates of return of publicly traded stock can provide substantial insight about investor risk versus return expectations and the resulting rates of return that investors can expect. These annual rates of return earned by investors are based on the following relevant amounts:

- Investments expressed as beginning of period cash outlays
- Return expressed as the net cash inflow for that period

Using this data, which is prepared in annual studies by Ibbotson Associates[1] and described in Chapter 8, investors can compare their expectations against the average historical performance of past investments in public securities.

---

[1] Ibbotson Associates, *Stocks, Bonds, Bills and Inflation*® Valuation Edition *2001 Yearbook* (Chicago: Ibbotson Associates, 2001).

Thus, the public company model computes the relevant current value based on relevant anticipated future net cash flow returns, with the relationship between them expressed as a multiple or percentage to quantify the company's risk. This procedure allows alternative investments to be analyzed and compared. Stock price movements reflect investor reaction to changes in either the company's expected net cash flow or risk, or both.

NONPUBLIC COMPANY VALUE CREATION MODEL

The secret to accurate valuation and return on investment analysis for nonpublicly traded entities, including divisions of public companies and thinly traded public companies, is to adapt the public security investment model to the unique characteristics of the nonpublic entity.

Investment in a nonpublic company is rarely evaluated properly for several reasons:

- Capital providers seldom know their true cash return. The traditional accounting measure of a company's earnings is seldom an accurate measure of the shareholder's return on investment. The first obstacle to accuracy occurs because the income data that is reported usually has been manipulated to achieve tax planning or other income distribution goals that disguise the entity's true economic performance. Second, accrual accounting methods produce an income that differs from cash flow. Alternative measures of return frequently are employed, including earnings before interest, taxes, depreciation, and amortization (EBITDA), earnings before interest and taxes (EBIT), and net income before taxes. These are not cash returns to investors because taxes and investments in working capital and fixed assets must be paid before cash is available to capital providers. Third, the cost of debt capital is shown as interest expense, but the cost of equity is excluded, so the company's return reflects some but not all of its financing costs. So capital providers are left uninformed about their real cash return.

- The accounting measure of "investment" that is traditionally used is generally irrelevant and misleading. Traditional return on investment analysis may compute the investment in a closely held business as the amount paid in by investors years ago. Even more common is to show investments at the book value of assets or stockholders' equity from the company's financial statements, but these amounts seldom reflect current value. To overcome the weaknesses of these first two measures, investments sometimes are shown at the appraised value of the tangible assets owned by the business. For a profitable company, doing this ignores general intangible value that may represent most of the value owned by the investor. So capital providers frequently use an incorrect value of their investment.

- The relative riskiness of the investment—the uncertainty that the future returns will be received—is not formally quantified. Although investors know that small and medium-size companies may carry substantial risk, they seldom understand how to translate that risk to a commensurate rate of return. As a result, capital providers seldom know what is an appropriate rate of return for their investment.

- Because expected returns are not accurately computed and risk is not quantified, the current fair market value of the investment is typically unknown. While such a business or business segment eventually might be sold to a strategic buyer, shareholders seldom know the value of their investment to potential strategic buyers considering expected synergies. Not knowing relevant stock values, capital providers may miss major investment or sale opportunities.

The preceding problems can be addressed by following these three steps.

1. *Measure return.* Estimate the company's true economic return, measured as its net cash flow to invested capital (NCF_{IC}).

This is the net cash flow available to debt and equity capital providers after all of the company's internal needs, including taxes and funding for working capital and capital expenditures, have been met. Adjustments to compute this are described in Chapter 6. To compute a realistic measure, review the company's historical performance, recognizing how future conditions may differ from the past. Nonoperating or nonrecurring income or expense items, such as a moving expense or gain on a sale of an asset, should be set aside if they do not reflect ongoing operating performance. Similarly, manipulations to income to minimize income taxes, such as paying above-market compensation or rent for real estate used by the company and owned by shareholders, should be adjusted to market levels.

The result is the expected net cash flows that current capital providers can remove from the business after having funded all of the company's cash flow needs. The rate of growth in the cash flow is a major value driver in almost every company.

To estimate the investment value of the company to a strategic buyer, recompute the cash flow to reflect all synergistic or integrative benefits, including revenue enhancements and expense reductions. These benefits are presented and analyzed in Chapter 5.

2. *Measure risk.*   Since every investment carries a unique level of uncertainty, this risk must be assessed and quantified to determine its effect on value. This measure of risk is the required rate of return or weighted average cost of capital (WACC). Following procedures that are described further in Chapters 8 and 9, estimate the rates that are appropriate to compute both the company's fair market value and its investment value. The resulting values reflect how the company's cash returns and risk profile would change if it were acquired and became a segment of a larger company.

The company's required rate of return reflects the risk or likelihood that the estimated net cash flows will be received in future periods. This risk typically declines substantially when the company is acquired by a larger buyer, and that lower risk increases value through use of a lower rate of return.

3. *Measure value.*   Using the estimated NCF_{IC} from Step 1 and the WACC from Step 2, estimate the current value of the entity, which is the risk-adjusted present value of its forecasted future cash flows, as explained in Chapter 7. This process should be done twice,

Do these three steps compute the value of equity, or the value of debt and equity?

Good question. The public company model described earlier computes equity value—the stock price. The three steps in the non-public company value creation model compute the value of debt *and* equity. This is done because we want to know what the whole company is worth, regardless of how it is financed. Chapter 6 clarifies these distinctions.

first to compute stand-alone fair market value and second to compute investment value. When several likely buyers exist, the investment value to each should be estimated considering the different risks and returns to each.

These results represent the company's fair market value as a stand-alone business and one or more investment values to strategic buyers. All values are shown at their relevant, current amounts based on market risks and expected net cash flow returns to capital providers.

To check the validity and accuracy of these value estimates, various market-based multiples of performance can be used, such as the well-known P/E multiple. This is done through application of the market approach, which is explained in Chapter 10. The market approach bases value on the price paid for similar alternative investments, and market multiples can be used as checks on both fair market value and strategic value.

Note how these three steps closely parallel the public security investment model. When evaluating investments in public securities, the expected returns on the investment (net cash flows in the form of dividends or appreciation) are considered first. Next market risks—in the economy, that specific industry, and the company—are examined in assessing the likelihood that the cash flows will be received. These return and rate-of-return variables are then combined to determine the appropriate price, which is the value for that security.

When investors in public company stocks witness events—competitive factors—that could influence the company's ex-

---

Does growth automatically create value?

Many shareholders and corporate executives are surprised to learn that value is not automatically created when a company increases its revenues or assets. Increased size does not necessarily lead to greater cash returns or reduced risk. Even profitable growth generally requires cash investments for working capital and fixed assets, both of which reduce the company's expected net cash flow. Therefore, growth increases value only when it reduces risk or creates positive net cash flows, after consideration of capital reinvestment requirements.

---

pected returns or risk profile, they may buy or sell the stock in response, which changes its market price. This process shows how expected changes in net cash flow returns and the rate of return affect stock value. Changes in the competitive position of a nonpublic company also affect its cash flow and risk profile, and ultimately its value. Investors should recognize these factors, analyze their effect on value, and adjust the company's strategy based on these new competitive circumstances.

MEASURING VALUE CREATION

The two key metrics to measuring value—the return and the rate of return—have been clearly identified. Conceptually, valuation creation now becomes obvious and fundamentally simple: Pursue strategies that raise the return, reduce the risk, or are a combination of the two. Application is more difficult, but to pursue value creation effectively, this theoretical goal must be understood.

Since value can be calculated as the present value of future returns discounted at a rate that reflects the level of risk, the mathematics of the valuation model (described in Chapter 7) is shown in Exhibit 2-1.

Assuming the return in the formula is a *constant* amount each year, the multiple period discounting computation in the exhibit can be reduced to the capitalization computation shown in Exhibit 2-2. This formula also is described further in Chapter 7.

Exhibit 2-1   Multiple-Period Discounting Valuation Method

$$V = \frac{r_1}{(1 + d)} + \frac{r_2}{(1 + d)^2} + \cdots + \frac{r_n}{(1 + d)^n}$$

where:

V = Value

 r = Return

d = Discount rate

n = Final year in forecast that extends to infinity

Exhibit 2-2   Single-Period Capitalization Valuation Method

$$V = \frac{r}{d}$$

To create value through an increase in the company's net cash flow to invested capital, consider the following example. Sample Company, which received an initial capital investment of $10 million five years ago, had invested capital at book value of $15 million at the end of last year on its balance sheet. The company's tangible assets were appraised as of that date to have a total value of $18 million. Based on a review of the company's recent historical financial statements and an estimate of its future performance, its NCF_{IC} for next year is expected to be $5 million. Assuming the company's weighted average cost of capital is 15%, and no material change in the company's net cash flow return is expected, Sample's current fair market value is computed in Exhibit 2-3.

Note first that this value exceeds the initial investment of $10 million, the book value of the $15 million, and the appraised value of the tangible assets of $18 million. Thus, the relevant value to the investor is the present value of the future returns, which reflects the current financial benefit the investment provides. The $33.3 million, however, reflects the expectation that only the current $5 million of net cash flow will be received in future years.

To provide growth, management proposes to promote a new product line that is expected to increase NCF_{IC} by $200,000 per year beginning in year 1, $300,000 in year 2, $400,000 in year 3, and $500,000 in year 4, after which the increased volume should

Exhibit 2-3   Calculation of Current Value through
               Single-Period Capitalization

$$\$33,333,333 = \frac{\$5,000,000}{15\%}$$

Exhibit 2-4   Calculation of Value Creation through
               Capitalization of Increased Returns

	Year 1	*Year 2*	*Year 3*	*Year 4*
Increase in Net Cash Flow to Invested Capital (NCF_{IC})	$200,000	$300,000	$400,000	$500,000
Capitalized Value of Increased Net Cash Flow $\left(\frac{NCF_{IC}}{d}\right)$	$1,333,333	$2,000,000	$2,666,667	$3,333,333
Present Value at 15% $\left(\frac{\frac{NCF_{IC}}{d}}{(1+d)^{n-1}}\right)$	$1,333,333	$1,739,130	$2,016,383	$2,191,721
Cumulative Value Created	$1,333,333	$3,072,463	$5,088,846	$7,280,567
Initial Value				$33,333,333
Total Value				$40,613,900

remain constant. This increased return is the net cash flow available to capital providers after paying all expenses and funding working capital and capital expenditure needs. Again assuming the company's cost of capital of 15%, the increase in value created by the new product line is shown in Exhibit 2-4.

The increased value calculated in Exhibit 2-4 occurs each year because the new product creates a *recurring* annual increase in the NCF_{IC}. This annuity is capitalized to determine the value

Exhibit 2-5   Calculation of Value Creation by Reducing
Cost of Capital

$$\$35,714,286 = \frac{\$5,000,000}{14\%}$$

Capitalized Value	$35,714,286
Less: Capital Investment	$-\$\ 1,000,000$
Total Value	$34,714,286
Less: Initial Value (Exhibit 2–3)	$-\$33,333,333$
Total Value Created	$\ 1,380,953

created in the forecasted period, and these amounts are then discounted to their present value. Thus, the increased NCF_{IC} increases value to capital providers.

Reducing the company's risk also can increase value. For example, assume that Sample Company cannot add the new product
line just described. Instead, the company will add a different product line that involves an initial investment of $1 million but pro-
duces no added cash flow. It will, however, shift sales to a new
customer base, create geographic diversification, and reduce
Sample's heavy reliance on a single customer. Management estimates this will reduce the company's risk, and its cost of capital,
from 15 to 14%, as will be explained further in Chapters 8 and 9.
The resulting affect on value is shown in Exhibit 2-5.

The increase in value computed in Exhibit 2-5 over the
amount originally determined in Exhibit 2-3 occurs because the
$5 million of NCF_{IC} is capitalized by 14% rather than 15%. This
lower rate reflects Sample Company's reduced risk, which reflects
the market's perception of a higher likelihood that the future return will be achieved. The increase in value also reflects the $1 mil-
lion capital expenditure required to add the new product line.
Thus, the reduced risk increases value to capital providers.

ANALYZING VALUE CREATION STRATEGIES

A company's value creating historical performance and future potential can be monitored through use of the return on investment
tool called the DuPont analysis. Developed by scientists at DuPont

> ## Can the company's risk profile change this much and can this change be accurately measured?
>
> Procedures to calculate rates of return are presented in Chapters 8 and 9. While they do involve judgment and reflect perceptions of anticipated future risk, the process of quantifying rates of return can be reliable and accurate, particularly for established businesses. In the middle market—companies with sales ranging from $10 million to several hundred million dollars—there is less stability than in the largest public companies. Therefore, the market price of these companies is much more volatile. For example, as explained further in Chapter 8, the volatility in the price of the smallest 10% of companies traded on the New York Stock Exchange is approximately 50% greater than in the largest 10% of those companies. So the risk profile of middle-market companies can change significantly. Information and techniques are available to measure and quantify the effect of these changes on stock value.

about a century ago to track that company's performance in its diversified investments, this analysis looks at profit margin and asset turnover as the building blocks to return on assets.

The DuPont formula involves the accounting measures of "return" and "investment" that this discussion has criticized as potentially misleading. It employs accounting measures of income and investment at book value that can distort performance and value. However, with proper adjustments and careful interpretation, the DuPont analysis can help to identify and quantify value drivers and ultimately develop strategies to improve return on investment and create value.

The DuPont analysis identifies the building blocks of profit margin and asset turnover that lead to return on net operating assets in the equation shown in Exhibit 2-6.

The profit margin, also known as return on sales, measures the margin of profit on a dollar of sales by comparing a measure of income to revenue. As previously discussed, nonoperating or nonrecurring items of income or expense should be excluded for the purpose of this analysis. Interest expense, net of its income tax benefit, should be added back to income to prevent financing costs from influencing the analysis of operating performance. The

Exhibit 2-6   DuPont Analysis

Profit Margin	Net Operating Asset Turnover	Return on Net Operating Assets
$\dfrac{\text{Net Income to I/C}}{\text{Sales}} \times$	$\dfrac{\text{Sales}}{\text{Net Operating Assets}} =$	$\dfrac{\text{Net Income to I/C}}{\text{Net Operating Assets}}$

Exhibit 2-7   Profit Margin Value Drivers

Value Drivers	Income Statement Accounts
Markets Customers Advertising and Marketing Policy Volume Pricing	Sales
Production Capacity Production Efficiency Product Design Raw Material Choices and Costs Labor Costs Overhead Costs and Utilization	Cost of Goods Sold
Warehousing and Distribution Costs and Efficiency Marketing, Advertising, and Selling Costs General Administration Policies and Costs	Operating Expenses
Attributes Strategies Rates	Income Taxes

result is the company's normalized net income after taxes but before financing costs, known as net income to invested capital (I/C). Strategies to improve profit margin include increasing revenues or decreasing expenses. The search to achieve these goals should focus management on analysis of profit margin value drivers, as shown in Exhibit 2-7.

In assessing each of these functional areas to improve profitability, management should refer to the company's strategic plan and the strengths, weaknesses, opportunities, and threats (SWOT) analysis, which is described further in Chapter 3. Those SWOTs should help both to identify and to assess the likelihood of improving profitability through changes in any of these functional areas.

Most managers and shareholders can clearly see the relationship between revenue enhancement or expense controls and profitability, and how this can lead to value creation. Far fewer see the importance of efficiency in asset utilization, known as *asset turnover*. This building block focuses on the capital employed relative to the sales volume generated. Improvements here can be achieved through strategies that increase revenues proportionately more than any accompanying increase in assets, or decrease assets proportionately more than any accompanying decrease in revenue. This conceptual goal can then be executed through improvements to the management of major assets, as measured by the accounts receivable collection period, inventory turnover, and fixed asset turnover. The primary resources and functions that comprise total assets are shown in Exhibit 2-8.

In assessing each of these activities to improve efficiency in asset utilization, management should return again to the SWOT analysis to determine the likelihood of improving performance in that activity, considering the company's internal capabilities and its external environment.

In traditional DuPont analysis, the profit margin measured as a percentage is multiplied by the asset turnover, expressed as a number of times, to yield the return on assets. This rate of return, expressed as a percentage, will receive less emphasis here than in the traditional analysis because of its reliance on accounting measures of "return" and "investment." In this focus on shareholder value, current and proposed strategies to improve profit margin and asset turnover should be analyzed to determine their effect on net cash flow and risk. The net cash flow is determined by sales volume, operating margins, tax rates, and investment requirements for working capital and fixed assets. Risk is reflected in the SWOT analysis and the company's competitive position given its strategic advantages and disadvantages. Risk is ultimately quantified through the weighted average cost of capital, which reflects the company's risk-adjusted cost of debt and equity and the relative amount of each

Exhibit 2-8   Asset Turnover Value Drivers

Value Drivers	Balance Sheet Accounts
Customer Base Industry Practices Credit Policy Collection Procedures Discounts and Allowances Credit Loss Exposure	Accounts Receivable and Collection Period
Supplier Capabilities Purchasing versus Handling versus Carrying Costs Customer Loyalty and Stock Out Risks Production Requirements Distribution Capabilities Obsolescence Threats	Inventory and Turnover
Supplier Base and Purchasing Power Industry Practices Payment Policy Cash Flow Capacity Discounts and Allowances Credit Availability	Accounts Payable, Accrued Payables, and Payment Period
Current and Anticipated Capacity Production and Scheduling Efficiency Warehousing and Distribution Efficiency Capital Constraints Vendor/Supplier Capacity and Reliability Make or Buy Options	Fixed Assets and Turnover

financing source employed. The components of this value creation analysis are summarized in Exhibit 2-9. The competitive analysis that supports the WACC is presented in Chapter 3, and the techniques to quantify the WACC are explained in Chapter 9.

The left-to-right flow in Exhibit 2-9 can be summarized as follows:

- Revenues less expenses yield the margin of profit on each dollar of sales.

Exhibit 2-9 Components of Value Creation

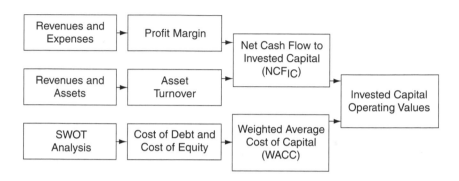

- Revenues versus assets reflects the sales volume achieved compared to the resources employed to reveal efficiency in asset utilization.
- Margin and turnover are combined to generate the NCF$_{IC}$, which is the cash return to debt and equity capital providers.
- The SWOT analysis considers the company's external environment and internal capabilities.
- The cost of debt and equity funds to the company is determined by its external environment and internal capabilities.
- The company's net cash flow return to debt and equity providers is discounted or capitalized by the WACC, which is its combined cost of debt and equity, to yield the operating value of the entity.

Once this information for a business has been gathered and organized, the key to value creation is to identify those strategies that most effectively improve net cash flow or reduce risk. In this process, managers frequently are tempted to stray toward strategies that create sales or asset growth without considering the effect on net cash flow. These growth strategies also frequently increase the company's risk profile as they move it away from its core business or into new and less familiar markets. So each strategy must be quantified in terms of its cash flow and risk consequences while

How do these value-building concepts compare to strategies generally referred to as "economic value added"?

They are quite similar. While some applications of economic value added employ proprietary adjustments and methodologies, the conceptual goals are always to pursue strategies that

- Increase net cash flow through some combination of increased revenues, decreased expenses, and more efficient asset utilization

- Reduce the company's risk, relative to its returns, and thereby decrease its cost of capital

management candidly assesses the company's ability to execute the strategy given competitive conditions.

Value creation in the nonpublicly traded entity should now be intuitively obvious. It employs the public company model but requires increased management attention and measurement precision in the absence of a published stock market price. The key is to pursue strategies that create cash flow and present the highest likelihood of success. Achieving these goals requires an understanding of, and relentless attention to, the risk and return fundamentals that have been described. To begin this process, we next look in further detail on how to analyze a company's strategic position to assess and quantify risk.

3

Competitive Analysis

We have established that a company's value is determined by its expected net cash flow and relative level of risk. To both measure value and manage valuation creation, we must accurately assess the competitive environment in which the company operates. Doing this includes analyzing both the external and the internal conditions that will influence performance. Many companies routinely perform these steps in their annual strategic planning process. What most nonpublic entities fail to do, however, is tie the results of their strategic plan to the ultimate goal of creating shareholder value. Whether valuing a company for merger and acquisition, performance improvement, or any other reason, competitive analysis is an essential step.

Many people see valuation as primarily a financial calculation. They analyze historical financial performance, position and cash flow, compute financial ratios, and compare them to industry averages. Based on this information, they prepare spreadsheets that forecast future performance. Armed with this data, they compute the company's value and often feel confident in their assessment.

This process overlooks a major weakness of financial statements: They portray the *results* of a company's financial performance but not the *causes*. A company's success is generally dependent on its ability to produce products or services efficiently, in appropriate quantity and quality, on time at a reasonable cost, and

Test Yourself on Risk and Value Drivers

Companies in many industries are valued based on multiples of earnings, cash flow, or revenue. A key point to remember is that the appropriate multiple for the target company depends on its strengths and weaknesses. Strong appraisal skills require an instinct for those factors that tend to influence these multiples up or down. Test yourself *from the buyer's and the seller's perspective* in assessing whether the following 20 factors would *generally* increase or decrease a company's value and resulting multiple. The answers are shown in the paragraph that follows the list.

1. Possess strong brand name or customer loyalty
2. Sales concentrated with a few key customers
3. Operate in a well-maintained physical plant
4. Operate in a small industry with a limited customer base
5. Generate a high sustainable net cash flow to shareholders
6. Have compiled or reviewed rather than audited financial statements
7. Possess competitive advantages such as technology, location, or an exclusive product line
8. Operate with deficient working capital and generally limited financial capacity
9. Generally favorable future economic and industry conditions
10. Operate with limited management on whom the company is heavily dependent
11. Sell a diverse mix of products to customers located in broad geographic markets
12. Sell commodity-type products that possess little differentiation from competitors
13. Operate in large, high-growth industry
14. Substantial excess capacity exists in the industry
15. High barriers in industry impede entry by new competitors
16. Continual threat posed by substitute products and technological obsolescence
17. Possess strong position in niche industry
18. Sell products through brokers, creating limited knowledge of or contact with product end users

19. Are either the most efficient low-cost producer or high-quality producer, or both
20. Possess history of litigation with customers, suppliers, and employees

When companies in an industry are selling, for example, at four to eight times some level of earnings, that range allows for major variation in value. The odd-numbered risk and value drivers listed above would generally move a company toward the higher end of the multiple range, while the even-numbered items generally have a negative effect, resulting in lower multiples. The significance of these drivers varies by company and the appraisal must subjectively weigh each. Finally, in assessing a driver, remember that while it may exist in an assessment of the company on a stand-alone basis, it may be eliminated through an acquisition, creating a synergistic benefit.

market, sell, and distribute them effectively at a sufficiently attractive price. This success depends on numerous external and internal factors that must be assessed as part of the valuation process. This chapter explains how to perform competitive analysis to assess a company's strategic position and ability to compete in its market against its peers.

LINKING STRATEGIC PLANNING TO BUILDING VALUE

Companies engage in annual strategic planning to provide purpose and direction for the business. In the first year of planning, the company establishes a mission, which in addition to defining the company's purpose, helps its management and employees to identify those key constituencies, often referred to as stakeholders, to whom the company is primarily accountable for its long-term success. A typical mission statement would read:

Our mission is to produce the highest-quality products and services for our *customers*, while generating the highest possible return on investment for our *stockholders,* while providing a safe, productive working environment for our *employees,* while operating as a constructive corporate citizen in our *community.*

The mission statement is intentionally general and, as demonstrated, can fit almost any for-profit entity. Management and employees can reconsider it annually to focus on exactly why the company exists and whom it must serve to be successful in the long term.

From this company-wide statement of purpose, the company's annual strategic plan develops. It begins with broad, long-term goals established by the board of directors and senior management. From this general direction, the planning process progresses throughout the organizational structure, with each business segment preparing intermediate and shorter-term objectives and plans, which must be consistent with the long-term corporate objectives established by the board. They are submitted, evaluated, resubmitted, and ultimately approved in a process that should provide the company with both direction and consensus at all management levels. Accompanying the plans at each segment level are budgets, which are financial expressions of how the goals, objectives, and targets will be achieved.

Throughout all levels of the planning process, an essential step is preparation of a competitive analysis. This analysis is typically done by evaluating the company's external environment and internal capabilities to identify any strengths, weaknesses, opportunities, and threats (SWOT) that exist. The external analysis examines those factors outside the company that will influence its performance and competitive position, including economic and industry conditions. The internal analysis considers the company's capabilities, including production capacity and efficiency, marketing, sales and distribution effectiveness, technological capability, and the depth, quality, and availability of management and employees. The SWOT analysis attempts to define the competitive environment in which the company operates to identify the optimum strategy for success considering these conditions. That is, the SWOT analysis enables management to formulate a strategy based on conditions in the industry and the capabilities of the company relative to its competition.

When preparing competitive analysis for a valuation, the same SWOT analysis should be performed. It identifies and assesses how the company operates, how it interacts with and relies on its suppliers and customers, and how it performs relative to its competitors. From this we determine how risky the company is relative to its competitors, considering the industry and economic conditions in which it operates. As the competitive analysis progresses, we identify the *causes* behind the *results* reflected on the company's financial statements. That is, we identify *why* the company performed the way it did given its competitive environment. And because investment is always forward looking, the competitive analysis ultimately is used to assess the company's *anticipated* performance. While history provides a track record, value is primarily a function of the future.

The factors that are identified in the competitive analysis are frequently referred to as value drivers and risk drivers. *Risk drivers* cause uncertainty for the company. *Value drivers* reflect the company's strengths that enable it to both minimize risk and maximize net cash flow returns. Cumulatively, identifying the risk and value drivers establishes the company's strategic advantages and disadvantages. They are ultimately quantified in the discount rate that reflects the company's overall level of risk and in the forecast of expected net cash flows, considering the company's competitive position.

ASSESSING SPECIFIC COMPANY RISK

The development of the discount rate is explained in Chapter 8. The primary element in this rate that incorporates the competitive analysis is known as unsystematic risk, which measures the company's specific risk relative to that of its peers. Unsystematic risk generally involves assessment at three levels:

1. Economic
2. Industry
3. Company

Competitive analysis begins at the macroenvironmental level. It proceeds to focus more specifically, first on the subject company's industry and then preferably on the subject company's subsection of that industry. The analysis then concludes with a review of the company itself. It is generally forward looking as it considers the future conditions in which the company must operate.

Macroenvironmental Risk

The examination begins by exploring the outlook for conditions in which all companies will operate. These conditions include political, regulatory, socioeconomic, demographic, and technological factors, but the primary focus is on the economic climate. Specific economic factors include the general rate of economic growth—gross national product or gross domestic product—and extends to the rate of inflation, interest rates, unemployment rates, and similar factors. The markets served by the company and its customer base frequently determine the breadth of this analysis. For example, a company that serves a national or international customer base must consider that economic climate, whereas when a company's customer base is primarily local, the state and local climate becomes the focus.

The extent of analysis of regulatory, political, cultural, and technological factors is dependent on the influence that these issues exert on the company's performance. Companies operating in industries such as health care, where regulatory influences traditionally have been substantial, require extensive examination on how these factors will affect overall performance. Similarly, these issues must be considered if major regulatory or political changes are anticipated. Technological changes also should be examined in proportion to their anticipated effect on a company's performance. Those companies that rely heavily on technology for growth and success or those that are particularly vulnerable to technological improvements require more concentrated analysis of these factors.

Most of the macroenvironmental factors are beyond the company's immediate control, but they all must be analyzed to assess their effect on its performance.

Industry Analysis

Analysis at the industry level examines the overall attractiveness of operating in a selected industry and the company's relative position versus its competitors in that industry. Whenever possible, broader industry definitions are more specifically defined. For example, the health care industry could be reduced to nursing homes and then, within that, personal care versus assisted living facilities. Similar industry subdivisions could reduce food services to restaurants, to fast food versus full menu, and then to with versus without alcoholic beverages. Keep in mind that the size of an industry affects the analyst's ability to make these subdivisions. Larger industries typically have trade or professional organizations devoted to industry research for their members' benefit.

Initially at the industry level and eventually extending to the company level, strategies must be formulated and implemented to direct the company toward success. The objective is to exploit the company's strategic advantages while minimizing the consequences of its disadvantages.

Various methodologies or frameworks for conducting strategic analysis have been developed. Probably the best known is described in *Competitive Strategy*[1] by Michael E. Porter; it provides a framework to analyze rivalry and structure within an industry. This includes analysis of barriers to entry and the threat of new entrants, the bargaining position and influence of customers and suppliers, and threats posed by substitute products or services. Porter describes generic strategies, including class leadership, differentiation, and focus, that represent the alternative strategic positions that companies may assume in an industry.

The purpose of the industry analysis is to identify and analyze how industry factors will affect a company's ability to compete. Since this analysis is forward looking, it examines the company's likely performance given its strategic advantages and disadvantages. The strategic analysis should recognize the concept of "positioning" based on varieties, needs, access, and trade-offs between these activities.

---

[1] Michael E. Porter, *Competitive Strategy* (New York: The Free Press, 1980).

Porter built on this model in many subsequent works, including his classic article, "What Is Strategy?"[2] In that article, Porter discussed "Reconnecting with Strategy," which explains the challenge for established companies to redefine their strategy as follows:

> Most companies owe their initial success to a unique strategic position involving clear trade-offs. Activities once were aligned with that position. The passage of time and the pressures of growth, however, led to compromises that were, at first, almost imperceptible. Through a succession of incremental changes that each seemed sensible at the time, many established companies have compromised their way to homogeneity with their rivals. The issue here is not with the companies whose historical position is no longer viable; their challenge is to start over, just as a new entrant would. At issue is a far more common phenomenon: the established company achieving mediocre returns and lacking a clear strategy. Through incremental additions of product varieties, incremental efforts to serve new customer groups, and emulation of rivals' activities, the existing company loses its clear competitive position. Typically, the company has matched many of its competitors' offerings and practices and attempts to sell to most customer groups.
>
> A number of approaches can help a company reconnect with strategy. The first is a careful look at what it already does. Within most well-established companies is a core of uniqueness. It is identified by answering questions such as the following:
>
> - Which of our product or service varieties are the most distinctive?
> - Which of our product or service varieties are the most profitable?
> - Which of our customers are the most satisfied?
> - Which customers, channels, or purchase occasions are the most profitable?

---

[2] Reprinted by permission of *Harvard Business Review* from "What is Strategy?" by Michael E. Porter, November–December 1996. Copyright© 1996 by the Harvard Business School Publishing Corporation.

- Which of the activities in our value chain are the most different and effective?

Around this core of uniqueness are encrustations added incrementally over time. Like barnacles, they must be removed to reveal the underlying strategic positioning. A small percentage of varieties or customers may well account for most of a company's sales and especially its profits. The challenge, then, is to refocus on the unique core and realign the company's activities with it. Customers and product varieties at the periphery can be sold or allowed through inattention or price increases to fade away.

A company's history can also be instructive. What was the vision of the founder? What were the products and customers that made the company? Looking backward, one can reexamine the original strategy to see if it is still valid. Can the historical positioning be implemented in a modern way, one consistent with today's technologies and practices? This sort of thinking may lead to a commitment to renew the strategy and may challenge the organization to recover its distinctiveness. Such a challenge can be galvanizing and can instill the confidence to make the needed trade-offs.

Industry analysis is an essential step in both the company's annual strategic planning process and in a business valuation. Management must clearly understand the relative attractiveness of an industry, the market and structural characteristics most likely to change that level of attractiveness, and the resources necessary to compete successfully in that environment. Industry analysis and strategic planning constitute a unique body of knowledge with which the business appraiser must be familiar in order to properly assess a company's likely performance. Those lacking this background should acquire the benefits that this insight can provide before addressing significant valuation or merger and acquisition decisions.

Company Analysis

The analysis of strengths and weaknesses within the company should take into consideration the external economic and industry factors that have been described. That is, the internal assessment should reflect the company's external environment, including SWOT.

A proper internal analysis will look at the company's historical performance, paying particular attention to the competitive factors—the *causes*—that created the *results* portrayed on the company's financial statements. With this history in perspective, the analysis then looks at anticipated future economic and industry conditions, how those conditions differ from the past, and the company's ability to compete in this expected environment. The DuPont analysis described in Chapter 2, with its focus on profit margin and efficiency in asset utilization, should be applied to forecasted future performance. Each of the company's major functional areas, including purchasing, design and production, sales, marketing and distribution, and general administration, should be evaluated from margin and asset efficiency viewpoints. This analysis should be done for each business segment to assess return on investment. Ultimately, the return should be quantified as net cash flow to invested capital and the rate of return as a weighted average cost of capital (WACC), with these factors determining value creation.

In assessing revenues, breakdowns must be made by product line, reflecting anticipated volume and prices, given external conditions and the company's internal competitive advantages and disadvantages. The other factors affecting the company's net cash flow include cost of sales, operating expenses, income taxes, and the funding of fixed assets and working capital. These factors also must be assessed in light of the company's internal capabilities and external environment. Internal capabilities, including purchasing, design and engineering, production, and accounting and data processing, should be assessed in light of the company's competition. A qualitative assessment of the company's history, personnel, production capacity, and technology versus that of its competition and factors identified in the industry analysis feed into the metrics measured by the DuPont analysis. From this, the company's ability to generate the forecasted return is evaluated and its risk profile measured against its likely competition is also assessed.

This returns us to the SWOT analysis, which was performed earlier in assessing external factors. A similar examination is now made of internal capabilities and limitations to identify the company's competitive advantages and disadvantages. The results of these internal strengths and weaknesses, when considered against the external opportunities and threats, are quantified in the forecast that supports the company's strategic plan. The risk profile that reflects the internal and external uncertainties in the plan are then quantified in the company's rate of return or WACC.

COMPETITIVE FACTORS FREQUENTLY ENCOUNTERED IN NONPUBLIC ENTITIES

Traditional financial analysis includes the measure of a company's profitability, financial leverage, and liquidity. The DuPont analysis, which was described in Chapter 2, analyzes profitability primarily as a function of profit margin and asset turnover. Financial leverage measures the extent to which the company is financed with debt. It is often combined with coverage ratios, which compare various measures of the company's income or cash flow against fixed debt payments that it must service. And liquidity ratios measure the company's ability to pay current debt with current assets. These factors affect companies of all sizes, whether they are publicly traded or privately held.

The following factors, which are discussed in more detail in Chapter 8, tend to be particularly important to nonpublic entities. Buyers and sellers must carefully distinguish the effect of each on stand-alone fair market value versus investment value to a strategic buyer. Many of these create substantial strategic disadvantages to the company on a stand-alone basis, but they are eliminated if the company is acquired and becomes a segment of a larger business.

- Lack of access to capital
- Ownership structure and stock transfer restrictions
- Company's market share and market structure of the industry
- Depth and breadth of management
- Heavy reliance on individuals with key knowledge, skills, or contacts

- Marketing and advertising capacity
- Breadth of products and services
- Purchasing power and related economies of scale
- Customer concentration
- Vendor and supplier relations and reliance
- Distribution capability
- Depth, accuracy, and timeliness of accounting information and internal control

Although business valuation involves many financial calculations, it is not primarily a financial activity, particularly when valuation is done for merger and acquisition purposes. The value estimate must consider the company's competitive environment. This analysis should closely parallel the SWOT analysis performed in annual strategic planning. From this investigation, the company's strategic advantages and disadvantages are identified and assessed to determine its optimum strategy for success. This must be done in computing both the company's fair market value on a stand-alone basis and its investment value to strategic buyers because the company's competitive position frequently changes dramatically in an acquisition. The process of quantifying these competitive factors into a rate of return is described in Chapters 8 and 9.

4

Merger and Acquisition Market and Planning Process

For buyers and sellers to be most effective in merger and acquisition (M&A), they should have an understanding of the volume, terms, and trends taking place in M&A to avoid being misled by transactions reported in the media. Most transactions involving privately held companies require only limited reports on the change in ownership, sale price, or strategic objectives. People usually hear only about the largest transactions involving major public companies. Yet such transactions make up only a small percentage of the total activity and may not present a representative picture of the M&A market. The following statistics, reported in the 2001 edition of *Mergerstat® Review*, provide valuable background and perspective. As the introduction to that source states: "Mergerstat® tracks formal transfers of ownership of at least 10% of a company's equity where the purchase price is at least $1 million and where at least one of the parties is a U.S. entity."[1]

---

[1] *Mergerstat® Review 2001* (Los Angeles: Mergerstat®, 2001).

Exhibit 4-1   Trends in Mergers and Acquisitions (1981 to 2000)

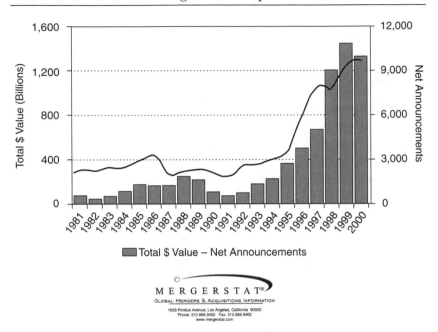

Source: Reprinted with permission from Mergerstat® (www.mergerstat.com).

As Exhibit 4-1 indicates, M&A activity in the United States increased steadily and dramatically throughout the 1990s in both volume and value.

Exhibit 4-2 illustrates the increasing importance of privately owned sellers, which increased as a percentage of the total transactions from 40% in 1990 to 57% in 1999. Clearly the heaviest activity is in the acquisition of privately held companies. While the average transaction price during the period from 1995 to 1999 ranged from approximately $187 to $421 million, the median transaction size during this time ranged from about $25 to $40 million, according to Mergerstat®. The magnitude of the middle market also becomes clearer with Exhibit 4-3, which shows that over two-thirds of the transactions in recent years have had a purchase price of less than $100 million. Of the privately owned sellers, the average purchase price during the period 1995 to 1999 ranged from $12 to $88 million, with the median purchase price ranging from $13 to $19 million. It is also noteworthy that over this five-

Exhibit 4-2   Composition of Net Merger and Acquisition
                Announcements (1991 to 2000)

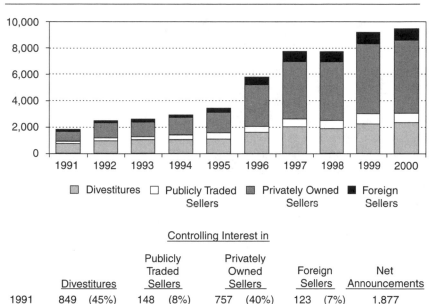

	Divestitures		Publicly Traded Sellers		Privately Owned Sellers		Foreign Sellers		Net Announcements
					Controlling Interest in				
1991	849	(45%)	148	(8%)	757	(40%)	123	(7%)	1,877
1992	1,026	(40%)	227	(9%)	1,119	(43%)	202	(8%)	2,574
1993	1,134	(43%)	221	(8%)	1,127	(42%)	181	(7%)	2,663
1994	1,134	(38%)	344	(11%)	1,324	(44%)	195	(7%)	2,997
1995	1,199	(34%)	447	(13%)	1,610	(46%)	254	(7%)	3,510
1996	1,702	(29%)	478	(8%)	3,137	(54%)	531	(9%)	5,848
1997	2,108	(27%)	603	(8%)	4,387	(56%)	702	(9%)	7,800
1998	1,987	(25%)	627	(8%)	4,445	(57%)	750	(10%)	7,809
1999	2,353	(25%)	746	(8%)	5,297	(57%)	882	(10%)	9,278
2000	2,501	(26%)	676	(7%)	5,511	(58%)	878	(9%)	9,566

MERGERSTAT®
GLOBAL MERGERS & ACQUISITIONS INFORMATION
1933 Pontius Avenue, Los Angeles, California 90025
Phone: 310.966.9492 Fax: 310.966.9462
www.mergerstat.com

Reprinted with permission from Mergerstat® (www.mergerstat.com).

year period, about three-fourths of all sellers had revenues of less
than $100 million.

   For privately owned sellers, this source cited two primary motives to sell. The first and most frequent reason was lack of a successor to take over the business. The second reason was increasing
demand for the company's products or services, causing the need
to sell to obtain adequate resources for expansion.

Exhibit 4-3   Net Merger and Acquisition Announcements
Purchase Price Distribution (1991 to 2000)

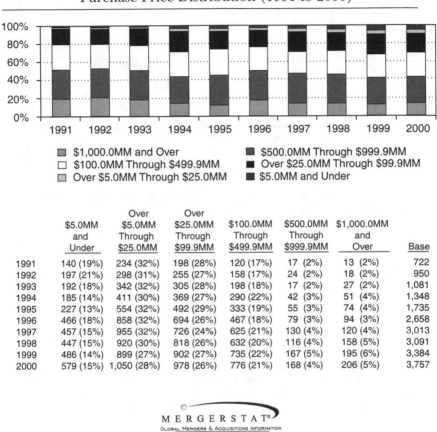

	$5.0MM and Under	Over $5.0MM Through $25.0MM	Over $25.0MM Through $99.9MM	$100.0MM Through $499.9MM	$500.0MM Through $999.9MM	$1,000.0MM and Over	Base
1991	140 (19%)	234 (32%)	198 (28%)	120 (17%)	17 (2%)	13 (2%)	722
1992	197 (21%)	298 (31%)	255 (27%)	158 (17%)	24 (2%)	18 (2%)	950
1993	192 (18%)	342 (32%)	305 (28%)	198 (18%)	17 (2%)	27 (2%)	1,081
1994	185 (14%)	411 (30%)	369 (27%)	290 (22%)	42 (3%)	51 (4%)	1,348
1995	227 (13%)	554 (32%)	492 (29%)	333 (19%)	55 (3%)	74 (4%)	1,735
1996	466 (18%)	858 (32%)	694 (26%)	467 (18%)	79 (3%)	94 (3%)	2,658
1997	457 (15%)	955 (32%)	726 (24%)	625 (21%)	130 (4%)	120 (4%)	3,013
1998	447 (15%)	920 (30%)	818 (26%)	632 (20%)	116 (4%)	158 (5%)	3,091
1999	486 (14%)	899 (27%)	902 (27%)	735 (22%)	167 (5%)	195 (6%)	3,384
2000	579 (15%)	1,050 (28%)	978 (26%)	776 (21%)	168 (4%)	206 (5%)	3,757

MERGERSTAT®
GLOBAL MERGERS & ACQUISITIONS INFORMATION
1933 Pontius Avenue, Los Angeles, California 90025
Phone: 310.966.9492   Fax: 310.966.9462
www.mergerstat.com

Source: Reprinted with permission from Mergerstat® (www.mergerstat.com).

Mergerstat® also presents pricing information in the form of median price to earnings (P/E) multiples offered for acquisitions of public and private companies. These multiples clearly increase with the size of the transaction and generally tend to be lower when the terms of sale call for a cash payment rather than for payment in the form of stock or some combination of cash, stock, and debt.

Exhibit 4-4 reveals the more popular payment terms employed in recent years. This increased use of cash is accompanied by a corresponding decrease in stock and some combination of

Exhibit 4-4   Payment Trends (1981 to 2000)

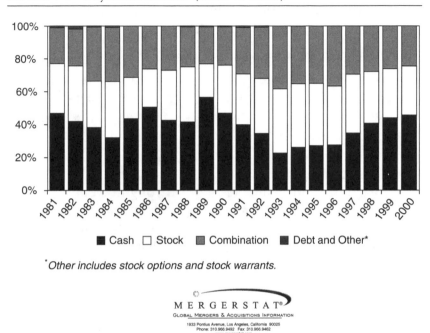

■ Cash   □ Stock   ▨ Combination   ■ Debt and Other*

Other includes stock options and stock warrants.

MERGERSTAT®
GLOBAL MERGERS & ACQUISITIONS INFORMATION
1933 Pontius Avenue, Los Angeles, California 90025
Phone: 310.966.9492 Fax: 310.966.9462
www.mergerstat.com

Source: Reprinted with permission from Mergerstat® (www.mergerstat.com).

payment, suggesting the market's increasing awareness of the riskiness of those payment forms.

The M&A data presented clearly emphasizes the importance of privately owned companies and middle-market-size companies in the U.S. economy, although transactions involving these companies receive less publicity than those concerning public firms. With these companies comprising such a large portion of total deal activity, it is essential that buyers and sellers understand how to both measure and build value in these businesses.

COMMON SELLER AND BUYER MOTIVATIONS

It is advantageous to know why the other side in a transaction is considering the deal. This knowledge should aid both in assessing the strength of one's negotiating position and in structuring the proposal to meet the other side's financial, strategic, and personal objectives. Common seller and buyer motivations include:

Common Seller Motives

- Personal desire to leave due to age, poor health, family pressure, burnout
- Owners' need for estate planning
- Lack of a successor, including conflicts among family members and owners or loss of key people
- Need for additional capital to finance growth
- Weak or declining performance or growing financial difficulties
- Presence of strategic disadvantages that cannot be overcome as a stand-alone business
- Market or industry conditions that create strong sale prices

Common Buyer Motives

- Expand product lines or geographic markets
- Obtain better growth opportunities
- Enhance profitability and cash flow through revenue enhancement or cost reduction
- Enhance competitive strengths or reduce weaknesses
- Acquire needed technology or capacity faster than through internal expansion
- Prevent competitors from entering that market
- Better employ surplus capital or management
- Diversify to minimize risk

WHY MERGERS AND ACQUISITIONS FAIL

Because most of the M&A activity in the United States involves privately held companies, data on the buyers' success in these transactions is limited. Much more information exists when the companies involved are public. The results of these transactions are described extensively in *The Synergy Trap: How Companies Lose the Acquisition Game,* by Mark L. Sirower, which, in addition to an in-depth analysis, includes a summary of acquisition performance in the United States over many years.[2] The general conclusion is that well over half of the acquisitions of public companies destroy value for buyers while sellers frequently are rewarded with the premiums they received.

There are numerous reasons why deals may fail, which, of course, vary by the transaction and circumstances involved. The most common causes tend to be:

- *Price paid is too high.* This frequently results from the failure to distinguish the *target* from the *investment.* Even the best company can be a poor investment if the price paid exceeds the present value of its anticipated future returns.

- *Make-it-happen pressure from the executive level.* This often results from executives' desire to move too quickly or to make their mark on the company without adequate analysis of the effects of the transaction on value.

- *Exaggerated synergies.* Anticipated revenue enhancements, cost reductions, operating efficiencies, or financing benefits are overestimated.

- *Failure to integrate operations quickly.* With the price for the synergies paid up front, they must be achieved on time to yield benefits and create value.

- *Failure to accurately assess customer reaction.* The newly combined company may force certain customers to seek a different source of supply to avoid buying from what has become a competitor or to avoid excessive reliance on one source of supply.

- *Failure to consider first-year negative synergies.* Mergers or acquisitions often cause disruptions, including name changes, additional regulatory requirements, strained shareholder relations, negative public perception of the effect on consumers or of closing facilities, and the cost of

---

[2] Mark L. Sirower, *The Synergy Trap: How Companies Lose the Acquisition Game* (New York: The Free Press, 1997).

severance packages and closing facilities, all of which should be quantified as part of the analysis.

- *Failure to estimate and recognize stand-alone fair market value.* For private companies that lack an established value, buyers may look only at investment value, including synergies, and ignore the target's lower value on a stand-alone basis.

- *Inconsistent strategy.* Inaccurate assessment of strategic benefits may occur.

- *Inadequate due diligence.* In the precombination phase, ineffective strategic planning or assessment of value drivers and risk drivers or pressure to win negotiations prevails over sound decision making.

- *Incompatibility of corporate cultures.* Lack of communication, differing expectations, and conflicting management styles all contribute to lack of execution.

- *Distraction from existing business.* Failure to anticipate or effectively react to competitors' response to the acquisition, including inattention to ongoing operations and loss of key personnel of acquirer or target, affect profitability.

- *Inadequate risk analysis.* Discussed in Chapter 6, this involves the failure to rigorously assess the likelihood of success of a transaction or to consider management discretion in future periods.

Much of the literature on M&A cite "CEO hubris," the desire to grow for the sake of growth, inexperience, and overly complacent corporate directors or shareholders as factors contributing to this poor track record. While much less information is available on the success of M&A activity involving closely held companies, many of these same conditions are present in middle-market transactions. In addition, there is an overwhelming misunderstanding of what value is, how it is created, and how it must be carefully measured and analyzed in M&A.

SALES STRATEGY AND PROCESS

As previously discussed, the success of buyers and sellers in negotiating a deal is dependent on understanding the transaction from the other side's perspective. Doing this includes recognizing their financial, strategic, and personal motivations and the process they are experiencing in the negotiation. The following discussion describes steps that a seller should go through *before* a transaction takes place.

Step 1: Identify Potential Consequences of Inaction

Most sellers have never sold a company. This inexperience, combined with the frequent emotional reluctance to sell, inhibits adequate preparation. Seller inexperience with the sale process typically causes underestimation of the consequences of lack of preparation. Too often they equate selling a company with the effort required to sell their inventory or home. The company, of course, is far more complex—financially, operationally, and emotionally—so much more preparation is needed to successfully complete the sale.

The principal consequence of inaction is lost opportunity. These losses occur most commonly on four fronts, and each can have huge long-term consequences to the seller.

1. Failure to address key nonfinancial issues
2. Failure to identify what drives value
3. Failure to recognize the importance of timing
4. Failure to prepare the company for a sale

Failure to Address Key Nonfinancial Issues

These most commonly concern "people" issues and usually include one or more of the following key groups: family members, other owners, and employees. Closely held companies frequently have one or more family members who work in the company, often in key management positions. Their financial and professional future may be greatly influenced by a sale decision, so these matters must be discussed. The key decision criteria here are often personal as well as financial, and painful choices are frequently required.

Partners and employees also may be affected favorably or unfavorably by the decision, and allowances for these personal and financial consequences may be necessary.

The natural inclination with these "people" issues is to ignore them, usually by postponing any decision at all. Ignoring issues seldom eliminates them, frequently exacerbates them, and often narrows options when the issues are finally confronted at a later date.

Failure to Identify What Drives Value

Business executives often are so immersed in the day-to-day challenges of running the company that they lose sight of the bigger value maximization goals that were described in Chapters 1 and 2. Without routine attention to what drives long-term value, particularly stand-alone versus strategic value, major sale opportunities may be missed. Unless the annual strategic planning process is tied to value creation, it frequently fails to drive value and return on investment.

Failure to Recognize the Importance of Timing

Companies and industries go through a natural progression of growth, development, and other changes that create strategic strengths and weaknesses. Recent worldwide trends in consolidation, reduced regulation, and globalization are only a few of the external factors that may create one-time opportunities that must be recognized to maximize return. Inattention to these factors may not only result in an excellent opportunity missed; it could render the company uncompetitive or unsaleable for more than tangible asset value.

Failure to Prepare the Company for a Sale

Because companies are operating entities that face changing competitive conditions, they are seldom ready on short notice to obtain the optimum sale price. Advanced planning, often over a period of years, may be necessary to capitalize on the company's strength and minimize its weaknesses. Inattention to the sale process usually prevents adequate planning.

The conclusion here should be clear: Inaction virtually guarantees lost opportunities and a lower sale price. Proactive planning, with a relentless focus on value, is a must.

Step 2: Identify Key Nonfinancial Issues

As briefly addressed in the last section, key nonfinancial issues are usually personal issues involving other owners or employees, some of whom may be family members or close friends. Often resolving these issues to the seller's satisfaction may carry negative financial consequences. When these issues are present, recognize that some decisions are made for reasons that cannot be justified financially. It may be helpful to separate these issues into categories, such as financial, strategic, and personal, then set goals based on their separate criteria in seeking an overall succession plan. Procrastination frequently results when shareholders attempt to apply a financial measure to a personal decision.

A common example of the difficulty that can arise occurs with confusion between ownership succession and management succession. While the former is easily accomplished without long-term consequences by transfer of shares through a gift or sale, the latter is far more complicated. Management succession requires careful assessment of the qualifications of the successor, and this transfer can have a huge influence on the future performance of the company.

Resolution of nonfinancial issues typically involves different measurement criteria and may necessitate professional consultation. An excellent reference source is *Passing the Torch: Succession Retirement and Estate Planning in Family Owned Businesses.*[3]

Step 3: Assemble an Advisory Team

While the logical, and often correct, first step for the business owner contemplating a sale is to contact the company's accountant, attorney, and banker, before doing so, consider the perspective and qualifications of these advisors. While they may be loyal and proven advisors on routine company matters, they may lack the expertise or experience to handle the sale of the business properly. Tax and legal advice is critical, so advisors, whether internal or external, should routinely handle M&A transactions. Also recognize that these trusted advisors may bring to the sale de-

---

[3] Mike Cohn, *Passing the Torch: Succession Retirement and Estate Planning in Family Owned Businesses,* Second Edition (New York: McGraw-Hill, Inc., 1992).

cision a natural reluctance to see it happen because of their resulting loss of a client. While this does not mean they would not provide appropriate advice, sellers need to be served by an enthusiastic, aggressive team that is determined to achieve their goals.

Other external advisors should include a valuation consultant and an intermediary. While the valuation and transaction advisory services are frequently provided by the same party—usually an investment banker—consider what skills they bring to the transaction. The intermediary may be great at the sale process but have little technical valuation knowledge. This could result in the seller not receiving the best advice about value maximization strategy, preparing the company for sale, or even on how to achieve the highest possible price. Conversely, the valuation consultant may possess little M&A experience or industry contacts, which are essential in the sale of certain kinds of businesses. In general, the more profitable a company is, the more helpful that the valuation and transaction advisors can be in achieving the maximum sale price as a function of the company's profits. Much of the value in this case would be intangible; here skilled advisors are essential. Less profitable or underperforming companies often sell at asset value, where little more than brokerage services are needed.

The independent valuation advisor often offers substantial benefits over having this service provided internally. A company's chief financial officer or controller may believe that, as a financial expert, he or she is competent to prepare a valuation. These skills require years of experience. Corporate executives, because of their involvement in the company's operations, may lose perspective in assessing key competitive factors. Less experienced appraisers also frequently have difficulty distinguishing between stand-alone fair market value and investment value in the valuation and analysis process.

Industry conditions also can influence the need for and choice of a transaction advisor. For some businesses, the biggest challenge is finding one or more qualified buyers. In other cases, it is assessing with which buyer the fit would be best or which can afford to pay the highest price. And in every case, deal structure and negotiation skills are essential.

As discussed further in Chapter 14, the seller must focus relentlessly on the after-tax cash proceeds received in the sale. Advisors may offer many options on how the sale is structured, with the maximum return potentially received in a wide variety of forms.

Therefore, tax advice is essential. Subsequent investment advice on how to handle the sale proceeds may also be required.

Step 4: Identify Likely Alternatives

Once the key nonfinancial issues have been identified and addressed and the professional advisory team is assembled, the next step for the seller is to identify the possible transfer alternatives. These typically include:

- Sale to an outside party
- Sale to an inside group
- Transfer through gifting
- Transfer through an estate plan

Each of these alternatives offers pros and cons to achieve the owner's financial and nonfinancial objectives. Naturally, they carry different risk and return consequences that should be fully explored with the advisory team. Again, it should be recognized that some of the owners' most important objectives may be nonfinancial, and these must be fully explored and discussed. Especially where family members are involved, there must be a candid assessment made of the company's ability to compete under a new management team. Where hand-picked successors are family members who are unlikely to succeed, these difficult issues should be addressed in advance to prevent likely future failure. Also recognize that decisions made for personal reasons may carry significant financial consequences. While the owners have the right to make these decisions, they also must recognize their effect on the sale price, the company, and its various stakeholders.

Step 5: Preparation and Financial Assessment of Alternatives

With the likely alternatives identified, the advisory team should make a more detailed assessment of the financial consequences of each alternative, including:

- *Evaluate legal issues in preparation for the sale.* This "legal audit" should include a review of the corporate bylaws, stock certificates, transfer restrictions, title to assets, ownership and protection of intellectual property, contracts in place, leases and debt covenants, and ongoing litigation.

- *Compute stand-alone fair market value and estimate investment value to assess the likely benefits to be achieved from a sale to a strategic buyer.* This synergy premium should be considered in assessing the financial consequences of other transfer options.

- *Address the need to prepare the company for a sale.* The valuation of the business will have identified the drivers that most heavily influence the company's value, and from this the timing of the sale can be considered. Economic and industry conditions may not be ideal at the present time, or the company may greatly benefit by pursuing short-term strategies that better position the company to achieve a maximum sale value. Preparation may take from up to a few months to a year but should allow the owners to present the company in the most advantageous possible way. Thus, to achieve the best possible price and terms, the seller should compute the stand-alone fair market value and estimate each potential buyer's investment value prior to committing to the sale process.

- *Reevaluate the tax issues and options that accompany each alternative.* Once again, while recognizing the seller's objective to achieve selective nonfinancial goals, he or she should focus on the after-tax proceeds that result from the sale, however it is structured.

- *Make a firm decision and stick to it.* Once the personal issues have been identified and addressed and the advisory team has identified the likely alternatives, including the personal and financial consequences of each and the steps necessary to achieve the desired value, a well-informed decision can be made. At this point, the owner should be comfortable with the decision, recognizing that most choices carry some unwanted consequences and that the best choice seldom achieves every goal.

- *Don't second guess.* Because entrepreneurs and others involved in middle-market companies frequently identify personally with the company and its success, the decision to sell frequently involves strong emotions. A sale is not by definition a failure, even if the company has been underperforming. It is a decision to achieve a variety of personal and financial goals that, if reached in a rational and systematic manner, simply represents sound management.

- *Prepare the company for sale.* Many of the details in the preparation and sale process are managed by the transaction advisor. Several points can be mentioned here that should be recognized in advance:

  — Strengthen the reliability of the financial statements, especially if the company is solidly profitable with a sound balance sheet. Do not give a buyer any reasons to doubt the company's reported performance. Have five years of audited financial statements prepared by a reputable accounting firm, with detailed supporting documents available for the due diligence process.

  — Clean house. Remove any bad debts, obsolete inventory, unused plant and equipment, and nonoperating assets that may create questions or doubts or impede the sale process. Resolve contingent liabilities and related legal and regulatory issues that are outstanding. Dress up the company physically, from repair and maintenance to painting and landscaping.

  — Maintain confidentiality while negotiating contracts or less formal agreements to keep key employees.

  — Rely on the intermediary. Often the negotiating process is long and difficult and requires hard bargaining. The seller does not want to expend valuable negotiating leverage early in this process. An intermediary should handle these initial steps, conserving the seller's negotiating capacity to the end of the process when it is needed most.

Step 6: Preparation of Offering Memorandum

An essential step in the sale process is preparation of the company's *selling brochure* or *offering memorandum.* This document presents the seller's strategic plan, including its long-term operating goals and objectives. While the selling brochure should be grounded in reality and defendable under intense scrutiny by buyers, it is also intended to present the most favorable, realistic picture of the company as an acquisition target.

A properly prepared offering memorandum presents more than details about the target and its industry. It provides insight into the seller's strategic position and potential, given industry circumstances. It also should indicate management's ability to design a coherent and effective strategy to maximize the company's performance and value.

A significant goal of the offering memorandum is a clear expression of the strategic advantages of the company as an acquisition candidate as well as what processes, skills, and proprietary systems can be transferred to the buyer. The unstated message in this description should be the justification for why potential buyers cannot afford to pass up this acquisition.

An offering memorandum consists of the following parts.

Executive Summary

Experienced M&A participants would agree that the most critical part of an offering memorandum is the executive summary. Intended to catch the potential buyers' attention, it must provide a compelling case for why the company is an attractive acquisition. In just a few pages, this summary should present the company's history and current market position, major products and services, technological achievements and capabilities, and recent financial performance. The company's strategic advantages should be emphasized, particularly how these can be exploited by an acquirer. Although descriptive, the well-written executive summary is a sales document that effectively promotes the company as an acquisition target.

Description of Company

This section of the selling brochure usually begins with a description of the company's history and extends to a forecast of its projected operations. It usually includes a detailed description of:

- Major product or service lines
- Manufacturing operations, capabilities, and capacities
- Technological capabilities
- Distribution system
- Sales and marketing program
- Management capabilities

- Financial position and historical performance
- Current capitalization and ownership structure

Market Analysis

The offering memorandum also should include a market analysis, which is a discussion of the industry or industry segment in which the company operates, including an overview of key industry trends, emerging technologies, and new product or service introductions. This assessment of the market typically describes the company's current position relative to its competition and strategic advantages that will allow it to maintain or improve this position. Key competitors are often described with a constant focus on the company's future and its strategy to grow and improve its performance.

Forecasted Performance

After this history of the company and strategic analysis, the brochure presents a forecast of future operations, including income statement, balance sheet, and statement of cash flows plus the assumptions that support this projection.

Deal Structure and Terms

The offering memorandum should present essential information about deal structure, specifics on any items excluded from the sale, and any restrictions on payment terms. For example, disclosure of any specific tangible or intangible assets that the seller intends to retain can be identified as well as restrictions on any debt that can be assumed by the buyer or the seller's willingness to finance any or all of the transaction.

The offering memorandum frequently is preceded by an initial "teaser" letter that may be narrowly or broadly sent to potential buyers. It provides a brief description of the company, which it may or may not specifically identify. The teaser provides only an overview of the company's finances. Its purpose is to stimulate interest, emphasizing where the company is, how it got there, and, most important, where it believes the company can go. It invites potential buyers to request additional information—the offering memorandum.

Exhibit 4-5 portrays a "Seller's Deal Timetable" that involves a 12-week sale process. This should be viewed as a goal—12 weeks

Exhibit 4-5   Deal Timetable

Develop and Implement Marketing Strategy	Solicit Initial Bids	Bid Evaluation and Detailed Due Diligence	Conduct Negotiations and Solicit Final Bids	Closing
• Collect data • Conduct due diligence • Prepare marketing materials • Prepare normalization adjustments and valuation • Select, prioritize candidates • Develop approach strategy • Determine list of potential buyers and gather detailed contact information • Obtain confidentiality agreement from all parties	• Continue calling process • Facilitate information flow between buyers and company to expedite buyers' evaluation • Select buyers to meet with management • Organize data room • Management meets with interested buyers • Buyers conduct preliminary financial, legal, and accounting due diligence	• Establish price • Establish form of consideration • Establish timing • Establish terms and conditions • Determine ability of buyer to complete transaction • Estimate prospects of combined entity • Select final bidders and conduct on-site due diligence • Distribute draft of definitive agreement and final bid request letter to interested parties	• Establish exclusivity • Prioritize key objectives • Negotiate and execute definitive agreement • Announce transaction • File regulatory documents (if necessary) • Obtain buyer shareholder approval (if necessary)	

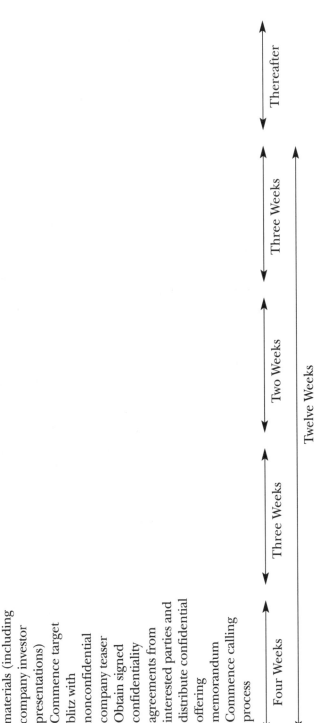

would be very fast. The timetable reflects the many steps in the sale process which emphasizes the importance of planning, preparation, and the benefits of good professional advisors.

For many middle-market shareholders, the sale of their company is the largest financial decision they will ever make. Businesses are complex entities involving people, products, customers, and technologies operating in continually changing industries, economies, and regulatory environments. Their strategic position and value is constantly changing. This value is difficult to measure in the first place, and owners should not only know what their company is presently worth on a stand-alone basis but what it could be worth to strategic buyers when synergistic benefits are considered.

Sale opportunities may be continually available at an attractive price. It is much more likely, however, that a buyer or an ideal population of likely buyers may have to be identified and enticed to consider an acquisition of the company. Anticipating the wants and needs of these prospective buyers, the target may have to be positioned to maximize its attractiveness. This process may require considerable time as well as careful timing to exploit ideal sale conditions in the industry or the economy.

The message here should be clear: Selling at an attractive price requires a lot of luck or, in most cases, careful advance planning. Failure to plan carefully greatly increases the likelihood that the owners will fail to achieve some or all of their financial and personal goals.

ACQUISITION STRATEGY AND PROCESS

The acquisition strategy should fit the company's overall strategic goal: increase net cash flows and reduce risk. In strategic planning over the long term, to achieve this goal shareholders and management frequently will face the choice of internal development versus merger or acquisition. To drive the company toward its strongest competitive position, resources constantly must be shifted from underperforming activities or those with less potential to those that provide greater benefits. In shifting resources, management can move them among existing operations, into developmental activities or into acquisitions.

The primary reason for acquiring or merging with another business is to produce improved cash flow or reduced risk faster or at a lower cost than achieving the same goal internally. Thus, the goal of any acquisition is to create a strategic advantage by paying a price for the target that is lower than the total resources required for internal development of a similar strategic position.

Forms of Business Combinations

Business combinations can take any of a number of forms. In an *acquisition,* the stock or assets of a company are purchased by the buyer. A *merger,* which is primarily a legal distinction, occurs through the combination of two companies, where the first is absorbed by the second or a new entity is formed from the original two. A less drastic form of combination is a *joint venture,* which typically involves two companies forming and mutually owning a third business , most often to achieve a specific limited purpose. The lowest form of commitment in a strategic combination would be an *alliance,* which is a formal cooperative effort between two independent companies to pursue a specific objective, or the *licensing* of a technology, product, or intellectual property to another organization. Thus, in terms of control, investment, and commitment, acquisition provides the strongest position, followed by a merger. When less commitment is desired, joint ventures, alliances, or even licensing arrangements can be adopted.

The planning process should identify the strategy behind combinations as well as the anticipated benefits from them. In assessing these benefits, the different types of potential acquisitions usually fall into one of the following categories:

- *Horizontal acquisitions.* By acquiring another firm in the same industry, the buyer typically aims to achieve economies of scale in marketing, production, or distribution as well as increased market share and an improved product and market position.
- *Vertical acquisition.* Moving "upstream" or "downstream," the buyer looks to acquire a supplier, distributor, or customer. The objective typically is to obtain control over a source of scarce resources or supply for production or quality control

purposes, improved access to a specific customer base, or higher value products or services in the production chain.

- *Contiguous acquisitions.* Buyers may see opportunities in adjacent industries where they can capitalize on related technologies, production processes, or strategic resources that may serve different markets or customer bases.

The strategic planning process described in Chapter 3 identifies the company's competitive position and sets objectives to exploit its relative strengths while minimizing the effects of its weaknesses. The company's M&A strategy should complement this process, targeting only those industries and companies that can improve the acquirer's strengths or alleviate its weaknesses. With the acquisition plan focused on this goal, management can reduce the cost and time involved in analyzing and screening investment opportunities that arise. Opportunities that fail to meet these criteria can be rejected more quickly as inconsistent with the overall strategic plan. Thus, acquisition should be viewed as only one of several alternative strategies to achieve a basic business objective. When less investment or commitment is preferred, alliances, joint ventures, or licensing agreements may be a more appropriate form of combination.

Typically, a major advantage of an acquisition over internal development is that it accomplishes the objective much quicker. In addition, the acquisition helps to reduce risk when the acquirer is moving beyond its core business. An established business brings with it one or more of the following:

- Track record
- Management
- Competencies
- Products
- Brands
- Customer base

Internal development may lack all of these benefits. The target also may carry weaknesses, which should diminish its stand-alone value. These attributes should be considered against the buyer's competencies to assess their effect on future performance.

Acquisitions also may provide "bounce-back" synergistic benefits that the acquirer can leverage by spreading that benefit over its larger base of business. These benefits will be described further in Chapter 5.

Acquisition Planning

The acquisition plan should tie very closely to the company's overall strategic plan. Whenever the acquisition plan starts to drift from the strategic plan, whenever its connection to the strategic plan tends to blur or become less well defined, stop! That is a clear warning to return to the company's basic strategy and goals and investigate whether this acquisition fits. Relentless discipline in this process is rewarded with less time and cost spent studying targets that are not a logical fit.

Step 1: Tie Acquisition Plan to Overall Strategic Plan

Maintaining focus also means requiring every proposal to pass the firm's primary value creating goal: It should increase net cash flow or reduce risk, or both, and the details of the forecast and valuation should support this conclusion.

From the company's strategic plan and the strengths, weaknesses, opportunities, and threats (SWOT) analysis that supports it, the company's competitive position—its strategic advantages and disadvantages—are identified. In a company's day-to-day operations, it attempts internally to improve on its strengths, eliminate or minimize its weaknesses, and take advantage of market opportunities. Business combinations, whether acquisitions, mergers, alliances, joint ventures, or licensing agreements, are generally undertaken to achieve the same goals, but typically faster or at a reduced cost. Thus, the acquisition plan originates in the strategic plan when objectives can be achieved more effectively through some form of combination rather than internal development. Acquisitions also may be made for defensive purposes, such as to keep a competitor out of a market, to eliminate a weak competitor that could be acquired and strengthened or that depresses prices, or to protect a technology.

Step 2: Form Effective Acquisition Team

The makeup of the acquisition team can influence its likely level of success. Teams tend to be more effective when comprised of managers from several functional areas, including marketing and sales, operations, distribution, and finance. Each of these disciplines provides a different focus on a target as these managers bring different concerns to the evaluation process. Teams comprised solely of financial executives often overlook operational issues, while those consisting only of generalists frequently exhibit a lack of attention to detail. For this reason, a blend of background and knowledge combined with open discussion of each member's concerns usually results in a more thorough and accurate analysis.

While larger companies have M&A or business development departments, those that lack this capacity internally may have to add external legal, tax, and valuation advisors. These outsiders often bring the added benefit of objectivity and creativity that internal team members may lack.

Step 3: Specify Acquisition Criteria

While the acquisition team's strategy should flow from the company's overall strategic plan, specific objectives for each acquisition should be required to both justify and focus the process. Typically, these objectives should lead to acquisition criteria and should leverage the acquirer's current strategic advantages, including surplus cash, management, technology, market strengths, or production capacity. Most strategic goals also include a minimum required rate of return on capital invested. The return should be measured as net cash flow with equal attention given to the timing of the cash inflows and their anticipated rate of growth. Adherence to specified goals and the company's track record of success also improves when managers' compensation is tied to the achievement of these specific measurements.

Typical acquisition criteria include parameters on the size, location, and market position of the target or its products as well as performance goals. For example, the required market position may be to be first or second in sales in a given market, or the high-quality or low price leader in the industry. In establishing this criteria, the target's current and forecasted growth must be assessed against these parameters.

The criteria also should be assessed from the perspective of risk tolerance. That is, management should consider the potential least favorable and most favorable outcomes and the company's ability to respond to downside conditions.

Step 4: Consider Target Weaknesses versus Acquirer's Strengths

As acquisition criteria are evaluated, managers should be encouraged not to quickly reject targets that display weaknesses. Companies frequently come on the market because of strategic disadvantages ranging from lack of capital to inadequate distribution. These limitations often have reduced the company's growth and returns, and, in the process, they decrease its value. This may make it a more attractive acquisition target, particularly when the buyer possesses the capabilities to eliminate the problem. Thus, the acquisition criteria must consider not only the strategic strengths and weaknesses of the target as a stand-alone but how it will perform when incorporated into the acquirer's operations. The acquisition parameters also should define whether the company will evaluate troubled companies and under what circumstances.

Step 5: Define Search Process

The acquisition strategy also should define the discovery or search process. Less aggressive companies may consider only those potential acquisitions brought to them by intermediaries or owners looking to sell. This approach probably will miss many opportunities, particularly those unknown candidates that are not being considered by any other buyer. The search strategy sources and resources should be defined, including establishment of the minimum information required to evaluate a candidate.

Step 6: Select Search Criteria and Find Target Companies

Following the decision to pursue mergers or acquisitions, set the criteria for the target of your hunt. In other words, *select the search criteria.*

The following are the primary criteria that should be on any criterial list:

- *Industry.* Generally this is the same industry or a similar industry to that in which the acquirer is currently active. A relevant question is whether only vertical acquisitions are of interest or if horizontal prospects are also to be considered.
- *Products or services.* Often acquirers desire products or services that have a significant presence in the market. Thus, they seek to acquire a target that has a better brand name or an expanded line of products or services, particularly higher value components or lines.
- *Revenues.* Revenues are usually evaluated based on size, and usually the target will be smaller than the acquirer.
- *Earnings.* Acquirers should decide if they require a desired minimum amount of earnings, or whether losses (see turnaround criteria) are also acceptable, if correctable. A target with losses will likely be dilutive to the acquirer's earnings in the short run; however, this is often less significant than indicated by the M&A market's fixation on whether earnings are immediately dilutive. Negative earnings can be corrected if they are a result of weak management or an inability to fund growth or to modernize plant. Often a target with correctable losses can be acquired at an attractive price.
- *Whether turnarounds are considered.* Turnaround situations can include anything from a target that has recently experienced losses to one in bankruptcy. Some acquirers are willing to look at turnarounds while others rule them out by policy. In a seller's market, when there are many buyers looking at every attractive company available to be acquired, the willingness to consider turnarounds can assist the acquirer. Usually there are fewer possible buyers for turnarounds, and the sellers tend to be more realistic about price. The more conservative prices paid for turnarounds also may provide the acquirer more time to achieve synergies.
- *Geographic area.* Most buyers want to acquire targets in a given geographic area. With the globalization of markets and the continuing reduction in trade barriers, acquirers are increasingly interested in targets throughout the world. The decision on where expansion should next take place should be based on the acquirer's overall strategic plan.

- *Whether target's management should be retained.* Most often this choice is influenced by the acquirer's depth of competent management. When a company has excess management worthy of a promotion, it may seek to acquire a region or product line for them. Growth strategies, however, should always be tied to value creation.

  When the M&A market is hot, the price required to acquire a successful company is higher. Often these higher prices can be justified only through an earnout used to bridge the higher price the seller feels is appropriate based on the future outlook versus the lower price the buyer feels is appropriate based on the target's current status and performance. Earnouts are discussed further in Chapter 14.

- *Private companies or public companies.* Generally, this choice is most dependent on whether the acquisition is consistent with the acquirer's strategic plan.
- *Ideal fit.* A target is usually an ideal fit when its product or service naturally fits the acquirer's marketing, sales, and distribution system and its geographic requirement. Such a fit allows fast and efficient integration. Buyers must be cautioned, however, that even the best fit remains a poor investment if the price paid is too high compared to the risk-adjusted returns.

Having selected the criteria to judge targets, the next step is to find prospective targets. The more common ways to locate targets include:

- *Industry contacts.* While hit and miss, targets sometimes are found through personal relationships within the desired industry. This process works better when the desired targets are in the same industry as the acquirer because this increases the number of companies and trade associations with which the acquirer has contacts.
- *Business intermediaries.* Business broker and investment banking firms represent companies available for acquisition as well as acquirers. Providing such firms with the acquirer's criteria informs them that the acquirer is looking and provides guidance as to what is desired. The acquirer should recognize that the use of intermediaries may

generate many inappropriate prospects. It can be expected to result in two types of pressure:

1. The intermediary's fee, or the major portion of the fee, is earned only when a deal occurs; hence, the intermediary's primary objective is to "make a deal happen."

2. Often the intermediary will create a sense of urgency, (i.e., a pressure for the acquirer to act in haste to avoid missing the deal).

Acquirers should resist these pressures, as well as the encouragement to bid a higher price than the analysis of the strategic benefits and synergies of the deal warrants. For nearly all acquirers there is, at any time, an ample number of possible acquisitions. Buyers should not be rushed into offering too much, acting too fast, or feeling the need to do any specific deal.

- *Searching for the right target.* With a well-defined criteria sheet, an acquirer can search for and approach companies to determine their level of interest. This process is more difficult than waiting for intermediaries to identify targets, but it often identifies targets that are not represented by any intermediary. Through this search, exceptional targets may be identified and competitive bidding against other buyers is avoided.

Some business valuation professionals and intermediary firms offer a service to locate and make the initial contact with companies not on the market but that fit your criteria. The advantages of outsourcing include:

- The task becomes a contracted performance with a time line in contrast to something the acquirer will do whenever the time can be found.

- When a valuation firm provides this service, it can use its familiarity with the company and contact with its executives to begin the process of estimating the target's stand-alone market value.

- The contact by the outsourced professional can sidestep the attempts of prospective targets to qualify the acquirer before the acquirer has determined his or her level of interest.

Understandably, targets want to know whether a potential acquirer is a cash buyer or wants management to stay. Early contacts by acquirers lead to the targets asking this type of question at a time when the buyer's focus should be on learning more about that specific target. Appraisers can easily deflect or delay these questions by explaining that at the time they lack the authority to address them.

Step 7: Establish Guidelines on Initial Contact Procedure

A search strategy also should provide guidelines on how contact with a prospect should be initiated, including control of:

- Who in the acquirer has access to this information
- What information about the acquirer may be released
- Strategic goals of the acquirer that can be discussed
- Personnel permitted to participate
- Authority to sign nondisclosure agreements
- Minimum information to request from the target

Many of these information related concerns can be simplified through use of an intermediary, which enhances confidentiality for both parties and frequently speeds the process. In gathering initial information, one option that may be attractive to both the buyer and seller is for the buyer to authorize preparation of a valuation of the target. In return for cooperation with the valuation, the buyer promises to provide the seller with a copy of the appraisal of the company's fair market value on a stand-alone basis. This information helps to educate the current owners on what their company is worth and, more important, why that value is appropriate. Armed with this information, the acquirer also can compute investment value inclusive of anticipated synergies, which enables the acquirer's management to make an informed decision on whether to proceed with negotiations.

Step 8: Establish Procedures to Review the Acquisition Team's Recommendation

Another step to implement in the acquisition process are checks on the negotiating manager's ability to close the deal. Too often acquisition team members, due to their proximity to the transaction, become emotionally involved and lose their objectivity. The company can protect itself from this process by establishing a committee to review acquisition team proposals or by designating a senior manager who must grant approval. This review process is a safeguard to prevent members of the M&A team from personally associating with the transaction and overpaying as a result.

With this acquisition planning strategy in place, the primary challenge is discipline. Rigorously examine each proposal to ensure its fit within the broader corporate strategy, then analyze that target's forecasted risks and net cash flow benefits relative to the price the company must pay to obtain them. Establish in advance of the negotiations the walk-away price where the project is rejected because the risk adjusted returns do not justify the price. Armed with this decision-making process, success in acquisitions is much more likely.

Step 9: Determine Tone of Letter of Intent

The letter of intent represents the parties' preliminary "agreement to agree." In tone and content, it can be either "hard" or "soft"; the latter option is recommended. This soft approach represents a good-faith intent to consider all issues when the letter is executed but to recognize that additional issues may (probably will) emerge that must be subsequently resolved. A soft letter often can be completed in a few drafts over a few weeks. "Hard" letters of intent usually must be much more detailed, require extensive negotiation at a relatively early stage in the purchase/sale process, and can take many revisions and weeks to reach agreement. They often resemble the definitive agreement that defines the final terms of sale.

DUE DILIGENCE PREPARATION

As part of the advance planning, both buyers and sellers should prepare for the inevitable due diligence that must precede any acquisition. Buyers should inform sellers with their letter of intent of the information that they will need. Sellers should begin this preparation in the initial stages of the sale planning process so that all necessary information is conveniently and promptly available for prospective buyers. Preparing for due diligence also will assist sellers to recognize buyers' concerns and issues that sellers must address to make the company as attractive as possible to prospective acquirers. Exhibit 4-6 provides a summary of a typical due diligence request list.

Merger and acquisition activity has been very heavy for middle-market-size companies. Although they receive much less publicity because the buyers and sellers are often privately held, as mentioned, these transactions constitute most of the deal activity in the United States.

In many respects, M&A activity for middle-market companies is not well organized. Many sellers, and to a lesser extent buyers, may be involved in just one transaction in their careers. Their legal, tax, valuation, and intermediary advisors also may possess limited expertise or experience. While some industries are consolidating with heavy M&A activity, in other industries prospective buyers and sellers frequently have difficulty identifying ideal prospects with which to do a deal.

These circumstances combine to emphasize the importance to buyers and sellers of understanding value and what drives it, knowing the market, and recognizing the advantages of advance planning and preparation to achieve successful deals.

Exhibit 4-6   Due Diligence Request List

A. Company Overview
_____ Resumés of key employees and division organization chart including all functional groups
_____ Most recent business plan and strategic planning documents
_____ Copies of published corporate literature and press articles
_____ Employment benefit plans, contracts, and compensation agreements that exist and/or are contemplated
_____ Employee head count (historical and projected)
_____ Copy of articles and by-laws and certificate of incorporation

(continued)

Exhibit 4-6   Due Diligence Request List *(continued)*

B. Ownership

_____ List of stockholders, option and warrant holders, including date of purchase/grant, price, number of shares

_____ Financing history, including shares, price, amount raised, dates

_____ Summary of recent stock option grants, if any, including shares, exercise price, dates

C. Historical and Projected Financial Information

_____ Five years of historical financial statements, by quarter

_____ Breakdown of sales by top 10 customers for the last 5 years

_____ Breakdown of sales by product line, including price and volume detail

_____ Breakdown of operating expenses by product line

_____ Summary of significant accounting policies

_____ Budget and marketing plan for at least one year

_____ Financial projections for at least one year

_____ Breakdown of significant historical and projected capital expenditures

_____ All management letters from auditors (if any), plus management responses (if any)

_____ Receivables aging analysis and bad debt experience

D. Products and Services

_____ Description of products and services

_____ Description of business model, pricing policies, volume projections

_____ Current market share data

_____ List of top suppliers

E. Sales and Marketing

_____ Discussion of sales and distribution by product line

_____ Sales force productivity statistics and sales plan for each department or product line for the most recent year

_____ Advertising and promotion plan and budget

_____ Current marketing materials and sample advertisements

_____ Web site statistics

F. Technology

_____ Description of technology processes

_____ Overview of process and historical and projected expenditures

_____ List and/or description of patents, licenses, copyrights, trade names, proprietary technology

_____ Description of licensed technology from outside parties

G. Other

_____ List of partnerships and affiliations, including any agreements

_____ Copies of bank loan agreements and lease contracts

_____ List of companies previously contacted and any documentation, including draft definitive agreements

_____ Outside legal and accounting team

5

Measuring Synergies

Buyers can destroy substantial value through merger and acquisition (M&A). That's the ugly, risky potential outcome that every buyer must have the discipline to confront continually. Since so much of the allure of M&A centers around synergy, this chapter addresses what it is and how to measure it.

The section "Acquisition Strategy and Process" in Chapter 4 emphasized that a company's acquisition plan should tie closely to the overall strategic plan of the business. At its core, that plan should drive the company to strategies that increase its net cash flow to capital providers and minimize its risk. The typical acquisition is actually a capital budgeting decision where the buyer acquires brands, processes, and technologies as well as tangible assets. Resources are allocated based on the anticipated future returns they are projected to generate, adjusted for the risk profile of the investment.

Acquisitions should be made to increase shareholder value. They may expand the company's products or markets, provide a new technology, increase its efficiency, or raise its growth potential. None of those results, however, should be the ultimate goal. The acquisition should increase shareholder value by reducing the company's risk or increasing its net cash flow to invested capital. This reminder of the company's essential purpose is made because potential acquisitions often create distractions that may cause managers to lose their focus on shareholder value.

To further emphasize this point, consider the return of investment implications when one public company pays a premium to buy another public company. When Buyco pays $90 per share to acquire 100% of Sellco, which had been trading for a market price prior to the acquisition of $60 per share, they are paying $30 per share more—a 50% premium—than what their shareholders would have to pay to acquire the same stock on the open market. Implicit in their acquisition decision is the message to their shareholders that they can create value above this premium through the acquisition. Thus, their decision is based on the assumption that it is in the shareholder's best interest to pay this premium *in advance* based on management's ability to deliver the expected synergies. For shareholders to end up better off in this scenario, management must create substantial returns to justify the premium paid. Success is not impossible, but such lofty goals, in light of investment alternatives, mandate sound acquisition valuation and analysis.

In addition to their focus on shareholder value, executives and board members also must recognize that M&A is usually the company's largest form of discretionary spending. Such a decision often has a greater effect on shareholder value than any other, and few other events in the life of a business can change value so quickly and dramatically. Acquisitions generally commit a company to the selected strategy for a long period of time. As implementation occurs, it becomes increasingly difficult to abandon that commitment, particularly if the market's initial reaction is negative. Finally, because the company has typically paid a premium over fair market value for the acquisition, it often is aiming to achieve difficult synergies, which creates a heightened level of uncertainty about the success of the investment.

SYNERGY MEASUREMENT PROCESS

These risks in M&A are not presented to discourage making acquisitions; rather the point is to impress on buyers the need to fully understand how to evaluate potential acquisitions with value creation as the goal.

Synergy Defined

Achieving synergy begins with a clear understanding of what it is. Defining synergy as "a combination of businesses that makes two plus two equal five" or "the wonderful integration benefits from combined strategies and economies of scale" is imprecise and misleading.

In his book, *The Synergy Trap: How Companies Lose the Acquisition Game,* author Mark L. Sirower provides the following definition and discussion of synergy:

> Synergy is the increase in performance of the combined firm over what the two firms are already expected or required to accomplish as independent firms.
>
> Where acquirers can achieve the performance that is already expected from the target, the net present value (NPV) of an acquisition strategy then is clearly represented by the following formula:
>
> NPV = Synergy − Premium
>
> In management terms, synergy means competing better than anyone ever expected. It means gains in competitive advantage over and above what firms already need to survive in their competitive markets.[1]

Thus, the acquiring and target firms already have built into their stock values investor's expectations of the increase in value that each company can achieve while operating as a stand-alone business. *Synergy is the improvement in excess of these anticipated improvements,* which makes success in the acquisition process a much more elusive goal. And the odds of successful achievement of this goal are generally reduced by the size of the acquisition premium paid. If most of the value-creating potential from the acquisition is paid to the sellers in the form of a premium, little potential value creation exists for the acquiring firm.

This fact raises the related issue of identifying which party, the buyer or the seller, creates the synergies. Typically, the buyer

---

[1] Mark L. Sirower, *The Synergy Trap: How Companies Lose the Acquisition Game* (New York: The Free Press, 1997, 2000), pp. 20, 29.

enables the competitive advantages of the combined enterprise, including revenue enhancements, cost reductions, or technology improvements, over the performance of the individual entities. So the synergy value is usually created by the buyer.

Exceptions do exist. When a target possesses a technology or proprietary process that the buyer can adapt and employ over its larger volume base, this "bounceback" synergy is created primarily by the seller. While the buyer brings the enhanced customer base over which the benefit can be extended, the target creates a benefit and value far beyond what it is worth as a stand-alone entity.

Sources of Synergy

Synergistic benefits generally result from four potential sources:

1. Revenue enhancements
2. Cost reductions
3. Practice improvements
4. Financial economies

Revenue Enhancements

Revenue enhancements may result from higher unit sales, which usually are achieved by the combined entity serving a broader market or offering an expanded product line, or both. Selected price increases also may be achieved, particularly when the combined entity creates strategic advantages, such as being the sole supplier for a technology or product.

Forecasted revenue enhancements should be viewed with caution. They are often dependent on many external variables, particularly customer and competitor response. Both may be difficult to predict, and, to a large extent, they are beyond the control of the combined entity. For example, customers may have a policy that prevents excessive reliance on any one source of supply. Competitor reaction also should be anticipated, including new product offerings and price discounts.

Revenue enhancements can be achieved when the combined company offers a broader line of products or services, often by leveraging the distribution system of the new entity. The expanded or improved product line also may qualify the combined company to compete for business that was not available to either the acquirer or the target operating as stand-alone businesses.

Cost Reductions

Estimates of the second synergy source, cost reductions, tend to be more predictable and reliable than revenue improvements. Through consolidation of functions, positions and related fixed assets and overhead are eliminated. The magnitude of this benefit tends to be larger when the target is similar to the acquirer in operations and markets served.

To succeed with cost reductions, particular attention must be paid in advance to job titles and account classifications. Because these tend to vary among companies, identifying which specific functions can be eliminated becomes more difficult. Salaries and wages, in particular, require vigilance because while positions may be cut, the individuals who held them sometimes survive in the new entity in a different department or job title.

Technology and Process Improvements

Process improvements occur when the combined entity adopts the most efficient or effective practices employed by the target or acquirer. These enhancements frequently result from technological or process improvements that can be leveraged over the broader base of the combined entity. The improvements can create enhanced revenues or cost reductions as well as more efficient operations or more effective marketing and distribution.

Financial Economies

The fourth synergy source, financial economies, is often misunderstood. The target's cost of capital can be reduced through acquisition by a larger company that eliminates many of the risks that exist in the target as a stand-alone business. These financial economies raise the investment value of the target but not its fair market value. The combination also may lower the combined entity's financing costs and may allow for efficiencies in lease terms, cash management, and management of working capital.

The value of a target, however, cannot be enhanced by attributing to it a lower cost of capital through use of more debt financing. Since any acquirer could achieve this benefit, such financial manipulations seldom have genuine value-creating potential.

The combined entity also may create certain tax benefits, such as use of net operating loss carryovers or the ability to incorporate in a jurisdiction that provides favorable tax rates. Acquirers are cautioned, however, to recognize that most financial economies cannot materially improve a company's strategic position and seldom should be the driving force behind a transaction.

KEY VARIABLES IN ASSESSING SYNERGIES

In assessing the potential savings from each of these synergy sources, members of an M&A team should focus relentlessly on three variables that can dramatically influence the accuracy of the estimated synergy and value calculation.

1. *Size of synergy benefit.* The synergy value should be quantified in a forecast of net cash flows that includes estimates of revenues, expenses, financing and tax costs, and investments in working capital and fixed assets. Each component of the forecast, particularly all estimated improvements, must be challenged rigorously. Acquisition team members must resist the natural inclination to buy into the deal emotionally, which so often leads to overly optimistic revenue and expense estimates. Each element in the forecast must be estimated accurately.

2. *Likelihood of achievement.* The business combination will project various benefits, some of which have a very high likelihood of success while others may be long shots. For example, the likelihood that the administrative costs associated with the target's board of directors can be eliminated is about 100%. Conversely, achieving certain sales goals against stiff competition is probably far less definite. These differences must be noted and allowed for in the forecast. Computing the probability of various outcomes, such as optimistic, expected, and pessimistic, or

through a Monte Carlo simulation, helps to quantify the range of possible outcomes. In particular, management should be sensitive to downside projections and their consequences.

3. *Timing of benefits.* The buyer's M&A team must recognize that while the acquisition usually occurs as a single transaction, its benefits accrue over the forecast period that may cover many years. The value of the acquisition and its success are critically tied to achieving the improved cash flows according to the forecasted time schedule. Any delays push cash flows farther into the future and reduce their present value. Temptations to accelerate the timing of revenue enhancements or cost savings must be avoided, with the timing of each assumption challenged just as the amounts are. The history of M&A is littered with stories of how unrealistic acceleration of improvements to enhance the attractiveness of an acquisition led to overestimation of synergy value. The M&A team that succumbs to this pressure is first and foremost fooling itself.

The clear point here is to stress the importance of objectivity and rigorous due diligence in the examination of forecasted synergies. Investors anticipate improvements in the performance of both the acquirer and the target in the values they establish for each company as stand-alone entities. The synergies related to the acquisition must reflect improvements beyond those already anticipated. The value of these synergies must exceed the premium over the acquirer's fair market value in order to create value. Thus, every forecasted synergy must be challenged aggressively in terms of the estimated amount, the likelihood of achievement, and when that benefit will occur. Companies that overlook this process are inviting unpleasant surprises and disappointment in the future.

SYNERGY AND ADVANCED PLANNING

The acquisition planning process described in Chapter 4 emphasized the need to tie the acquisition plan to the company's overall strategic plan. Within this context, each acquisition should be

Exhibit 5-1   Sirower's Cornerstones of Synergy

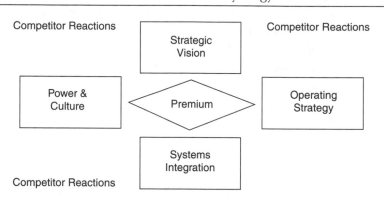
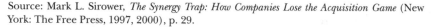

Source: Mark L. Sirower, *The Synergy Trap: How Companies Lose the Acquisition Game* (New York: The Free Press, 1997, 2000), p. 29.

evaluated in light of the likelihood of achieving the forecasted synergies. Mark L. Sirower describes the "Cornerstones of Synergy" as four elements of an acquisition strategy that must be in place to achieve success with synergies. As shown in Exhibit 5-1, lack of any of the four dooms the project, according to Sirower.

Sirower's cornerstones include:

- *Strategic vision.* Represents the goal of the combination, which should be a continuous guide to the operating plan of the acquisition.
- *Operating strategy.* Represents the specific operational steps required to achieve strategic advantages in the combined entity over competitors.
- *Systems integration.* Focuses on the implementation of the acquisition while maintaining preexisting performance targets. For success, these should be planned in considerable detail in advance of the acquisition to achieve the timing of synergy improvements.
- *Power and culture.* With corporate culture changing with the acquisition, the decision-making structure in the combined entity, including procedures for cooperation and conflict

resolution, must be determined and implemented. Success in the integration requires effectiveness throughout the newly combined organization which forces the need for clarity of purpose.

Synergy has acquired almost a mythical reputation in M&A for the rewards that it reputedly provides. Watch out for these rewards. They may indeed be a myth.

Business combinations can provide improvements, but these must be in excess of the improvements that investors already anticipate for the acquirer and target as stand-alone companies. These anticipated stand-alone improvements are the first hurdle that any combination must surpass. When the acquirer pays a premium to the target's shareholders, the present value of any benefits provided by the combination must be reduced by this premium. Thus, the higher the premium paid, the lower are the potential benefits to the acquirer. Acquirers also must recognize that in handing over initial synergy benefits to the seller in the form of the premium payment, they have left themselves the challenge of achieving the remaining synergies, which are often the most difficult.

Synergies must not be mythical. They must be harshly contested, accurately forecasted, and appropriately discounted net cash flows that reflect their probability of success under carefully constructed and reviewed time schedules.

6

Valuation Approaches and Fundamentals

Accurate valuation requires appropriate application of the available approaches to determine value, a clear understanding of the exact investment in a business that is being sold or acquired, and a clear measure of the returns that the company generates. Therefore, to enhance precision in the valuation process, this chapter introduces: (1) The three valuation approaches, (2) The invested capital model to quantify the investment in the business to be valued, (3) The net cash flow to most accurately measure the company's return to capital providers, (4) The adjustments to the company's financial statements to most accurately portray economic performance, (5) The mathematical techniques to manage investment risk.

BUSINESS VALUATION APPROACHES

Businesses vary in the nature of their operations, the markets they serve, and the assets they own. For this reason, the body of business valuation knowledge has established three primary approaches by which businesses may be appraised, as illustrated in Exhibit 6-1.

Within each of the approaches, there are methods that may be applied in various procedures. For example, we may use a

Exhibit 6-1   Business Valuation Approaches

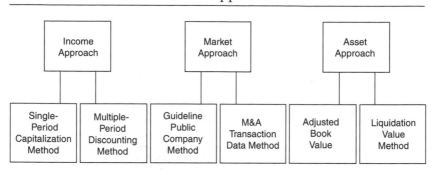

discounted cash flow procedure within the multiple-period discounting method within the income approach.

The income approach is described in Chapter 7, with Chapters 8 and 9 devoted to development of appropriate rates of return within that approach. Chapters 10 and 11 introduce the market approach and asset approach. Business valuation theory requires that the appraiser attempt to use each of the three approaches in every appraisal assignment, although doing so is not always practical. For example, a company may lack a positive return to discount or capitalize, which may prevent use of the income approach. Use of the market approach may not be possible because of the lack of similar companies for comparison. The asset approach, in the absence of the use of the excess earnings method (which is generally not employed for merger and acquisition appraisals), cannot accurately portray general intangible or goodwill value that is not shown at market value on a company's balance sheet. Thus, each of the approaches bring constraints that may limit its use or effectiveness in a specific appraisal assignment. It is even more important, however, to recognize that each approach brings a unique focus on value and what drives it. While the income approach most often looks at future returns discounted to reflect their relative level of risk, the market approach establishes value based on the price paid for alternative investments, while the asset approach establishes value based on a hypothetical sale of the company's underlying assets. The strengths and weaknesses of each methodology, the nature of the appraisal assignment, and the circumstances present in the company being appraised and the industry in which it operates determine which of the approaches can be used and the relative reliability of the results from application of that approach. How to evaluate these results is discussed in Chapter 13, and Exhibit 13-1 provides a summary of the circumstances in which each approach is generally most applicable.

In providing this overview of the approaches to business valuation for merger and acquisition, this discussion assumes, unless stated to the contrary, that the business being appraised is a viable, going concern. Those companies intending to liquidate or that are in long-term decline may require different assumptions and valuation procedures.

USING THE INVESTED CAPITAL MODEL TO DEFINE THE INVESTMENT BEING APPRAISED

For merger and acquisition, the investment in the company is generally defined as the *invested capital* of the business, which is the sum of its interest-bearing debt and equity. This quantity is computed in Exhibit 6-2.

Subtracting the payables from the current assets yields the company's net working capital. Nonoperating assets are also removed, with a corresponding decrease in owner's equity. This leaves the net operating assets that are used in the business and the interest-bearing debt and equity—the invested capital—that is used to finance them.

Keep in mind that all of the company's general intangible characteristics, including employees, customers, and technology, will be included in the calculation of the value of invested capital. Invested capital is also referred to as the enterprise value of the company on an operating basis because the whole business—including the net operating tangible and intangible assets—is being appraised. A major reason why invested capital, rather than just equity, is valued for merger and acquisition is to prevent potential distortions that could be caused by variations in the company's

Exhibit 6-2   Computation of Invested Capital

Balance Sheet	
Assets	*Liabilities*
(Nonoperating assets excluded)	Payables Interest-Bearing Debt *Equity*
Total Operating Assets*	Total Liabilities and Equity*
Less: Payables	*Less:* Payables
Net Operating Assets	Invested Capital

* All operating assets and liabilities should be adjusted to market value.

capital structure. Invested capital is frequently referred to as a *debt-free model* because it portrays the business before the relative levels of debt and equity are determined. The objective is to compute the value of the company before considering how operations are financed with debt or equity. Each buyer may choose to finance the company in a different way. This choice, however, should not affect the value of the business. Its operations should have the same value regardless of how they are financed. Also note that any debt related to the acquisition is excluded from invested capital because the value should not be distorted by financing choices.

Since the invested capital model portrays the company on a predebt basis, the company's returns—income or cash flow—must be calculated before debt, and its cost of capital or operating multiples must consider both debt and equity financing sources. These points will be described in Chapters 9, 10, and 11 after further discussion on returns and rates of return.

WHY NET CASH FLOW MEASURES VALUE MOST ACCURATELY

As we discussed in the first two chapters, value creation in a business ultimately can be defined as the risk adjusted net cash flow that is made available to the providers of capital. Whether the company's stock price increases as a result of a new technology, an improved product line, more efficient operations, or a similar reason, all of these will produce increased cash to capital providers. Thus, value inevitably can be traced to cash flow, which is why in the context of valuation a commonly used phrase is "Cash is king." Investors and managers are used to seeing a company's performance expressed as some level of earnings—before or after interest or taxes. The first difficulty with earnings, of course, is that it does not represent the amount that can be spent. As such, earnings frequently fail to show the true amount that is available to capital providers. For example, a company may have an impressive earnings before interest and taxes (EBIT), but if most or all of this is consumed in interest, taxes, or reinvestments into the company for the working capital or capital expenditures needed to fund anticipated operations, there may be no cash return available for capital providers.

For closely held companies, earnings often are presented as net income before or after taxes. Because this is a return to equity—after interest expense has been recognized—it reflects the present owner's preferences for relative levels of debt versus equity financing. Buyers want an accurate picture of the true operating performance of the company prior to the influence of financing, so returns to invested capital rather than equity should be presented.

Computation of Net Cash Flow to Invested Capital

Because financial statements usually are prepared in compliance with generally accepted accounting principles (GAAP) for reporting to external parties, net cash flow to invested capital (NCF_{IC}) does not appear anywhere in the statements, including the statement of cash flows. It can, however, easily be computed, as Exhibit 6-3 illustrates.

In reviewing this computation, the benefits of net cash flow become more apparent. It represents the amount that can be removed from the business without impairing its future operations because all of the company's internal needs have been taken into consideration. This is why net cash flow is frequently referred to as "free cash flow."

NCF_{IC} is the only return that accurately portrays the company's true wealth-creating capacity. It reveals the company's

Exhibit 6-3   Net Cash Flow to Invested Capital

Math Symbol	Component
	Net income after taxes
+	Interest expense, net of income tax (interest expense $\times$ [1−t])
=	Net income to invested capital
+	Noncash charges against revenues (e.g., depreciation and amortization)[a]
−	Capital expenditures (fixed assets and other operating noncurrent assets)[a]
+ or −	Changes in working capital[a,b]
+	Dividends paid on preferred shares or other senior securities, if any[c]
=	Net cash flow to invested capital

[a] In a forecast, these amounts should be at levels necessary to support anticipated future operations, not simply averages or actual amounts from the past or next year's expected amounts.

[b] Remember that the invested capital model is "as if debt free," so any interest-bearing debt in the current liabilities should be removed. Generally speaking, doing so will reduce the dollar amount of the growth in working capital.

[c] In most appraisals this item is zero because usually there are no preferred or other senior dividend-receiving classes of securities.

return before principal and interest on debt to prevent distortions that could be caused by different borrowing levels. It is a measure of cash flow rather than earnings because investors can spend only cash, not earnings. NCF_{IC} is the net return after taxes and also after providing for the company's internal need for capital expenditures and working capital. Thus, it represents the true cash flow available to providers of debt and equity capital, after payment of taxes and the company's internal reinvestment requirements.

As will be explained further in Chapter 7, the company's net cash flow can be forecasted in discretely identified future years or for a long-term period. In computing the net cash flow for the long-term or terminal period, specific relationships between components in the net cash flow computation almost always should be maintained. Capital expenditures should exceed the depreciation write-off of prior period capital expenditures to reflect inflation and growth. Similarly, the change in working capital should cause a decrease in net cash flow, because the cash outflow required to fund increases in accounts receivable and inventory should exceed the cash inflow provided by increases in accounts payable and accrued payables.

FREQUENT NEED TO NEGOTIATE FROM EARNINGS MEASURES

The M&A market, particularly for middle-market and smaller businesses, is seldom well organized. As mentioned earlier, many participants are involved in only one transaction during their entire career, and most advisors—accountants, attorneys, and bankers—seldom encounter such transactions. The lack of an organized market and inexperienced participants often leaves sellers hunting for potential buyers and buyers searching through contacts and industry associations or mailing lists for potential companies in which to invest.

In this environment, expectations are often unrealistic and misinformation abounds as participants look for shortcuts or simple formulas to compute value quickly and conveniently. Values based on multiples of EBIT or earnings before interest, taxes, depreciation, and amortization (EBITDA) usually fill the resulting void. Sellers, in particular, like these measures because they produce relatively high return numbers that look and sound impressive. The problem, of course, is that these are not real returns because income taxes and the company's internal reinvestment needs have not yet been paid. That is, neither EBITDA nor EBIT represents cash that could be available to capital providers.

So how does either party—a seller who wants to know what a company is really worth, regardless of negotiating strategy, or a buyer negotiating with a seller who is quoting such numbers— handle the likely confusion that will be present? The key is to consistently make all value computations using net cash flow to invested capital. With this process the party will be employing the true return available to capital providers along with the most accurate and reliable rates of return. When sellers or their intermediaries quote unsubstantiated EBIT or EBITDA multiples, buyers must demand an explanation of how the multiples were determined. The informed participant, whether buyer, seller, or intermediary, generally will recognize the lack of justification for unrealistic multiples and, more important, be able to explain why they do not accurately reflect value.

Among the most common ways that EBIT or EBITDA multiples distort value include:

- *Inaccurate return*—the computation of EBIT or EBITDA is unrealistic in comparison to historical or future performance, considering likely industry and economic conditions.

- *Confusion of strategic value with fair market value*—investment bankers or brokers may quote an EBIT multiple that was derived from one or a few transactions where the buyer paid a particularly high price. Unusual synergies unique to that transaction may have justified that multiple, but it seldom represents "the market," particularly where such synergies are not available to other buyers.

- *Inappropriate guideline company*—selection of multiples from public companies that are much larger or industry leaders that are not sufficiently similar to the target company for an appropriate comparison.

- *Inappropriate date*—selection of multiples from a transaction that is not close to the appraisal date and that may reflect different economic or industry conditions. Similar distortions can occur by mixing returns and multiples—for example, deriving a multiple for net income and applying it to EBIT.

- *Choice of average multiple*—indiscriminately using the mean or median multiple derived from a group of companies when the target company may vary substantially from the average of that group.

The solution: When savvy investors find they must negotiate from earnings multiples, they determine value using NCF_{IC} and then express that value as a multiple of EBIT or whatever other measure of return the other party prefers to use in the negotiating process.

The second compelling reason to choose net cash flow rather than a measure of earnings results from the choices available in developing a rate of return. This rate, or its inverse, a multiple, is applied to the return in a discounting, capitalization, or multiplication process to compute value. The reliability of the value determined is clearly dependent on the accuracy and dependability of the two primary variables in the equation, the return and the rate of return or multiple. The public markets provide the basis for highly reliable, long-, intermediate-, and short-term rates of return on net cash flow based on many years of historical experience. In the U.S. market, this data dates back to 1926 and reflects actual cash returns that creditors and investors have received and the resulting rates of return that have been earned on their investments. These rates reflect buyers' *prospective* choices—that is, the *current* prices paid for the anticipated *future* net cash flow returns on investment. This data provides appraisers with an excellent perspective on investors' risk versus return expectations and an accurate indication of their required rates of return on investments with varying levels of risk.

It is important to emphasize that no similar historical rate of return data is available on the other return measures that are frequently reported, including EBITDA, EBIT, net income before taxes, and net income after taxes. None of these measures reflects net cash returns that actually could be available to shareholders. And all are merely measures of historical performance with no investment amount attached to them. As such, there is no way to tie these historical results to prices that investors paid for the anticipated future return on those investments. Chapter 8 illustrates potential errors and distortions from use of historical rates.

FINANCIAL STATEMENT ADJUSTMENTS

Adjustments to a target's financial statements, commonly referred to as normalization adjustments, convert the reported accounting information to amounts that show the true economic performance, financial position, and cash flow of the company. Differences between amounts shown on the financial statements and market values most commonly result from one or more of the following causes:

- Elections to minimize taxes, including excess compensation, perquisites, rent, or other above-market payments made to owners or other related parties
- Adjustments required to change the basis of accounting, including conversion from cash to accrual or from one inventory or depreciation method to another
- Adjustments for nonoperating and/or nonrecurring items, including asset surpluses or shortages, personal assets carried on the company's balance sheet, or personal expenses paid by the business, and items of income or expense that are not part of ongoing operations
- Differences between the market value of assets and the amounts at which they are carried on the company's books

The significance of many of these normalization adjustments is greater in the valuation of smaller companies. Midsize or larger businesses may have characteristics that require adjustment, but the effect may be immaterial. For example, $100,000 of above-market compensation could result in a significant change in value to a company with $1 million of annual sales, but it may be immaterial to a business with sales of $50 million. Smaller companies also more frequently have financial statements that have been compiled or reviewed, rather than audited, or use the cash rather than the accrual basis of accounting. Thus, smaller companies frequently require more adjustments and the relative impact of the adjustments tends to be greater.

Adjustments can be made to both the income statement and the balance sheet, or one can be adjusted without a corresponding change to the other. For example, a nonrecurring gain or loss can be removed from the income statement without any required adjustment to the balance sheet.

Most often in merger and acquisition the buyer is acquiring a controlling interest in the target. This gives the buyer the authority to control and, if desired, manipulate the company's income. Minority owners, however, generally lack the authority of control. For this reason, the first category of adjustments listed above is referred to as the "control adjustments" and generally should be made only when a controlling interest in a company is being appraised. Typical control adjustments include:

- Above- or below-market compensation, in any form, paid to controlling shareholders
- Above- or below-rent paid on real estate or equipment owned by the controlling shareholder and leased to the company
- Related or favored parties on the payroll who are paid above or below market compensation
- Assets such as automobiles, airplanes, condos, memberships, and so on that are owned and/or paid for by the business for the benefit of controlling shareholders but that would not need to be provided to an arm's length employee hired to provide the same services
- Insurance premiums for policies on which the corporation is not the beneficiary
- Above- or below-market-rate loans to and from the corporation to controlling shareholders

In those less common M&A valuation circumstances where the target is a minority equity interest, the decision not to make control adjustments to income may result in a very low or zero value for that minority interest. This low value often reflects the disadvantages of the minority owner versus that of the control owner. (The value of the minority interest can be increased by provisions in a shareholder agreement that restrict the majority owner's access to the company's cash flow.) Alternatively, the return to the controlling shareholder can be used after control adjustments and then a minority interest discount can be applied to the resulting value. Doing this is not recommended and frequently distorts value because the minority interest discount may not reflect the magnitude of that particular company's minority versus control income difference. These adjustment points are discussed further in Chapters 11 and 12.

Adjustments to the Balance Sheet

Adjustments to the balance sheet primarily reflect the need to convert assets from book value to market value. In the context of the going concern enterprise, market value is usually the value of the asset "in place in use" as opposed to either the historical cost and depreciation-based book value or value in contemplation of a liquidation. Asset surpluses or shortages also must be considered; industry norms often are used to determine the desired balance. Nonoperating assets, such as airplanes or condominiums for the owner's personal benefit or real estate not used in the company's operations, should be removed from the balance sheet, with the net effect of these changes charged to an equity account, most typically retained earnings. When real property used by the business is owned by related parties, the rent paid should be compared to market rates to determine if adjustments to income are required. Whether these assets will be included in a sale also should be considered.

Specific adjustments to balance sheet accounts are listed and explained in detail in Chapter 11.

Adjustments to the Income Statement

Adjustments are made to the income statement to convert the company's reported financial performance to its true economic performance. Buyers typically purchase a business to obtain the company's future returns. These returns usually are portrayed in a forecast when the acquisition is under consideration so buyers can assess the company's historic performance and, more importantly, its future. The forecast frequently requires the following income statement adjustments:

- *Nonrecurring revenue or expense items.* One-time revenue or income sources, such as a gain on a sale of assets, insurance proceeds, a large sale to a customer under circumstances that are not expected to recur, or a gain from a property condemnation should be subtracted from the company's income because they do not reflect the ongoing profitability of the business.

- *Nonrecurring expense or loss items.* Expenses not expected to recur, such as losses on sale of assets, moving expenses, restructuring costs, or other one-time charges that do not reflect the company's ongoing performance should be added back to income.

- *Nonoperating items of income or expense.* Interest or dividend income beyond amounts earned on transactional-level cash balances, rental income on assets not used in the business, and nonoperating expenses such as charitable donations or expenses for activities that are not part of the company's core business should be added or subtracted from income.

- *Owner perquisites.* Payments made by the company to shareholders or other parties favored by them in the form of salaries, bonuses, and fringe benefits of any kind that are above or below market rates should be adjusted to market levels. When such individuals are paid a market-rate compensation but fail to provide adequate service that is required by the company's operations, no adjustment should be made if the buyer anticipates replacing that person with a competent substitute.

Adjustments to the target's historical income statements are made to allow more accurate interpretation of historical performance and also to help to identify any inappropriate items that may be included in a forecast. These adjustments should be considered in both the income and the market approaches in choosing the return stream used to compute the company's value.

MANAGING INVESTMENT RISK IN MERGER AND ACQUISITION

Much of Chapters 8 and 9 are devoted to deriving discount rates that accurately reflect the risk associated with a specific investment. Based on the underlying theory of the Capital Asset Pricing Model, these techniques allow business appraisers to determine an appropriate rate of return for an investment given general economic, industry, and specific company conditions. While these techniques are clearly the most accurate in assessing the cost of capital for a business and gauging general company and market risk, additional risk analysis tools are available. M&A investment decisions, with appropriate computation of rates of return, constitute a variation of capital budgeting analysis to which more advanced statistical techniques can be employed to further inform management of the possible outcomes from an investment decision.

Traditional Statistical Tools

Business valuation techniques assess company and market risk. For example, the data cited later in this book develop discount rates based on the probability-weighted statistical expected value for each increment of return. In addition, various traditional statistical parameters are used in evaluating investment risk, including:

- *Expected value*—is a weighted average of the forecasted returns with the weights being the probabilities of occurrence.

- *Variance and standard deviation*—variance is a standard statistical measure of the variation of the distribution around its mean. The standard deviation is the square root of the variance. It is the conventional measure of the dispersion or the "tightness" of a probability distribution. The tighter the distribution, the lower this measure will be, and the wider the distribution, the higher it will be. In the normal bell shaped distribution, approximately 68% of the total area of the distribution falls within one standard deviation on either side of the mean. From this we conclude that there is only a 32% chance that the actual outcome will be more than one standard deviation from the mean. Similarly, the probability that the outcome will fall within two standard deviations of the mean is approximately 95% and the probability that it will fall within three standard deviations is over 99%.

- *Coefficient of variation*—is a statistical measure of the relative dispersion of a distribution. It is computed as the ratio of the standard deviation of a distribution to the expected value of the distribution and measures the risk per unit of expected value.

An effective method for evaluating uncertainty is the *decision tree*, so-called because the resulting chart resembles a tree with its trunk on the left and it branches extending toward the right. Each "fork" in the decision tree represents an event or a decision from which two or more outcomes are possible. By assigning a probability of occurrence to each branch, an expected value can then be calculated for each terminal branch of the tree.

Monte Carlo Simulation

While traditional statistical techniques frequently accompany M&A decisions, Monte Carlo simulation (MCS) is sometimes appropriate. In a merger or acquisition analysis, value is usually a "best estimate" single valuation, similar to budgeting for routine business decisions. (A range of values can also be determined, but this is not often seen in valuations for M&A.) Typically a spreadsheet analysis can demonstrate how the value would change if various inputs would change. The valuation reflects the best judgment for each of the inputs; however, it may also be useful to consider the following questions to supplement the valuation results:

- The valuation result is the best estimate available, but how likely is it that the target company is worth more than the investment value? In other words, if we base our decision on that value, what is the chance of success? How much would we have to reduce the price to yield, say, an 80% chance of success?
- How much plus/minus variation from the traditional value is realistically possible?
- Which variables or decisions in this analysis create most of the risk? And which create most of the opportunity? Of those that are controllable, how much can we reduce the risk and increase the opportunity by taking preemptive action?
- In a friendly acquisition, how can we use the data derived from our risk analysis to negotiate a better deal?

MCS is a statistical technique that can be used to assess the uncertainties inherent in a forecast. While decision trees are useful for assessing uncertainties and problems that have a limited number of decisions and alternatives, MCS may be helpful when the number of decisions are much more numerous. MCS originated in the field of nuclear physics and derived its name because it employs techniques similar to those used in games of chance.

The MCS process involves these steps:

- Identify the problem's critical elements—those variables that can cause significant swings in the valuation

- Quantify the uncertainty associated with each variable through a probabilistic approach
- Develop a model to describe the relations among the elements

The results of the model are then used to assess the potential for achieving various results, such as estimated synergies or operational targets, as well as to identify areas of risk and opportunity. While MCS may provide answers to important questions, it requires substantial training and experience to apply correctly. And the reliability of its results is heavily dependent on the ability to accurately quantify the uncertainty of key variables, so the results must be carefully assessed.

Real Option Analysis

Traditional capital budgeting techniques require that uncertainties related to an investment be identified and quantified in advance. Because of the long-term and speculative nature of M&A investments, however, the company may encounter continually changing conditions, including variations in the project's risk profile or the emergence of new information. When an investment involves substantial uncertainty, whether in markets, technology, or competition, and there is a likelihood of continually evolving new information and changing competitive conditions, management may need decision tools that allow them to react as conditions change. The use of *real options* allows management to account for uncertainty as it gradually emerges over the life of an investment by valuing business strategies as chains of options or a series of decisions. *Real option analysis (ROA)* ties computation of the value of an investment to the expected way it will be managed in the future, with this future decision process guided by continual knowledge of the investment's value as it varies over time.

Investors and managers may encounter scenarios where traditional valuation methodologies generate inadequate or negative returns and values. Most commonly, these returns accompany substantial future uncertainty, which leads owners and managers to conclude they should not fully commit to an investment. While that investment may offer potential for attractive returns, rapidly changing market conditions, technical developments, and similar uncertainties render the returns too unlikely (too much of a long shot) to merit a full investment at the present time.

Traditional valuation methods, such as the multiple period discounting method, rely on forecasted investments and returns over a discrete number of periods, discounted at a fixed cost of capital. In the real world, management could react to new information or changing market conditions as they occur. Recognizing new strategic advantages and disadvantages, they would alter their strategy. Traditional valuation models that reflect circumstances and facts known at the outset of a potential investment cannot reflect this *management flexibility* to change course over time. The traditional model would generate an inadequate or negative value that concludes the forecasted benefits are inadequate given the investment risk.

Real options, which view the investment as a series of choices rather than a single decision, are based on the financial options that are routinely traded in public stock markets. Financial option theory, primarily the Black-Scholes Option Model,[1] was developed to determine the equilibrium value of a stock option. These options *give the holder the right, but not the obligation,* to make a purchase at an agreed on price before an agreed on future date. Thus with the option, the investor has purchased the opportunity to share in the upside potential of an investment's performance while limiting the downside risk. Investors will only choose to exercise the option after considering future information that was unavailable at the time of the investment. If unfavorable conditions exist at the future date, the option is not exercised and the option cost is forfeited.

Quite logically, ROA was initially adopted in industries where very large investments were required, payoffs occurred over many years, and the likelihood of failure in any specific project was high. These conditions exist in oil and gas exploration as well as mining, where most initial searches do not result in a positive return. Similar conditions exist in sectors of the pharmaceutical industry, where the likelihood of success at the outset of a research and development effort is quite low.

In some circumstances, this real option risk management methodology may serve as a strategic investment tool to assist in

---

[1] Fischer Black and Myron Scholes, "Pricing of Options and Corporate Liabilities," *Journal of Political Economy* 81 (May–June 1973), pp. 637–654.

analyzing M&A targets or investments in start-up companies or research and development.

As with the use of MCS, ROA option analysis only works effectively in selected circumstances and requires substantial knowledge and experience for proper application. ROA may offer benefits in the following situations, each of which should first be evaluated using the traditional techniques:

- Substantial uncertainty exists
- Required investments are large and frequently commit the company to a course of action that is difficult or expensive to reverse
- There is a high likelihood that new information or competitive conditions will emerge from which management could increase value by changing strategy
- Most of the investment benefits will be derived from future rather than current returns

Since these criteria exist in many if not most M&A investments, ROA is most often used to evaluate start ups or acquisitions that may substantially change the manner in which the acquirer or target conduct their operations. In these circumstances, most of the value resides in the future direction of these companies and their growth potential rather than their ongoing operations. Similarly, initial investments in research and development are often made on a "platform" basis, not to achieve an immediate return, but to create the opportunity to make follow on investments or develop new product options as further information emerges. In each of these cases, the value tends to center on the company's future rather than current products and operations.

Investment in a real option typically involves the acquisition of a package of rights to a license, patent, or similar benefit. This investment usually constitutes a smaller initial outlay, but allows management to be proactive to favorably influence the value of their option. That is, investors who have made a relatively small initial outlay can then take steps to influence the return on an investment, its risk profile, its holding period, or its value during that period, all of which affect the value of their real option. This methodology recognizes and quantifies this management flexibility by identifying the key factors that affect value and risk over time. The real option provides its holder with the opportunity to react to uncertainties as they unfold by either exercising the option or declining to do so. In the process, management can proactively decide to:

- invest further
- expand operations or markets
- increase uncertainty through, for example, an investment in a new market
- change the return on an investment through variations in revenues or expenses
- extend the option period
- sell and withdraw from the investment entirely
- do nothing

With the financial option, the key variables in the Black-Scholes Option Method that effect value are:

- time to expiration
- risk-free interest rate
- exercise price
- stock price
- uncertainty of stock price movements
- dividends

These same criteria can be applied to real options in M&A or similar investment decisions with slight variations in the economic variables. For example, the exercise price is comparable to the present value of the committed operating costs of the project while the stock price is the equivalent of the present value of the expected returns from the project. Similarly, dividends are analogous to the payout or decline in the value of the investment during the holding period.

So, management could attempt to improve its strategic position and create value by influencing one or more of the real option variables. For example, they could try to extend the level or duration of regulatory barriers or invest in additional technology during the expiration period. They could also affect the exercise price or stock price by changing the company's cost structure to effect its revenues, expenses, and ultimately cash flow. In many new and emerging markets, management can actually encourage competitor investment and innovation to speed the development of new markets, products, or customers, or invest further to create additional hurdles for competitors. Thus with real option investments, greater uncertainty can actually *increase* the value of an option. With the option providing the ability but not the obligation to exercise, increased uncertainty may bring with it additional opportunities that are not yet well enough defined for an investment decision. The option provides the flexibility to management to wait for further information after which it can either exercise the option at what appears to be the optimum time or decline to exercise at all. Thus, real option analysis captures and quantifies the investor's ability to pay an upfront fee to acquire the flexibility or right to make an additional future investment at a price defined today, but only after analyzing future information that may make the investment more or less attractive.

While traditional valuation theory can be highly accurate and effective in assessing company and market risk, some M&A decisions may be clarified through use of additional analytical tools. *MCS and ROA, however, require expertise and experience for proper application.*

Accurate business valuation requires precision in measuring both the investment and the return on investment. In M&A, invested capital is most often the quantity being valued, and net cash flow provides the most accurate indication of the company's performance. To make sure that the company's financial statements accurately portray the company, normalization adjustments may have to be made to the income statement or the balance sheet to eliminate the effects of nonoperating and nonrecurring items or nonmarket base compensation to shareholders.

Risk management techniques are also available for use in valuation for M&A. Most commonly these involve traditional statistical parameters that include expected value, variance, standard deviation, coefficient of variation, and decision trees. Where substantial risk exists and specific variables can be accurately quantified, MCS and ROA, when properly applied, may provide managers with additional information for decision making.

7

Income Approach: Using Rates and Returns to Establish Value

The theory of the income approach is compelling: The value of an investment is computed as the present value of future benefits discounted at a rate of return that reflects the riskiness of the investment. That makes great sense and applies to almost any operating business that generates a positive return.

Successful application of the income approach is more difficult, of course, because each of the key determinants of value—the return and rate of return—must be estimated. In the process of making these estimates, the analyst should carefully analyze the key variables, including prices, volume, and expenses that affect the return, and the risks that each carries. Investments made without the rigor and detail of this process are frequently those that overlook major costs or risks, or carry assumptions that are unrealistic and would not have withstood careful investigation.

WHY VALUES FOR MERGER AND ACQUISITION SHOULD BE DRIVEN BY THE INCOME APPROACH

The income approach is employed much more often to compute value for merger and acquisition than either the market or asset approaches. The acquirer is investing now to get future net cash flows that are uncertain, that is, carry risks, and the income approach conveniently quantifies these key determinants of value.

Conversely, the market approach usually employs price to earnings or similar multiples of a return of the latest historical period rather than an estimate of the future. Market multiples also tend to be less precise than the accuracy that can be achieved through the income approach with forecasted returns and a discount rate. For example, a price-to-earnings (P/E) or earnings before interest and taxes (EBIT) multiple that is applied to a single year's earnings cannot accurately reflect anticipated variations in those earnings over future years. When properly employed, multiples reflect general investor preferences and are often quoted by industry sources or sellers. Analysts should understand them and compare their results to the primary conclusion, which should be calculated through the income approach.

As discussed in more detail in Chapter 4, acquisition analysis should be an integral component of the company's overall strategic plan, which is supported by a budget and forecasted financial statements. Just as the budget forces managers to quantify and defend the financial consequences of their plan, the forecasts and underlying assumptions employed in the income approach to determine value require the same analysis and defense. Whether acquisition benefits arise from revenue enhancement, cost reductions, process improvements, or lower capital costs, the income approach will quantify the assumption and allow it to be debated and evaluated. The income approach also clearly quantifies the timing of these anticipated benefits and reflects how value declines as benefits are pushed farther into the future.

This approach also allows buyers and sellers to compute a company's stand-alone fair market value and its investment value to one or more strategic buyers. With this distinction clearly portrayed, buyers and sellers can easily see synergistic benefits and make informed decisions.

Merger and acquisition valuations may include application of probability or real option analysis. Each of these analysis can be conveniently incorporated into the forecast structure used in the income approach. The forecast also can easily be modified or updated as circumstances change, and forecasts provide an excellent budget that encourages postinvestment analysis and control.

When studying the income approach, the following question inevitably arises: Does the value determined by the income approach include the value of the tangible assets owned in the business, and if so, how?

The values determined by the income approach and the market approach *do* include the value of all tangible and intangible assets employed in the operation of the business. The business uses these assets to generate its return and could not produce that return if these operating assets were not available. Therefore, the value determined by the income and market approaches includes the value of the tangible and intangible operating assets owned by the business.

If the business owns excess operating assets or nonoperating assets, these assets can be valued separately, and this value can be added to operating value to determine the value of the whole enterprise. This process is discussed in Chapter 11.

TWO METHODS WITHIN THE INCOME APPROACH

Although this discussion of the income approach has assumed use of a multiple-year forecast, a forecast of only one year also can be used. This difference in the number of years—one versus multiple—creates the distinction between the two primary methods within the income approach.

Single-Period Capitalization Method

The first and simpler method involves the capitalization of the return for a company for one year, which is why it is called the *single-period capitalization method* (SPCM). Since this method involves computing value based on the return of only one year, it can produce a reliable value only if the return chosen is representative of the company's anticipated long-term future performance. Therefore, analysts should not automatically use the return for the latest historical year or an average of recent years if these are not an accurate indication of the future. The rate of growth in the single-period return is computed through the capitalization. This mathematical process requires a second critical assumption: that the return will grow approximately at the selected annual rate to infinity.

The formula for the SPCM is:

$$PV = \frac{r_0\,(1 + g)}{d - g}$$

where:

PV $=$ Present value

r $=$ Historical or current-year return used as a base return, without the next year's growth

g $=$ Proxy for long-term sustainable growth

d $=$ Discount rate

d−g $=$ Capitalization rate

The key variables in this formula, r, g, and d, will be discussed in detail in Chapter 8. At this point, recognize that the discount rate reflects the riskiness of the investment while the long-term growth rate reflects how the return is expected to grow annually to infinity. Thus, the capitalization rate, computed as d− g, is derived from the discount rate as a function of these two factors. Capitalization rates also can be expressed as a multiplier or multiple by dividing 1 by the capitalization rate. Capitalization rates can be derived from stock market prices in the market approach (which will be explained and illustrated later). This source for these rates is not recommended, however, because of the volatility of market multiples and the stronger reliability of capitalization rates derived from discount rates. Exhibit 7-1 illustrates these relationships and shows how variations in the capitalization rate affect value and the related size of the multiplier.

As with many simple formulas, users must understand the underlying assumptions or they may substantially distort value. The formula can employ a historical, current, or forecasted return, and frequently the forecasted return is computed as shown in the exhibit by

Exhibit 7-1   Illustration of Capitalization Computations

To Calculate Value:

$\dfrac{\$ \text{Return}}{\text{Capitalization Rate}}$	=	$ Value
$\dfrac{\$1,500,000}{15\%}$	=	$10,000,000

To Convert a Capitalization Rate to a Multiplier:

$\dfrac{1}{\text{Capitalization Rate}}$	=	Multiplier
$\dfrac{1}{15\%}$	=	6.67 times

Effect of Different Capitalization Rates on Value:

			Multiplier
$\dfrac{\$1,500,000}{30\%}$	=	$5,000,000	3.33
$\dfrac{\$1,500,000}{20\%}$	=	$7,500,000	5.00
$\dfrac{\$1,500,000}{10\%}$	=	$15,000,000	10.00
$\dfrac{\$1,500,000}{8\%}$	=	$18,750,000	12.50
$\dfrac{\$1,500,000}{5\%}$	=	$30,000,000	20.00

multiplying the latest period's return by $1 + g$, the anticipated long-term growth rate.

The SPCM is simple and convenient, so it is used often as a way to determine an initial indication of value. It also must be recognized that the cap rate can be the reciprocal of the well-known price earnings multiple when historical earnings is the return stream chosen.

The key to proper application of the SPCM is to never lose sight of the critical assumptions that underlie this method. The less real-

Which return on investment would you prefer, 20% or 40%?

The choice may depend on the definitions of "return" and "investment." Return is the benefit to the investor and is usually some measure of income or cash flow. Investment generally is common stock equity, invested capital, specific assets, or another security, such as preferred stock or a stock option. To avoid error, the return must be matched correctly with the rate of return as shown in the sidebar.

Watch out for distortions. For example, using the single-period capitalization calculation and the 20% equity cap rate below, $10,000,000/20% yields a $50,000,000 equity value, while $12,000,000/20% yields a $60,000,000 equity value, and $20,000,000/20% yields a $100,000,000 equity value. The $50,000,000 equity value is the only correct choice. The other values result from matching a capitalization rate of return that applies to net cash flow with different returns. Remember, it is imperative to match the return with the correct rate of return.

Using Rates of Return to Compute Equity Value

Return on Equity	Amount	Equity Value
Net income before taxes	$20,000,000	$20,000,000/40% = $50,000,000
Net income after taxes	$12,000,000	$12,000,000/24% = $50,000,000
Net cash flow to equity	$10,000,000	$10,000,000/20% = $50,000,000

istic these assumptions are for a particular company, the less reliable will be the results of the SPCM. The return employed in the computation—the numerator—must be a realistic measure of the company's long-term sustainable performance. Also, the growth rate, g, must be a realistic expectation of that company's ability to achieve annual growth in that return to infinity. Where material variations in annual growth are likely, the SPCM becomes less accurate and can substantially distort value.

Multiple-Period Discounting Method

An alternative to the simplicity of the SPCM is the *multiple-period discounting method* (MPDM). Through use of a multiple-year forecast, this method overcomes both of the potentially limiting SPCM assumptions. The forecasted future returns, which typically range from 3 to 10 years, can portray future returns that may not be representative of the company's anticipated long-term performance. It also can accurately reflect variations in the return over the life of the forecast, from, for example, changes in revenues, expenses, or capital expenditures. Thus, when material return variations are anticipated, the MPDM should be employed and the SPCM rejected. At the same time, it should be recognized that the methods will generate identical results if the returns forecasted in the MPDM reflect the long-term growth rate used in the SPCM computation.

Because M&A decisions normally involve large amounts of money and carry long-term consequences for buyers and sellers, the MPDM generally should be used unless the subject company has very stable earnings and constant growth is the likely outcome.

As commonly developed, the MPDM has two stages. The first is a forecast of a specific number of years, and the second stage is a method for estimating the terminal value, that is, the value for all years after the forecasted period. The MPDM is portrayed mathematically as

$$PV = \frac{r_1}{(1+d)^1} + \frac{r_2}{(1+d)^2} + \frac{r_3}{(1+d)^3} + ... + \frac{r_n}{(1+d)^n} + \frac{\dfrac{r_n(1+g)}{d-g}}{(1+d)^n}$$

where:

  PV = Present value

    r = Return—generic term for whichever type of earnings or cash flow is selected

    d = Discount rate

    g = The long-term sustainable growth rate

    n = The last period in the forecast which should be a sustainable, long-term return

 d−g = Capitalization rate

Note the implicit *end-of-year convention* assumes the return is received at the end of each year. For start-up companies or ventures into emerging industries, it may be difficult to forecast with a high level of confidence beyond just a few years. Conversely, for established companies in mature industries, relatively accurate forecasts can be made for periods as long as 7 to 10 years. While there is no prescribed number of years to forecast, it should extend long enough to reflect anticipated variations in the company's return, and it should end with a stable or sustainable return.

Once a stabilized return is achieved, the MPDM capitalizes all returns beyond the forecast period as the *terminal value*. As portrayed in the equation above, the terminal value is computed by increasing the stabilized return in the final year of the forecast by the anticipated long-term growth rate as of the end of the forecast, capitalizing that return, and then computing the present value of the capitalized return as of the end of the forecast period.

Several questions frequently emerge about the MPDM formula.

- How long should the forecast be?

    The forecast should be long enough to portray all anticipated variations in the company's return and until a stabilized return is achieved. The stabilized or sustainable return is necessary because it is used in the terminal value computation, which should reflect long-term relationships between the various elements in the company's return.

- Why do we discount the capitalized value in the terminal computation?

    The terminal value represents the value of all of the future returns beyond the discretely forecasted period. This capitalized value then must be discounted, using the end-of-year present value factor for the final period in the forecast.

- What proportion of the total value should the terminal value be?

    There is no correct answer to this question because the terminal value will vary depending on the particular circumstances, such as the long-term growth rate, of each investment. The relative size of the terminal value increases as the forecast period decreases and becomes increasingly less important as the forecast lengthens. Depending on the discount rate, after a forecast of about 10 years, the terminal value is much less significant.

The MPDM formula assumes that the returns generated by the investment are received by the company at the end of each period. Since most investments generate returns that are received throughout the year, the MPDM formula often is revised by the *midyear discounting convention* and is portrayed in the following equation:

$$PV = \frac{r_1}{(1+d)^{.5}} + \frac{r_2}{(1+d)^{1.5}} + \frac{r_3}{(1+d)^{2.5}} + \dots + \frac{r_n}{(1 \mid d)^{n-.5}} + \frac{r_n(1+g)}{\dfrac{d-g}{(1+d)^n}}$$

where:

PV $=$ Present value

r $=$ Return—generic term for whichever type of earnings or cash flow is selected

d $=$ Discount rate

g $=$ The long-term sustainable growth rate

n $=$ The last period in the forecast, which should be a sustainable, long-term return

d$-$g $=$ Capitalization rate

The midyear convention assumes the return is received evenly throughout each discretely forecasted year. A minority of practitioners prefer to use the midyear convention in the computation of the terminal value, in which case the discount factor would change in the above equation from n years to n $-$ .5 years.

ESTABLISHING DEFENDABLE LONG-TERM GROWTH RATES AND TERMINAL VALUES

In both the SPCM and the MPDM, the computation of value is influenced by the size of g, the long-term growth rate of the company's return. Both computations assume that the return will grow at this rate forever, so an unrealistic growth rate can substantially distort value.

The factors most commonly considered in determining the growth rate include:

- General economic conditions
- Growth expectation for the company's industry, including consideration of growth expectations for industries in which the company's products are sold
- Synergistic benefits that could be achieved in an acquisition
- The company's historical growth rate
- Management's expectations as to future growth considering the company's competitive condition, including changes in technology, product lines, markets, pricing, and sales and marketing techniques

In evaluating these factors, it is essential to keep in mind that the SPCM and the terminal value in the MPDM involve perpetual models—they assume the returns extend to infinity. A good way to begin selection of the long-term growth rate is with consideration of macroeconomic factors. In the United States, for example, population growth is less than 2%, and growth in gross national product is usually less than 3%. Thus, the weighted average growth rate of all industries is about 3% in the long term. With this macroeconomic benchmark in mind, move to the specific industry and determine its historical and forecasted long-term growth. From that, if appropriate, move to that segment of the industry in which the target company operates and perform a similar analysis. While national data can be used for companies that sell nationwide, smaller firms that operate regionally or locally should be analyzed based on the performance in these specific areas. Remember that the growth rate chosen is applied to the company's return—earnings or cash flow—so product mix, prices, and margins should be used to assess the reasonableness of the growth rate chosen.

Companies that possess a track record of double-digit growth reflect competitive advantages that have allowed them to capture market share and grow rapidly. When these competitive factors suggest that continued very high growth should be anticipated for the foreseeable future, this result should be reflected in a forecast for that high-growth period. This high-growth performance logically should decline as competitors enter the market, introduce new technologies, and bring cost savings and pricing pressure that eliminate the company's strategic benefit. Rates of growth also tend to decline as companies increase in size.

Values are frequently inflated by long-term growth rates that suggest a company will maintain its competitive advantages forever. For example, in an industry that is growing at an annual rate of 3%, an SPCM or MPDM computation that includes a long-term growth rate of 10% assumes that the target company will perpetually grow at over three times the industry rate, capturing additional market share forever. Sellers or their agents frequently attempt to inflate value through unrealistically high long-term growth assumptions, so these numbers always should be reviewed.

In summary, long-term growth rates should not always be 3%. The forecast should, however, be scrutinized carefully with rigorous attention to the details that most affect growth, including markets, products, volume, and prices. Where unsustainable growth is anticipated, it should be reflected in the forecast of MPDM.

The explosive effect on value from what may appear to be modest changes in the long-term growth rate is illustrated in Exhibit 7-2.

Exhibit 7-2   Effects on Varying Long-Term Growth Rates on Value in the SPCM

Key Facts		
Annual Return:	$6 million	
Discount Rate:	15%	
Long-term Growth Rates:	3%, 6%, 9%	

3% Growth	6% Growth	9% Growth
$\dfrac{\$6\text{ million}}{15\% - 3\%} = \$50\text{ million}$	$\dfrac{\$6\text{ million}}{15\% - 6\%} = \$66.7\text{ million}$	$\dfrac{\$6\text{ million}}{15\% - 9\%} = \$100\text{ million}$

The income approach is the most widely used technique to value businesses for M&A because it is appropriate for almost any enterprise that generates a positive return. This approach is grounded in widely accepted economic theory that value can be computed by discounting future economic benefits at a rate of return that reflects their relative risk. The challenge in this process is to develop reliable returns and rates of return to use in computing the value. Both of the methods within the income approach, SPCM and MPDM, offer advantages. While the SPCM is quick and convenient, the MPDM allows for more detail and accuracy. The value generated by either method is dependent on the choices made for the returns and rates of return used in the formula, and each requires selection of a realistic long-term growth rate. While selection of the returns and the particular benefits of use of net cash flow to invested capital were described in Chapter 6, Chapter 8 explains how to develop defendable rates of return.

8

Cost of Capital Essentials for Accurate Valuations

A *discount rate*, also known as a cost of capital or a required rate of return, reflects risk, which, simply stated, is uncertainty. It is the rate of return that the market requires to attract funding to an investment. Discount rates are determined by the market of alternative investment choices available to the investor with the rates varying over time as economic and risk characteristics change.

Cost of capital is further described in the SBBI *Valuation Edition 2001 Yearbook:*

> The cost of capital (sometimes called the expected or required rate of return or the discount rate) can be viewed from three different perspectives. On the asset side of a firm's balance sheet, it is the rate that should be used to discount to a present value the future expected cash flows. On the liability side, it is the economic cost to the firm of attracting and retaining capital in a competitive environment, in which investors (capital providers) carefully analyze and compare all return-generating opportunities. On the investor's side, it is the return one expects and requires from an investment in a firm's debt or equity. While each of these perspectives might view the cost of capital differently, they are all dealing with the same number.

The cost of capital is always an expectational or forward-looking concept. While the past performance of an investment and other historical information can be good guides and are often used to estimate the required rate of return on capital, the expectations of future events are the only factors that actually determine the cost of capital. An investor contributes capital to a firm with the expectation that the business's future performance will provide a fair return on the investment. If past performance were the criterion most important to investors, no one would invest in start-up ventures. It should also be noted that the cost of capital is a function of the investment, not the investor.

The cost of capital is an opportunity cost. Some people consider the phrase "opportunity cost of capital" to be more correct. The opportunity cost of an investment is the expected return that would be earned on the next best investment. In a competitive world with many investment choices, a given investment and the next best alternative have practically identical expected returns.[1]

Because businesses are usually financed with both debt and equity, a cost of each must be determined. Debt is less expensive than equity because it tends to be less risky and the interest cost of debt is usually tax deductible. Returns on equity are not guaranteed, so they are more risky than debt and more difficult to quantify. Exhibit 8-1 portrays key distinctions between the characteristics of debt and equity, particularly in closely held corporations.

These differences in the rights and accompanying risks of capital providers cause commensurate differences in the cost of each source of capital. The resulting capital costs, or rates of return, are used to determine the value of the business. A lower-risk investment requires a lower rate of return, and the lower rate generates a higher value in the multiple-period discounting method (MPDM) or single-period capitalization method (SPCM) computation. Conversely, for a higher-risk investment, shareholders require a higher rate of return, which leads to a lower value, as illustrated with the SPCM in Exhibit 8-2.

---

[1] Ibbotson Associates, *Stocks, Bonds, Bills and Inflation*® Valuation Edition *2001 Yearbook* (Chicago: Ibbotson Associates, 2001).

Exhibit 8-1   Comparison of the Characteristics of Debt
                 Versus Equity

Characteristics	Corporate Bonds or Loans—Lesser Risk to the Investor	Common Stock— Greater Risk to the Investor
Safety of Principal	Guaranteed principal protection when held to maturity, although bond market values vary with interest rate levels.	No principal protection.
Income	Guaranteed fixed annual interest return.	Dividend payments dependent on financial condition, management preferences, and board approval.
Liquidation Preference	Priority in liquidation frequently exists over general creditors and over all equity holders.	Last priority in liquidation behind all creditors and other equity holders.
Collateral Provided	Often, depending on nature of loan and provisions.	Rarely.
Management Control	No management control, but creditor approval may be required for certain corporate actions.	Degree of control depends on size of interest, voting rights, and prevailing legal restrictions and agreements.
Appreciation	No potential for return beyond fixed interest payment.	Potential for return limited only by company performance, but may vary depending on degree of control, ownership structure, and legal restrictions and agreements.

Source: Frank C. Evans, "Making Sense of Rates of Returns and Multiples," *Business Valuation Review* (June 1999), pp. 51–57. Reprinted with permission from *Business Valuation Review*, Copyright © 1999.

Exhibit 8-2   Effects of Varying Rates of Return on Value

Higher risk and required rate of return yields lower value	Medium risk and required rate of return yields middle value	Lower risk and required rate of return yields higher value
$\dfrac{\$6\ \text{million}}{24\%} = \$25\ \text{million}$	$\dfrac{\$6\ \text{million}}{18\%} = \$33.3\ \text{million}$	$\dfrac{\$6\ \text{million}}{12\%} = \$50\ \text{million}$

Conclusion: The level of risk must be accompanied by a commensurate rate of return which affects value. The higher the risk and associated rate of return, the lower the value will be.

COST OF DEBT CAPITAL

A company's cost of debt is usually its after-tax interest rate, assuming the company is profitable so that the interest expense can be deducted. When the company's long-term debt is carried at approximately the current market rate of interest, then the book value and the market value of that debt are the same. When, however, the company carries debt securities that have interest rates that are materially above or below market rates as of the valuation date, the market value of the debt may vary from its book value, and adjustments should be made for the difference. Since this seldom occurs, particularly in closely held companies, this discussion assumes that the market value and book value of the debt are the same unless it is specified to be different.

Interest rates that reflect relative levels of investment risk that does not pertain to any specific date or economic conditions are illustrated in Exhibit 8-3.

Exhibit 8-3   Cost of Debt

U.S. Government Treasuries (Risk-free Rate)		Other Government Debt Instruments	Higher-Grade Corporate Bonds	Lower-Grade Corporate Bonds	Secured Loans to Privately Held Companies		Unsecured Loans to Privately Held Companies
5%	6%	7%	8%	9%	10%	11%	12%

COST OF PREFERRED STOCK

The cost of preferred stock is typically the market yield, which is the dividend rate of return on the security. Preferred stock can carry features that can make it callable, convertible, cumulative, or participating, all of which can affect the rate of return on the security.

COST OF COMMON STOCK

The cost of common stock, which is generally referred to in this discussion as "equity," is more difficult to determine because it carries no fixed return and its market value can vary dramatically. For this reason, the cost of common stock usually is expressed as the total of several elements, and every equity discount rate will include the following three fundamental components:

1. *Risk-free rate*—the rate on an investment free of default risk. The common proxy for this component for long-term investments is the rate of return on long-term U.S. Treasury Bonds.
2. *Equity risk premium*—the addition to the risk-free rate of return for the increased risk inherent in equity over debt.
3. *Specific company premium*—the adjustment to the rate for the specific risk profile of the subject company.

Typical costs of common stock, which do not pertain to any specific date, industry, or economic condition, are illustrated in Exhibit 8-4.

Exhibit 8-4   Cost of Common Stock

Large-Cap (S&P 500) Public Company	Mid-Cap and Lower-Cap Public Company	Micro-Cap Public Company	Larger/Stronger Private Company	Venture Capitalists and Smaller/ Weaker Private Company			
10%	15%		20%	25%	30%	35%	40%

FUNDAMENTALS AND LIMITATIONS OF THE CAPITAL ASSET PRICING MODEL

The cost of equity for public companies usually is quantified through the capital asset pricing model (CAPM), a branch of capital market theory that describes and quantifies investor behavior. An extensive discussion of CAPM is available in finance textbooks.

The CAPM can be used to determine the cost of equity in a privately held company, with the most common application being for those businesses that are viable candidates to become public companies. The CAPM often is inappropriate for valuing private companies because the assumptions that underlie it are either inconsistent with or not sufficiently similar to investor circumstances surrounding such an investment. To emphasize this point before reviewing the elements of the CAPM, consider the following assumptions that underlie it:

- All investors are single-period expected utility of terminal wealth minimizers who choose among alternative portfolios on the basis of each portfolio's expected return and standard deviation.

- All investors can borrow or lend an unlimited amount at a given risk-free rate of interest and there are no restrictions on short sales of any asset.

- All investors have identical estimates of the expected values, variances, and covariances of returns among all assets (i.e., investors have homogeneous expectations).

- All assets are perfectly divisible and perfectly liquid (i.e., marketable at the going price).

- There are no transactions costs.

- There are no taxes.

- All investors are price takers (i.e., all investors assume that their own buying and selling activity will not affect stock prices).

- The quantities of all assets are given and fixed.[2]

---

[2] Jay Shanken and Clifford W. Smith, "Implications of Capital Markets Research for Corporate Finance," *Financial Management* 25 (Spring 1996), pp. 98–104.

It should be obvious that many of the assumptions underlying the CAPM do not fit the typical investment in a closely held company. Such investments are seldom fully diversified, are often highly illiquid, and frequently carry significant transaction costs, and many times investor behavior is motivated by tax considerations. For example, while CAPM assumes a fully diversified portfolio, it is applied in valuation to assess the value of an investment in a single company. This distinction necessitates inclusion of the specific company risk premium in the modified CAPM (MCAPM) that is discussed later in this chapter. These differences make the CAPM less effective in appraising closely held business interests, particularly of smaller companies. However, in order to quantify the cost of equity capital effectively, the mechanics of CAPM must be understood. They are summarized below and begin with recognition of the three factors essential in the development of a discount rate:

1. Risk-free rate
2. Equity risk premium
3. Specific company risk premium

The CAPM formula quantifies these as follows:

$$R_e = R_f + B(ERP)$$

where:

R_e = Rate of return expected—the proxy for the market's required rate

R_f = Risk-free rate of return—a fixed return free of default risk

B = *Beta*—a measurement of the volatility of a given security in comparison to the volatility of the market as a whole, which is known as systematic risk

ERP = Equity risk premium—long-term average rate of return on common stock in excess of the long-term average risk-free rate of return

Simply stated, the required rate of return on equity—the cost of common equity capital—is equal to the sum of the risk-free rate

Exhibit 8-5   CAPM Derivation of a Cost of Equity

	Basic Data		
R_f	as of the appraisal date	=	6.0%
B	based on analysis of public companies in that industry	=	1.2
ERP	historical average	=	7.0%

CAPM Computation

$$R_e = R_f + B(ERP)$$
$$14.4\% = 6.0\% + 1.2(7.0\%)$$

plus the equity risk premium, as modified by beta. While the equity risk premium quantifies the higher return that investors require for the added risk of equity over the risk-free rate, beta theoretically measures systematic specific company risk. Beta quantifies *systematic risk* as the volatility in the market price of the subject stock versus the overall riskiness or volatility of the stock market. The beta for public companies is routinely reported by several data sources, although there are slight variations on how each source computes it. So for the stock of public companies, which have a market price that can be tracked continually compared to the movement of the market as a whole, the required rate of return, or R_e, demanded by investors can be computed accurately by CAPM. To compute the cost of equity of a larger privately held company, or a thinly traded public company that carries a market price that may not accurately express investor expectations, CAPM also can be used. In this procedure, analyze the betas—the expressions of volatility—of a portfolio of public companies that are similar to the target company; from that analysis an appropriate beta for the target can be derived.

   An application of CAPM to derive a cost of equity capital is illustrated in Exhibit 8-5, which does not apply to any specific company, date, or economic conditions.

   This computation can be interpreted as follows. The risk-free rate or cost of safe money as of the appraisal date is 6%, and on average over the long term, investors in large-cap stocks required an equity risk premium (ERP) of 7% over the long-term average risk-free rate. Although the market as a whole reflected systematic risk of 1.0, a study of the volatility, as measured by beta, of specific public companies reveals that those companies are more volatile than the overall market. Based on the similarity of the subject company to the sample of public companies from which the beta was derived, the overall market rate of return of 7% is increased by 20% to 8.4%. When added to the risk-free rate, this yields a required rate of return on the common stock in the subject company of 14.4%.

Public companies are usually much larger and more diversified than closely held companies. As a result, establishing an appropriate beta that expresses the risk profile of the closely held target based on the volatility of a group of public companies in that industry is very difficult, if not impossible. Usually CAPM requires too many factors about the subject company to be quantified through beta.

MODIFIED CAPITAL ASSET PRICING MODEL

To overcome these limitations, the modified CAPM was developed, which includes two additional premiums that add precision to the process of estimating a required rate of return.

The MCAPM is expressed as:

$$R_e = R_f + B(ERP) + SCP + SCRP$$

where:

R_e = Rate of return expected—the proxy for the market's required rate.

R_f = Risk-free rate of return—a fixed return free of default risk.

B = Beta—a measurement of the volatility of a given security in comparison to the volatility of the market as a whole, which is known as systematic risk.

ERP = Equity risk premium.

SCP = Small-company premium—increase in the required rate of return to compensate for the risk associated with smaller size.

SCRP = Specific company risk premium—increase or decrease in the required rate of return caused by specific strengths or weaknesses within the subject company, which is known as unsystematic risk.

The SCRP, also known as *alpha,* is intended to reflect *unsystematic risk,* which is the risk that emanates solely from the target company rather than the market. In the MCAPM, it can be difficult to distinguish between those risk factors that are captured in the beta (which reflects systematic risk in the market) from those that should be included in the alpha (reflecting risk that is specific only to the subject company).

The MCAPM is most effective in developing a cost of equity capital when a group of public companies that are reasonably similar to the target can be identified. When a population of, say, three to six similar public companies is available, analyze their operating and financial characteristics and compare them to the target. Assess the systematic risk reflected in their betas considering conditions within that industry or segments of it, and then analyze specific company factors or alphas. When this information is available, the cost of equity can be computed from the MCAPM with reasonably reliable results.

An application of MCAPM to derive a cost of equity capital is illustrated in Exhibit 8-6, which does not apply to any specific company, date, or economic conditions. The source of the SCP and SCRP are explained later in this chapter under "Summary of Ibbotson Rate of Return Data."

The results of this MCAPM computation is an equity cost of 23.4%, which is 9% higher than the results of the CAPM application in Exhibit 8-5, which totaled 14.4%. The 9% difference results from application of the SCP and the SCRP factors in the MCAPM computation. The illustration in Exhibit 8-6 assumes that a smaller, more risky business is being valued that requires a 9% additional rate of return over the larger company profiled in Exhibit 8-5, which was less risky and had a required rate of return of 14.4%.

BUILDUP METHOD

An alternative to using CAPM or MCAPM to determine a cost of equity is the buildup method, which recognizes the same three fundamental elements of any cost of equity:

1. Risk-free rate
2. Equity risk premium
3. Specific company risk premium

Exhibit 8-6   MCAPM Derivation of a Cost of Equity

Basic Data		
R_f	as of the appraisal date	= 6.0%
B	based on analysis of public companies in that industry	= 1.2
ERP	historical average	= 7.0%
SCP	historical average	= 4.0%
SCRP	determined through informed judgment	= 5.0%

MCAPM Computation

$R_e = R_f + B(ERP) + SCP + SCRP$
$23.4\% = 6.0\% + 1.2(7.0\%) + 4.0\% + 5.0\%$

The buildup model conceptually follows the MCAPM formula but eliminates the beta factor by assuming a beta of one, which is the overall market's average volatility. Therefore, all differences in the risk profile of the subject company compared to the market as a whole must be reflected in the size premium and the specific company premium. Implicitly this assumes that a company's specific risk factors that would cause its beta (if it had a beta) to be greater or lesser than one will be captured in the SCRP. Mathematically, this formula would appear as follows:

$$R_e = R_f + ERP + SCP + SCRP$$

Although each factor in the formula was previously defined, they will be described in more detail. The most common reference source for this market data is *Stocks, Bonds, Bills and Inflation*® Valuation Edition *Yearbook,* published annually by Ibbotson Associates.

Risk-Free Rate

This rate, theoretically free of the risk of default, is most commonly expressed in the U.S. market as the rate of return on U.S. Treasury Bonds of 20-year duration. Ibbotson selected this 20-year duration for its studies, which start in 1926, for several reasons:

- Ibbotson wanted a long-term time horizon.
- Ibbotson wanted to include the Great Depression, as it was part of what could happen in the long-term.

- The year 1926 was the oldest year for which there were reasonably reliable records of the details needed for the study.
- The 20-year U.S. Treasury Bond was the longest-term bond.

Ibbotson also develops risk premiums for shorter time horizons, but for the fair market value or investment value on a going-concern basis of a business, these long-term rates are almost always used to reflect the long-term nature of these investments.

Equity Risk Premium (ERP)

This premium recognizes the additional risk over the risk-free rate associated with investing in a portfolio of large publicly traded common stocks, commonly known as the large-cap stocks.

Small-Company Risk Premium

The SCP reflects the additional increment of risk associated with investing in the common stock of smaller public companies. Over the long term, smaller-cap stocks have been much more volatile but have provided higher returns than larger companies, which is why small-cap stocks and funds are popular with some investors.

Specific-Company Risk Premium

The SCRP component reflects the risks specific to the company and its industry. While it is determined judgmentally, it can be both accurate and defendable. It should reflect the analysis of the competitive conditions in which the company operates, including external industry factors and internal company factors not captured in the return to which the rate will be applied. The ability to relate the competitive analysis of the company to the selection of this premium is critical to establishing a credible and defendable rate of return for use in valuing a business.

Risk and value drivers and their importance vary by company. For example, poor inventory turnover could cripple the profitability of a retail or wholesale business, but it may be immaterial to a service company. Recognizing that judgment is always required, the following is a list of common specific-company risk factors and a brief discussion of each.

- *Lack of access to capital.* Especially when comparing closely held companies to their public counterparts, remember that they frequently face limits in the amount of debt or equity capital that they can raise. This fact also must be considered in assessing their growth prospects or ability to diversify. Also note that when an owner personally guarantees a business loan, the company's effective interest rate probably exceeds its stated rate.

- *Ownership structure and stock transfer restrictions.* The stock of privately held companies, without a public stock market for trades, often is unmarketable, particularly for minority ownership interests. Shares of stock in closely held companies frequently carry restrictions that tightly limit the conditions under which they can be transferred. Rights of first refusal at a specified price are common, and minority shareholders in particular often face restrictions that severely limit the marketability of their investment.

- *Company's market share and the market structure of the industry.* Smaller companies frequently operate in niche industries or segments of industries where market share can be a significant, strategic advantage. Market leaders may possess special strength, such as a proprietary technology that gives them brand awareness or pricing power. The structure of the industry also must be examined. For example, a company with a 20% market share may be able to dominate an industry when no other company possesses more than 5% of the market. However, a 20% market share where two competitors each control 40% leaves the company in a much weaker position.

- *Depth and breadth of management.* Smaller and even middle-market companies frequently possess gaps in their management team, leaving them weak in one or more functional areas. These factors must be assessed in considering the company's strength at core functional levels, including quality control, production capability, marketing and sales capacity, and so on.

- *Heavy reliance on individuals with key knowledge, skills, or contacts.* It is not unusual in smaller companies to have one person or a few individuals possess essential technical knowledge, production skills, or customer contacts. This characteristic commonly increases the risk profile of a small or middle-market company in comparison with larger businesses because the company's success is tied to the presence of these key individuals.

- *Marketing and advertising capacity.* Smaller companies that compete against much larger rivals or national chains often lack the financial capacity or marketing expertise to properly inform their potential customer base about the advantages that they offer. Independent retailers, for example, may have as good or even better prices than the national chains against which they compete. The chains, however, possess the capacity to promote the image of their low pricing, which is a competitive advantage that the independents usually lack. Thus, due to their inability to inform their potential customers , the independents may lose market share even when they possess superior products, customer service, or prices.

- *Breadth of products and services.* Specialty companies frequently derive their strength from focusing in niche markets, but this product concentration creates risks from lack of diversification and overdependence on limited markets. Some specialty companies may find their largest customers adopt a policy to deal only with suppliers who offer a broad range of products, forcing them to either expand their product offerings or sell out to a bigger company.

- *Purchasing power and related economies of scale.* Due to their size, smaller companies often cannot achieve the cost or production efficiencies of their larger competitors. Whether through quantity discounts or spreading capacity costs over higher volumes, larger companies possess distinct advantages in certain operations and markets.

- *Customer concentration.* This problem plagues many small and middle-market companies, which frequently grow and prosper by providing exceptional service to their largest customers. In the process, however, they sometimes become overly reliant on these customers, who constitute too great a percentage of their total sales.

- *Vendor and supplier relations and reliance.* In order to specialize and create certain competitive advantages, smaller companies frequently subcontract major operations or production components to suppliers on whom they may become overly dependent. Lack of control over the timing, quality, or pricing of needed resources is a common result.

- *Distribution capability.* Larger companies with broad product lines typically possess regional or national distribution systems to protect their market share and product image. Independents frequently must rely on brokers or face much higher distribution costs as a percentage of sales. For example, independent food manufacturers that supply grocery chains lack the ability of broad-line national companies to influence in-store shelf spacing decisions and as a result receive the least attractive locations. This lack of direct access to customers may limit the independent's ability to provide customers with the necessary attention and services to retain their loyalty. Lack of direct customer contact also prevents feedback on evolving customer wants and needs and limits branding potential.

- *Depth, accuracy, and timeliness of accounting information and internal controls.* Public companies face heavy accounting reporting requirements to regulatory agencies, which in the process generally improves the information that is available to their management. Such data is frequently lacking in smaller businesses, a fact that may hamper management's assessment of performance, and potential buyers may also question the quality of this data.

Caution should be exercised when considering these SCRP factors. Some may have been considered in the selection of the growth rate or in the returns through a higher cost of sales or operating expenses. The objective of this care is to avoid double counting by incorporating the same factor in both the rate and the return. A similar concern for avoiding double counting should be observed when qualifying any applicable discounts and premiums.

In addition to the foregoing list of factors that are often particularly important to small and middle-market companies, every business should be evaluated in terms of profitability and growth. These issues are reflected primarily in the forecast of the company's return in either the SPCM or the MPDM. More important, the factors that cause these results need to be carefully examined in determining the SCRP.

SUMMARY OF IBBOTSON RATE OF RETURN DATA

This discussion has liberally referred to the *SBBI Valuation Edition Yearbook* (SBBI), published by Ibbotson Associates, which serious appraisers carefully study.

An understanding of the general process used in the annual Ibbotson Equity Risk Premium Series studies helps to explain several points made in this chapter and in Chapters 6 and 7, including why these rates, without further adjustment, are applicable only to net year's net cash flow to equity. The research assumes that a portfolio of large company stocks, such as the large-cap stocks of the New York Stock Exchange (NYSE) or Standard & Poor's 500, was purchased on January 1 of each year beginning in 1926 and sold on December 31 of each year. Each year's investment would have a rate of return based on the aggregate increase in the portfolio's share values plus dividends that were paid in that year. This process is repeated for each year from 1926 through the most recently completed year. These annual returns are the return of the market, or R_m. For each of the same years, the income return for the 20-year U.S. Treasury Bond, called the R_f, is determined. Subtracting the R_f from the R_m for each year produces the equity risk premium for each year. The ERPs for all years are totaled and divided by the number of years to indicate the long-term arithmetic average ERP. This is the rate of return shown for the ERP in each *SBBI Yearbook*.

A similar process is used for the small-company premium (SCP) using NYSE companies or companies from the major U.S.

Exhibit 8-7   Size-Decile Portfolios of the NYSE/AMEX/NASDAQ
Size and Composition (1926-2000)[a]

Decile	Historical Average Percentage of Total Capitalization	Recent Number of Companies	Recent Decile Market Capitalization (in thousands)	Recent Percentage of Total Capitalization
1 - Largest	63.13%	237	$11,757,098,230	72.56%
2	14.07%	262	1,797,427,043	11.09%
3	7.64%	285	864,872,122	5.34%
4	4.78%	327	546,712,821	3.37%
5	3.26%	364	400,422,531	2.47%
6	2.37%	412	286,627,260	1.77%
7	1.72%	482	221,635,399	1.37%
8	1.27%	517	137,729,312	0.85%
9	0.97%	869	116,702,549	0.72%
10 - Smallest	0.80%	1,927	74,292,170	0.46%
Mid-Cap 3–5	15.68%	976	1,812,007,474	11.18%
Low-Cap 6–8	5.36%	1,411	645,991,971	3.99%
Micro-Cap 9–10	1.76%	2,796	190,994,719	1.18%

[a] Historical average percentage of total capitalization shows the average, over the last 75 years, of the decile market values as a percentage of the total NYSE/AMEX/NASDAQ calculated each year. Number of companies in deciles, recent market capitalization of deciles, and recent percentage of total capitalization are as of September 30, 2000.

Source: © CRSP University of Chicago. Used with permission. All rights reserved. *Stocks, Bonds, Bills and Inflation*® Valuation Edition *2001 Yearbook*, © 2001 Ibbotson Associates, Inc. All rights reserved. Used with permission.

exchanges, divided into 10 groups based on total market capitalization. Each group, called a decile, contains 10% of the total companies traded in that year on the NYSE. The SCP is calculated by taking the actual return of each decile and subtracting the return predicted by CAPM. As shown in Exhibit 8-9, the betas increase as the deciles get smaller. This increase reflects the greater volatility of the return of smaller companies, so the returns estimated by CAPM also increase. Even as betas increase, however, they do not explain fully the returns achieved by these deciles, especially the smallest ones. To clarify the factors influencing the SCP, the return due to beta is removed to isolate the SCP due solely to size and exclusive of any specific riskiness of the company.

Three tables from the *Valuation Edition 2001 Yearbook* are shown as Exhibits 8-7 through 8-9, with the caution that every reader should consult the text itself to thoroughly understand the material presented. In reviewing these exhibits, consider:

Exhibit 8-8   Size-Decile Portfolios of the NYSE/AMEX/NASDAQ, Largest Company and its Market Capitalization by Decile (September 30, 2000)

Decile	Market Capitalization of Largest Company (in thousands)	Company Name
1-Largest	$524,351,578	General Electric Co.
2	10,343,765	National City Corp.
3	4,143,902	Reader's Digest Association, Inc.
4	2,177,448	Engelhard Corp.
5	1,327,582	Price Communications Corp.
6	840,000	Student Loan Corp.
7	537,693	APAC Customer Services Inc.
8	333,442	IHOP Corp. New
9	192,598	SCPIE Holdings Inc.
10-Smallest	84,521	Fibermark Inc.

Source: © CRSP University of Chicago. Used with permission. All rights reserved.
Stocks, Bonds, Bills and Inflation® Valuation Edition *2001 Yearbook,* © 2001 Ibbotson Associates, Inc. All rights reserved. Used with permission.

- Exhibit 8-7 shows that on September 30, 2000 the largest decile of public companies comprise over 72% of the total market value of all NYSE companies, which emphasizes the dominance of the largest public firms.

- It is also obvious from Exhibit 8-7 that the microcap stocks, deciles 9 and 10, comprise only 0.72% and 0.46%, respectively, of the total market capitalization of pubic companies. But Exhibit 8-8 shows that the ninth-decile stocks possess a total equity value of up to $192,598,000, and the tenth-decile stocks of up to $84,521,000, so most of the microcap stocks probably are bigger than most privately held companies.

- From Exhibit 8-9 notice that the beta for decile 1, the largest public companies, is 0.91, which indicates that these largest companies are more stable than the market as a whole. Conversely, decile 10, which is further divided by size into 2 halves, has betas of 1.43 and 1.41, which shows these

Exhibit 8-9   Long-Term Returns in Excess of CAPM Estimation
for Decile Portfolios of the NYSE/AMEX/NASDAQ,
with 10th Decile Split (1926–2000)

	Beta	Arithmetic Mean Return	Realized Return in Excess of Riskless Rate	Estimated Return in Excess of Riskless Rate	Size Premium (Return in Excess of CAPM)
1-Largest	0.91	12.06%	6.84%	7.03%	−0.20%
2	1.04	13.58%	8.36%	8.05%	0.31%
3	1.09	14.16%	8.93%	8.47%	0.47%
4	1.13	14.60%	9.38%	8.75%	0.62%
5	1.16	15.18%	9.95%	9.03%	0.93%
6	1.18	15.48%	10.26%	9.18%	1.08%
7	1.24	15.68%	10.46%	9.58%	0.88%
8	1.28	16.60%	11.38%	9.91%	1.47%
9	1.34	17.39%	12.17%	10.43%	1.74%
10a	1.43	19.11%	13.89%	11.10%	2.78%
10b-Smallest	1.41	24.56%	19.33%	10.91%	8.42%
Mid-Cap, 3–5	1.12	14.46%	9.23%	8.65%	0.58%
Low-Cap, 6–8	1.22	15.75%	10.52%	9.45%	1.07%
Micro-Cap, 9–10	1.36	18.41%	13.18%	10.56%	2.62%

* Betas are estimated from monthly portfolio total returns in excess of the 30-day U.S. Treasury bill total return versus the S&P 500 total returns in excess of the 30-day U.S. Treasury bill, January 1926–December 2000.

** Historical riskless rate is measured by the 75-year arithmetic mean income return component of 20-year government bonds (5.22 percent).

† Calculated in the context of the CAPM by multiplying the equity risk premium by beta. The equity risk premium is estimated by the arithmetic mean total return of the S&P 500 (12.98 percent) minus the arithmetic mean income return component of 20-year government bonds (5.22 percent) from 1926–2000.

Source: *Stocks, Bonds, Bills and Inflation*® Valuation Edition *2001 Yearbook*, © 2001 Ibbotson Associates, Inc. All rights reserved. Used with permission.

companies to be about 42% more volatile than the market as a whole.

• This volatility, which is generally interpreted to indicate risk, is reflected in Exhibit 8-9 in the arithmetic mean return of companies from each decile. As the companies become smaller and their volatility increases, their returns over the long term also increase, reflecting investor demands for higher returns to compensate for the higher risk that they accept.

- Exhibit 8-9 further reveals that the long-term arithmetic mean return on the largest public companies was 12.06% at the end of 2000. This return gradually increases with each successive decile, with the largest proportionate increase in the smaller half of the 10th decile, where the average long-term return is 24.56%, while the average return for microcap stocks was 18.41%. This reflects the confidence company size gives to investors and the higher returns they demand from companies that lack size.

INTERNATIONAL COST OF CAPITAL

It has long been known that investment risk will vary from country to country based on political, regulatory, and economic conditions. This variance from the U.S. norm can be minimal, such as for England, or substantial, such as for developing nations. Adjusting the rate of return for this country-risk factor may not be precise, but even an approximate adjustment assists in the development of a rate of return applicable to a given country.

The following is an overview of the international cost of capital adjustment methods, together with sources of more specific information.

Country Risk Component

This approach adds an additional risk component to the rate of return developed for investments in the United States through the CAPM or the buildup method. The procedure used by many practitioners is to obtain the country-risk component from the *International Country Risk Guide*.[3]

Converting CAPM to a Country-Specific Format

To convert CAPM to a country-specific format, one needs a risk-free proxy for the country, a beta specific to the country, and a

---

[3] *International Country Risk Guide* (East Syracuse, NY: The PRS Group, 2001). *www.prsgroup.com*.

country-specific equity risk premium. The risk-free rate for each country used to develop the country-specific equity risk premium is often selected from the income return on each country's long-term government bond, as provided by the International Monetary Fund. The country-specific beta is estimated by comparing the volatility of a country-specific index to the volatility of the world market comprised of the index of various countries; for example, the S&P 500 for the U.S. index. To a varying degree, from country to country, this process is limited by the availability of data over a historical period long enough to make the equity risk premium sufficiently reliable.

It is not recommended that this process be attempted from the limited data and description contained in this book. For more information on this process, contact Ibbotson Associates at *http://valuation.ibbotson.com* to obtain copies of their *International Equity Risk Premia Report and International Cost of Capital Report.*

Simply adding a country risk component to a cost of capital is a less complex process than the country-specific conversion of the CAPM. If a rate of return for an investment in another country is needed, obtain the details from each of the above sources (and perhaps others that may become known) before deciding on the best procedure for the country-specific investment under consideration.

HOW TO DEVELOP AN EQUITY COST FOR A TARGET COMPANY

The foregoing discussion describes three methods for determining a required rate of return on common stock in a private company, CAPM, MCAPM, and the buildup method. The CAPM method is seldom ever appropriate because of its underlying assumptions. If in studying the market one has identified several publicly traded companies that are sufficiently similar to the target, MCAPM may be an acceptable methodology. When this data is available, a beta for the target company is derived from the betas of the guideline companies. In the CAPM or MCAPM formula, the ERP is multiplied by B to reflect the risk characteristics of the guideline public companies, including the risk profile of the industry in which they operate. After studying the relative strengths and weaknesses of these companies and comparing them to the target, further adjustments should be made for size and specific company risk factors, which are expressed as the SCP and SCRP premiums in the MCAPM formula.

In the application of this formula, even experienced appraisers struggle to distinguish between the amount of risk that is captured in the beta compared to that which is expressed in the SCP and the SCRP. As a result, the size of the SCRP adjustment is usually smaller when used in MCAPM than when used in the buildup method where there is no security-specific beta factor. To avoid this confusion or the potential of double counting factors, many simply employ the buildup method instead of MCAPM.

When the buildup method is used, the beta is assumed to be one so it is eliminated from the computation. If the target company appears to have an equity value of less than $100 million, one of the 10th-decile size premiums is probably the more appropriate choice for the SCP. For companies with equity values below $200 million, the combined 9th-and 10th-decile or microcap premium would most likely be more appropriate for the SCP. For even larger companies, selection of a low-cap premium or use of the MCAPM methodology is an alternative.

Once the size premium is determined, the analyst has established a base rate of return of either about 18% if the microcap premium is used or about 19 to 25% with the 10th-decile premiums, which should be understood to mean: If an investor acquires a broad portfolio of microcap or 10th-decile-size companies, holds that investment for the long term, and makes the average return earned over approximately the last 75 years in the United States, that investment will earn a net cash flow return (after corporate taxes but before the investor's personal taxes) of either 18 or 19 to 25% while enjoying the high liquidity of a public security.

The investment in the target company must be considered against that benchmark. Most closely held companies are smaller than microcap-size public companies, and most possess less management depth, narrower product lines, smaller markets and customer bases, and less access to capital. With this in mind, review the external and internal analysis of the target, identify the specific risk drivers and value drivers of the target, and compare them against the appropriate public company decile benchmark. From this, each risk driver or value driver of the target company can be quantified to determine the SCRP.

Less experienced appraisers are naturally confused about the magnitude of the SCRP adjustment. That is, should a specific value driver or risk driver cause the SCRP to change by 1%, 2%, or more? To provide a sense of perspective, look at the conclusions that the market—millions of investors spending billions of dollars over a period of 75 years—have made. What the market has essentially said is that the cost of relatively safe money, R_f, which includes an assumption of inflation, was about 6% at the end of 2000. Investors have further stated through their actions that they will accept the greater risk of ownership of large-cap-size common stocks but only if they receive the ERP, approximately an additional 6 to 7% in the long term (conclusions are different in the intermediate and short term), or about twice the risk-free rate. Through history, investors have further stated that they will assume the additional risk of buying much smaller tenth-decile-size public stocks, but that they demand an additional 5 to 10% in return for taking that additional step up the risk ladder. Thus, investors in the market have moved from risk-free investments, to big public company stocks, to small public company stocks in approximately 6 to 8% increments. With the size of these relative risk increments as a guide, the selection of the specific company premium is the appraiser's assessment of the size of the final step that the investor takes, versus other market alternatives, when buying the target company.

One final point should be made in considering these rates. The target is most often a private company and the investor is most often acquiring a controlling interest in it. Yet the rates of return just quoted are for publicly traded securities where investors typically own minority interests. Any differences in control versus lack of control should be calculated in the relevant returns to which the rate will be applied or, when appropriate, in any discounts and premiums that may be applied later in the appraisal process. They should not be reflected in the derivation of these equity rates of return.

Buyers and sellers often are surprised to see equity capital costs of 25% or even higher. This can lead to doubt or disbelief in these rates and to the following questions:

> In the latter half of the 1990s, the average P/E multiples for S&P 500-size U.S. companies has been about 25 times, which implies a required rate of return of 4%. Why would anyone invest in common stock, even of an S&P 500-size company, to earn a return of only 4%? Are the much higher equity discount rates for closely held companies that result from the MCAPM or buildup methods of about 25% realistic?
>
> The journey from 4 to 25% is very logical if taken in steps that recognize the distinctions between the alternative investments. Begin by recognizing the advantages that S&P 500 companies have in terms of size, market share, access to capital, depth of management, breadth of product lines, brand names, and distribution systems, which often extend worldwide. When compared with the typical closely held company, even one of middle-market size, these differences tend to be very large.
>
> Next, consider growth expectations. Investors do not buy stock at 25 times annual earnings expecting to earn 4%. Instead, they expect the stock to increase in value with the high implied growth rate continuing for something less than an infinite number of periods. As discussed in Chapter 7, the short-term versus long-term differences in the anticipated growth rate are a scenario that the SPCM cannot effectively portray. The reciprocal of the capitalization rate used in the SPCM, which is a P/E multiple, suffers from the same limitations. The competitive advantages that some large corporations possess provide long-term growth potential, but the duration of this advantage probably lies somewhere in the range of 4 to 10 years, rather than infinity. However, with the stock market's traditional reporting mechanism being a multiple of a single year's earnings, high P/E multiples may result. The clear factor driving the multiple is the

implied earnings growth and its resulting stock value appreciation.

Technical errors also create confusion. The 4% rate computed as the reciprocal of the P/E multiple of 25 is actually a capitalization rate, not a discount rate, for historical earnings, not for future net cash flow. Because P/E multiples, like capitalization rates, are applied to a single year's return, they reflect anticipated growth.

Exhibit 8-10 reconciles the 4% rate that results from a P/E multiple of 25 with an equity discount rate of approximately 25%. The key "unknown" needed to explain much of the difference is the implied long-term growth increment of 10% for large company stocks.

Determining an appropriate cost for the specific elements of capital in a business is one of the most complex areas in the valuation process. The cost of equity in a privately held company is least understood because it lacks both an ongoing market price and a fixed rate of return. The required rate of return or discount rate for common stock in a privately held company can be determined precisely through application of the appropriate methodology and selection of appropriate market-based rates of return. Professional judgment is required to quantify specific company risks. This process is greatly aided by experience. In establishing the equity discount rate, the strategic strengths and weaknesses of the target that were identified and assessed in the competitive analysis of the company and the industry are quantified as the rate of return that is used to discount or capitalize the estimated future returns of the company to determine its value. Thus, the discipline of rigorously evaluating and determining the equity cost can result in an accurate valuation that reflects the risk and value drivers identified for that target.

Exhibit 8-10   Conversion of a Public Company P/E Multiple to a
                  Discount Rate for Net Cash Flow to Equity for a
                  Closely Held Company

Typical S&P 500 public company P/E multiple	25 times
Conversion of P/E multiple to cap rate for historical earnings (1/25 times)	4%
Conversion to cap rate for future earnings by multiplying by one plus implied growth rate for next year of 5%	X 1.05
Cap rate for future earnings	4.2%
Conversion from net earnings to net cash flow to equity cap rate based on long-term relationship between them calculated to be 20%	1.20
Cap rate for future net cash flow to equity	3.5%
Conversion to discount rate for next year's net cash flow to equity by adding implied growth rate of large public company	+10.0%
Discount rate for future net cash flow to equity before premiums for size and specific company risk factors (approximates arithmetic mean return for large cap stocks)	13.5%
Tenth decile premium from 2000 Ibbotson's *Stocks, Bonds, Bills and Inflation*®	4.5%
Premium for specific risk factors typical of a closely held company	7.0%[a]
Discount rate for future net cash flow to equity	**25.0%**

[a] An increment is included in the 7% to recognize the risk associated with the difference in investment liquidity between private closely held companies and the freely and actively traded S&P companies. This difference is commonly recognized through the application of a lack of marketability discount applied to the indicated value. It is provided for in this exhibit as that difference is part of the reconciliation of the public P/E to the ultimate private rate of return, amended through an application of a lack of marketability discount.

Source: Frank C. Evans, "Tips for the Valuator," *Journal of Accountancy* (March 2000), pp. 35–41. Reprinted with permission from the *Journal of Accountancy*, Copyright© 2000 by American Institute of CPAs. Opinions of the authors are their own and do not necessarily reflect policies of the AICPA.

9

Weighted Average Cost of Capital

Chapter 6 introduced the concept of invested capital, which is the total of the company's interest-bearing debt and equity. Also known as enterprise value, this is the quantity most commonly used in a merger and acquisition to define the investment in the company that is being appraised. As emphasized previously, because operations are usually financed with debt and equity, its discount rate should include the cost of both debt and equity, which is referred to as the weighted average cost of capital (WACC). Therefore, when using either the single-period capitalization method (SPCM) or the multiple-period discounting method (MPDM) to compute the value of invested capital, a return to debt and equity is discounted or capitalized by the cost of debt and equity, the WACC.

The WACC reflects the combined cost of debt and equity with the weights of these capital sources based on their market value rather than book value. Typical WACC rates are shown in Exhibit 9-1; note that they do not pertain to any specific date, industry, or economic conditions.

The company's WACC declines as it employs more of the lower-cost debt with proportionately less of the higher-cost equity. Once the WACC applicable to the approximate optimum capital structure is achieved, additional debt causes the WACC to rise, reflecting the added risk higher financial leverage creates.

Exhibit 9-1   Weighted Average Cost of Capital

Large Cap (S&P 500)	Mid-Cap to Micro-Cap	Larger/stronger private company	Venture capitalists and smaller/weaker private company		
5%	10%	15%	20%	25%	30%

One of the more common finance questions relates to whether and how variations in the relative level of debt affect the value of a company. The presence of little or no lower cost debt could create an artificially expensive all-equity WACC, even after allowing for the absence of financial leverage. That many privately held companies avoid debt may reflect the failure by some investors to recognize that equity capital bears a cost, that is, requires a return, and that the added risk associated with equity capital demands a higher rate of return than debt. However, one should also recognize the increased flexibility and the decreased risk that an all-equity capital structure creates, which may make the company more attractive to some buyers.

In considering the effect of financial leverage, continuously focus on those characteristics that create value for the business. Capital is only one of many factors of production, and it is often relatively easy to replicate. For this reason, value is seldom significantly increased or decreased by variations in the capital structure of a business. That is, investors generally cannot manipulate value in a material fashion through adjustment to the capital structure of the company. Remember, buyers can refinance operating debt at their own lower-cost debt financing, so they will not pay a premium price to acquire a leveraged company.

To prevent these potential distortions in value, employ the invested capital model rather than equity model to determine value on a predebt basis, that is, before financing considerations. Further, it is usually informative to compare the debt-to-equity ratio of the subject company to industry standards—but only if these standards are based on market values, not book values—to get a better understanding of market practices. In the process, however, remember that because privately held companies usually lack the access to capital that is available for a public firm, they may have less debt capacity.

ITERATIVE WEIGHTED AVERAGE COST OF CAPITAL PROCESS

Determining the appropriate debt-to-equity weightings to use in the WACC computation is generally simple for publicly traded corporations because the market value of the debt and equity is readily available information. The market value of the debt of a public company is usually equal to the book value unless a note or bond carries an interest rate that differs substantially from current market rates. Equity value can be determined by multiplying the company's stock price times the number of shares, and the resulting market values of the debt and equity determine their weights in the WACC computation.

The debt and equity discount rates previously discussed are inserted into a block format to compute the WACC in a computation that students usually see in their first college finance course. In valuing closely held businesses, however, the computation can be more complex and errors are commonly made. So we begin with a simple illustration of the WACC and build on it to emphasize how to avoid the pitfalls that can occur.

Exhibit 9-2 contains the fundamental data that will be used in several computations that follow, and Exhibit 9-3 shows the initial computation that yields a WACC of 14.4%.

Because a privately owned company lacks a going market price for its stock, the market value of equity, and the resulting debt-equity weightings, cannot be determined. And if the wrong debt and equity weights are used in the WACC computation, distortions to value can occur, as Exhibit 9-4 illustrates, based on the data from Exhibits 9-2 and 9-3.

The computation in Exhibit 9-4 yields an invested capital value of $4.4 million, from which is subtracted the interest-bearing debt of $0.8 million to yield what appears to be a correct equity fair market value of $3.6 million. Further study of the data, however, reveals that the conclusion contradicts the 40 to 60% debt-to-equity weightings on which the computation is based. That is, the

Exhibit 9-2   Iterative Process for a Typical Corporation
(Fundamental Data)

Total Assets	$2,200,000	
Other Liabilities (trade and accrued payables)	$200,000	
Interest-Bearing Debt	$800,000	
Total Liabilities	$1,000,000	
Equity	$1,200,000	

Debt-Equity Mix (at book values)

Interest-Bearing Debt	$800,000	40%
Equity	$1,200,000	60%
Invested Capital	$2,000,000	100%

Net Cash Flow Available to Invested Capital	$500,000
Forecasted Long-Term Growth Rate	3%

Exhibit 9-3   Weighted Average Cost of Capital

Applicable Rates

Equity Discount Rate 20%
Nominal Borrowing Rate 10%
Tax Bracket 40%

Capital Structure at Book Values

Debt 40%
Equity 60%

Computation of WACC

Component	Net Rate	Ratio	Contribution to WACC
Debt @ Borrowing Rate $(1-t)$	6.0%	40%	2.4%
Equity	20.0%	60%	12.0%
WACC Applicable to Invested Capital Based on Book Values			14.4%

Exhibit 9-4   Single-Period Capitalization Method: Net Cash Flow
               Available to Invested Capital Converted to a Value
               for Equity (amounts rounded), Second Iteration

Net cash flow available to invested capital	$500,000	
WACC cap rate (14.4% − 3.0%)	.114	
Fair market value of invested capital		$4,400,000
Less: Interest-bearing debt		$800,000
Indicated fair market value of equity		$3,600,000

Exhibit 9-5   Debt-Equity Mix, Second Iteration

Invested capital	$4,400,000	100%
Debt	$800,000	18%
Equity	$3,600,000	82%

Computation of WACC
Second Iteration

Component	*Net Rate*	*Ratio*	*Contribution to WACC*
Debt @ Borrowing Rate (1− t)	6.0%	18%	1.1%
Equity	20.0%	82%	16.4%
WACC Applicable to Invested Capital			17.5%

40% debt and 60% equity weightings from Exhibit 9-3 produced
the $3.6 million equity value, which equals 82% of the resulting
$4.4 million value of invested capital. At this point in the compu-
tation we do not know what the appropriate debt-to-equity weightings should be, but we should recognize that they cannot simultaneously be 40 to 60% and 18 to 82%.

The solution is to perform a second iteration using the new
debt-to-equity mix of 18 to 82%.[1] As illustrated in Exhibit 9-5, this

---

[1] The authors gratefully acknowledge the pioneering development of this procedure
by Jay B. Abrams. "An Iterative Valuation Approach," *Business Valuation Review,* Vol. 14,
No. 1 (March 1995), pp. 26–35; and *Quantitative Business Valuation: A Mathematical Approach for Today's Professionals* (New York: McGraw-Hill, 2001), Chapter 6.

Exhibit 9-6   Single-Period Capitalization Method: Net Cash Flow
Available to Invested Capital Converted to a Value
for Equity (amounts rounded), Second Iteration

Net cash flow available to invested capital WACC cap rate (17.5% − 3.0%)	$500,000 14.5%	
Fair market value of invested capital		$3,400,000
Less: Interest-bearing debt		$800,000
Indicated fair market value of equity		$2,600,000

Exhibit 9-7   Debt-Equity Mix, Third Iteration

Invested Capital	$3,400,000	100%
Debt	$800,000	24%
Equity	$2,600,000	76%

Computation of WACC Third Iteration			
Component	*Net Rate*	*Ratio*	*Contribution* *to WACC*
Debt @ Borrowing Rate (1− t)	6.0%	24%	1.4%
Equity	20.0%	76%	15.2%
WACC Applicable to Invested Capital			16.6%

yields a WACC of 17.5%, which is much higher than the 14.4%
WACC originally computed.

The debt and equity weights that result from the new WACC
cap rate of 14.5% in Exhibit 9-6 are shown in Exhibit 9-7. Once
again a contradiction results, but the magnitude of the distortion
has been reduced.

Exhibit 9-7 leads to the need for a third and, in this case, final iteration in Exhibit 9-8 with the resulting debt-to-equity
weights in Exhibit 9-9.

Exhibit 9-8   Single-Period Capitalization Method: Net Cash Flow
            Available to Invested Capital Converted to a Value
            for Equity (amounts rounded), Third Iteration

Net cash flow available to invested capital	$500,000	
WACC cap rate (16.6% − 3.0%)	13.6%	
Fair market value of invested capital		$3,700,000
Less: Interest-bearing debt		$800,000
Indicated fair market value of equity		$2,900,000

Exhibit 9-9   Debt-Equity Mix, Third Iteration

Invested Capital	$3,700,000	100%
Debt	$800,000	22%
Equity	$2,900,000	78%

   This third iteration produced debt and equity values, and corresponding weightings of 22% debt and 78% equity that were approximately consistent with the 24% debt and 76% equity weightings on which the underlying WACC computation was based. For
simplicity, amounts in this illustration were rounded, and additional iterations could continue to reduce the remaining variation.
The essential conclusion is that the debt and equity weights used in
the WACC must produce consistent debt and equity values, or the
debt-to-equity weights are not based on market values.[2]
   Although this example used the SPCM to demonstrate that
the iterative process will achieve the desired results, multiple iterations are used most often in application of the MPDM. With its
multiple-year forecast, it involves more computations, but conceptually the process is the same.

---

[2] David M. Bishop and Frank C. Evans, "Avoiding a Common Error in Calculating the
Weighted Average Cost of Capital," (Fall 1997), pp. 4–6. Reprinted with permission
from *CPA Expert*, Copyright© 1997 by American Institute of Certified Public Accountants, Inc.

SHORTCUT WEIGHTED AVERAGE COST OF CAPITAL FORMULA

There is a shortcut to this iterative process when using the SPCM. The fair market value of equity is the dependent variable in the following formula in which the remaining factors are typically known.

$$E_{FMV} = \frac{NCF_{IC} - D(C_D - g)}{C_E - g}$$

where:

E_{FMV} = Fair market value of equity

NCF_{IC} = Net cash flow to invested capital

D = Total interest-bearing debt

C_D = After-tax interest rate

C_E = Cost of equity

g = Long-term growth rate

Although the return in this formula is net cash flow to invested capital, it could be a different return, such as net income to invested capital. Any change in this return must be accompanied by a commensurate change in the cost of that return to prevent distortions to the value of equity. Use of a different return is illustrated in the case study in Chapter 16.

This formula is presented with the data from the preceding example inserted to demonstrate the outcome:

$$2,800,000 = \frac{500,000 - 800,000\,(.06 - .03)}{(.20 - .03)}$$

The resulting equity value of $2.8 million can be added to the $800,000 of interest-bearing debt to yield the fair market value of invested capital of $3.6 million. In the weighted average cost of capital block format in Exhibit 9-10, this yields weightings of approximately 22 and 78% and a resulting WACC of 16.9%. This computation reflects the result that could have been achieved by the iterative process previously shown in this chapter, had it performed additional iterations and not rounded numbers.

Exhibit 9-10   Computation of WACC

Component	Net Rate	Ratio	Contribution to WACC
Debt	.06	22%	1.3%
Equity	.20	78%	15.6%
WACC Applicable to Invested Capital			16.9%

Exhibit 9-11   Single-Period Capitalization Method to Confirm Validity of WACC Weights

Net cash flow available to invested capital	$500,000	
WACC cap rate (16.9% − 3.0%)	13.9%	
Fair market value of invested capital	$3,600,000	100%
Less: Interest-bearing debt	$800,000	22%
Indicated Fair Market Value of Equity	$2,800,000	78%

To confirm these results, a long-term growth rate of 3% is subtracted from the WACC of 16.9% to yield the capitalization rate of 13.9%. Capitalizing the NFC_{IC} by 13.9% generates the values and debt equity percentages shown in Exhibit 9-11, which produce the same debt-equity ratios used to derive the WACC.

Thus, the shortcut formula generates consistent fair market value debt and equity weightings and eliminates the need to perform multiple iterations with the SPCM. Formulas that simplify, however, seldom eliminate the need for common sense and informed judgment. In this case, carefully review the outcome to determine if the resulting debt and equity weights appear to be consistent with the general trend and structure in that industry. Also recognize that the formula employs specific costs of debt and equity that must be appropriate for the resulting debt-equity weightings and capital structure. If, for example, the capital structure produced by the formula includes heavy financial leverage, the associated costs of the debt and equity may have to be adjusted to recognize this outcome.[3]

---

[3] Frank C. Evans and Kelly L. Strimbu, "Debt & Equity Weightings in WACC," *CPA Expert* (Fall 1998), pp. 4–5. Reprinted with permission from *CPA Expert*, Copyright© 1998 by American Institute of Certified Public Accounts, Inc.

COMMON ERRORS IN COMPUTING COST OF CAPITAL

In applying these costs of capital principles, several questions frequently arise where erroneous answers could lead to poor investment choices:

- As a shortcut to performing the iterative process in computing the WACC, can I use industry average debt-to-equity weightings from a source such as Robert Morris Associates (RMA) Annual Statement Studies?

  These industry debt-to-equity averages are most commonly derived from actual unadjusted balance sheets submitted to that industry source, including RMA. Aggregating the data, however, does not eliminate the problem that the weightings are based on book values rather than market values. The private company financial statements used to generate the averages probably reflect the typical attempts by owners to minimize income taxes or achieve other objectives. Any such strategy could change the book value of equity versus its market value, which is primarily a function of anticipated future cash flows. So these sources should not be used because they do not reflect market values.

  Industry averages typically reflect historical rates of return computed based on accounting information. Because investments are future oriented, use of historical rates to reflect investor choices can cause serious distortions to value. To illustrate, assume two returns on equity from RMA (actually, in RMA this ratio is identified as pretax income/new worth), 40% from a more profitable industry and 10% from a less profitable one. Computing value from these rates using a single-period capitalization computation, assuming a return of $1,000,000, yields the following results:

$$\frac{\$1,000,000}{40\%} = \$2,500,000$$

$$\frac{\$1,000,000}{10\%} = \$10,000,000$$

Note that the use of the *higher* 40% rate of return from the more profitable industry produced the *lower* value, while the *lower* rate of return from the less profitable industry produced the *higher* value! This demonstrates the potential distortion to value that can result from using historical measures of earnings compared to dubious book values. As explained in Chapter 2, valid rates are derived by comparing current cash investments at market value against the future cash returns received—dividends and/or capital appreciation—on those investments. The resulting rates reflect a price paid at market value compared to an actual cash return.

One source of market-based rates of return is *Cost of Capital Yearbook* published by Ibbotson Associates. This annual publication, which is heavily influenced by large-cap-size companies, contains industry financial information related to revenues, profitability, equity returns, ratios, capital structure, cost of equity, and weighted average cost of capital based on market values rather than book values.

- How much influence should the target company's capital structure—whether it has more or less financial leverage—have on the value of the company?

  The target's existing capital structure should not materially influence its investment value to the buyer. Buyers have alternative sources of financing operations, and capital is usually an enabler, rather than a creator, of value. Since strategic buyers bring capital to the transaction, the target's capital structure is seldom of great importance to the buyer. If the target is illiquid or has excessive debt, these weaknesses could reduce its stand-alone fair market value. Conversely, if the target carries low-cost financing that could be assumed by the buyer, this could increase its value. Aggressive buyers also may look to the assets owned by the company as a source of collateral to finance their acquisition, although this is a financing rather than valuation consideration.

- Should buyers use their own company's cost of capital or hurdle rate in evaluating a target, rather than computing an appropriate WACC for the target?

Wise buyers and sellers enter into a transaction knowing both the fair market value of the target on a stand-alone basis as well as the approximate investment value to each potential strategic buyer. Determining the fair market value requires computation of the target's WACC to calculate what the company is worth to its present owners as a stand-alone business.

To determine the investment value to a strategic buyer after adjusting the forecasted earnings or net cash flow to reflect consideration of synergies, begin with the buyer's cost of capital. From this rate, which reflects all of the buyer's strengths, adjustments should be made, taking into account the risk profile of the target. For example, a large company with a WACC of 12% may look at three different targets with varying levels of risk and apply WACCs to them of 14, 16, and 18% to reflect their varying levels of risk to that buyer, given its overall WACC of 12%. In short, the role of the WACC is to provide a rate of return that is appropriate to the perceived investment risk, not to reflect the buyer's risk profile or cost of capital.

The acquirer that uses the same hurdle rate in assessing the value of every acquisition implicitly assumes that each carries the same level of risk, which is seldom true. A single rate will tend to undervalue safer investments that merit a lower rate and overvalue riskier investments that require a higher rate.

Investments bring substantial differences in their levels of risk. To maximize value, buyers and sellers must be able to identify and quantify risk. In merger and acquisition, this is primarily done through application of the income approach, where risk is expressed through a cost of capital.

There is a substantial body of financial theory available to quantify the costs of debt and equity capital sources and to deal with them on a combined basis through a weighted average cost of capital. When these procedures are applied properly, risk can be measured accurately and, in the process, managed to maximize returns.

10

Market Approach: Using Guideline Companies and Strategic Transactions

While market multiples are widely quoted as a source for determining value for merger and acquisition (M&A), it is quite likely they are misused most of the time. With this introduction, we are not discouraging the use of multiples; rather, we are suggesting caution when using multiples to avoid distorting value.

Because many people working in merger and acquisition have little education or experience with market multiples, this chapter reviews the fundamental steps in the process and offers suggestions and cautions along the way.

The market approach is based on the *principle of substitution*, which states that "one will pay no more for an item than the cost of acquiring an equally desirable substitute." Thus, with the market approach, value is determined based on prices that have been paid for similar items in the relevant marketplace. Expert judgment is needed for interpretations of what companies are considered to be "similar" and what markets are "relevant." Expertise helps in choosing what multiple to use to gauge the company's performance. Knowledge is also required to properly determine whether the market multiples reflect value on a control or lack of control basis. Finally, substantial judgment is necessary to determine what multiple is appropriate for the target company, which could be the mean or median multiple derived from the range of multiples of a group of companies, or a multiple within or outside of that range.

The market approach relevant to valuation for M&A includes two primary methods: the M&A transactional (transaction) and the guideline public company (guideline). They result from different kinds of transactions and yield different types of value, so their distinction must be clearly understood. A variety of multiples or ratios also can be used to compute value with either method. These are described in the "Selection of Valuation Multiples" section of this chapter.

The value determined by the market approach, like the income approach, includes the value of the tangible assets used by the company in its operations. If the business owns excess operating assets or nonoperating assets, these assets can be valued separately, and this value can be added to operating value to determine the value of the whole enterprise. This process is discussed in Chapter 11.

MERGER AND ACQUISITION TRANSACTIONAL DATA METHOD

The transaction method looks at the prices paid, typically by public companies, to acquire a controlling interest in a business. The buyers in these transactions often are publicly traded companies because closely held businesses usually do not reveal financial information when they make acquisitions. These transactions are often strategic, where the buyer is acquiring a company in the same or a similar industry in which it currently operates to achieve various synergies or other integrative benefits. Thus, the price paid most commonly reflects investment value to that specific buyer rather than fair market value, which assumes a financial buyer.

For the transaction method to yield an appropriate indication of value, the transactional data must relate to companies that are reasonably similar to the target being valued. In addition, the synergies anticipated in the acquisition of the target must be similar enough to those reflected in the transaction data to achieve a reasonable basis for comparison. Thus, it is helpful to have an adequate number of strategic transactions that generate a range of multiples that can be analyzed. When working with strategic transactions, the buyer's motivations may not be fully understood. Buyers may make certain acquisitions purely for defensive reasons—to keep a major competitor out of a market. Similarly, the price paid for a target may seem unusually high in comparison with its potential benefits, but that acquisition may position the buyer to make incremental profits elsewhere. And prices and corresponding multiples may increase dramatically during an industry consolidation and decrease just as quickly. Again, strategic transactions must be analyzed carefully for this reason.

Because transaction data reflects acquisition of a controlling interest, it generates value on a control basis that is generally appropriate for direct comparison with other M&A transactions. Strategic acquisitions and resulting multiples also may reflect synergies and other benefits that are different than those available in the transaction under consideration, so caution is urged in comparison of data.

Similarly, it is wise to study an industry carefully to identify those factors that are driving M&A activity in it. These circumstances may be short term in nature, in which case they temporarily drive up values and multiples when buyers are taking advantage of temporary opportunities. This was seen, for example, in the dramatic increase in the price of health care practices for a period of years during the 1990s brought about by changes in managed care and other regulations. Regulations changed, however, and values quickly declined. Thus, temporary aberrations may occur that must be analyzed to assess their long-term effect on value.

A real benefit of transaction data is that it reveals information about what well-informed strategic players in an industry are doing and the prices they have paid in strategic transactions. When adequate information exists, these transactions also provide indications about selected value or risk drivers for these companies.

To illustrate application of the transaction method, assume that the target is a cement manufacturing company that came on the market in the middle of 2000. The target's sales are approximately $300 million, with high profits by industry standards, primarily state-of-the-art manufacturing facilities, adequate raw material reserves, but only modest growth capacity as a stand-alone business. A study of the cement industry as of that date reveals:

- Commodity nature of products impede company and product differentiation.
- Economies of scale create both revenue and cost synergy potential.
- Broader customer base and geographic market served provide protection from geographic or industry downturns.
- Strong recent pattern of merger and acquisition activity in the industry.
- Recent passage of new federal highway spending bill presages increased cement construction from more stable infrastructure market.
- Generally low stock prices create M&A bargains.

Given these industry conditions, the transaction data in Exhibit 10-1 was gathered from a publicly available source.

When the companies involved are publicly traded, substantial information can be obtained from public sources about the nature and terms of the transactions, prices paid, and resulting multiples. The first three transactions in the exhibit were consummated; the last was an offer that ultimately was rejected by the seller.

These transactions indicate that substantial premiums— probably in the range of 40% above fair market value—were being paid by strategic buyers for targets in this consolidating industry. From this initial information, a thorough investigation of the buyer and the seller is necessary to assess their circumstances, intentions, and options as of the transaction date. It should be clear, however, that buyers and sellers operating in this market would benefit substantially by possession of this data and the details behind each of these transactions as they move forward in their negotiations.

Many of the issues discussed thus far regarding industry circumstances, company size, market position, and other competitive factors must be considered. For example, the last transaction listed was an unsuccessful offer made by Lafarge Corporation, the second largest company in the world in that industry, bidding for Blue Circle Industries, the third largest. Whether details on a

Exhibit 10-1   Cement Industry Strategic Aquisitions

Date	Buyer	Seller	Premium
11/4/99	Cementos Portland, S.A.	Giant Cement Holding, Inc.	51%
1. Terms of sale: All cash			
2. Price paid equals $195 per ton of capacity			
3. Price paid reflects 6 times forward EBITDA			
9/2/99	Dyckerhoff Aktiengesellschaft	Lone Star Industries, Inc.	45%
1. Terms of sale: All cash			
2. Price paid equals $235 per ton of capacity			
3. Price paid reflects 8 times forward EBITDA			
3/30/98	Southdown, Inc.	Medusa Corp.	27.5%
1. Terms of sale: Buyer's stock			
4/27/00	Lafarge Corp[a]	Blue Circle Industries	43%
1. Terms of sale: All cash			

[a] Latest offer rejected by Blue Circle as of 4/28/00, with offer elapsing 5/5/00

potential transaction between two companies of this size is relevant in determining the value of a much smaller target requires further analysis. This data does, however, clearly indicate pricing patterns for strategic buyers in this industry as of this approximate date.

Buyers and sellers should be particularly cautious of transaction multiples quoted by intermediaries. These multiples are first presented to sellers by intermediaries as part of their proposal to represent the seller in the sale. The investment bankers or brokers then use the same multiples in presenting the company to prospective buyers, justifying its offering price based on these multiples. Both buyers and sellers can be misled by the seller's representations if the strategic transaction or transactions on which the multiples are based are not representative of the current market or adequately similar to the target company. Without adequate similarity, the impressive multiples may not be possible, and both buyers and sellers need to recognize this potential for distortion.

GUIDELINE PUBLIC COMPANY METHOD

The guideline method determines value based on the price at which similar public companies are traded on public stock exchanges. As with the transaction method, value is determined through the use of multiples that compare the transaction price to some measure of operating performance or financial position. The result usually reflects value on a minority marketable basis (it could be control marketable, depending on the return used) because the guideline company shares being traded are minority interests in securities that are readily marketable. Since merger and acquisition most commonly involves acquisition of a controlling interest in a privately held company or a division of a public company, adjustments may be necessary to reflect differences in control and marketability between the guideline companies and the target. In the United States, since 1996 more than 16,000 public companies are required to report electronically with the U.S. Securities and Exchange Commission (SEC). Access to this public company data is readily available through the SEC's Electronic Data Gathering and Retrieval system (EDGAR). This database includes SEC Form 10-K annual reports, SEC Form 10-Q quarterly reports, and other material disclosures. In addition, commercial electronic databases are available that summarize this information. Thus, the guideline method is becoming much more widely used because of the increased convenience in gathering and analyzing the data on public companies.

The first challenge that arises in use of the guideline method is to identify an adequate number of public companies that are similar enough to the target to provide a reasonable basis for comparison. EDGAR allows searches by Standard Industry Classification (SIC) code and North American Industry Classification System (NAICS) code, and commercial databases allow for searching and screening the data through use of many other parameters, such as sales volume or income level. These online sources also provide convenient summaries of this data that permit users to survey companies quickly and conveniently based on operational or performance criteria. Thus, if the initial search generates 25 potential guideline companies, a review of this summary data often can eliminate a substantial number of potential guidelines that fail to meet subsequent tests for appropriateness. Once the population of guidelines is reduced to 10 or 12, further analysis of each can be made with the goal of optimally having about four to seven companies to serve as proxy for the market.

Depending on the characteristics of the target, many searches will be less successful. Because of the target's size, industry, or product line, very few or no guideline companies may be available for comparison. When initial searches do not generate an adequate list of guidelines for comparison, the criteria of the search can be broadened to additional NAICS or SIC codes or to a broader definition of the industry. Such a decision, however, always requires care and judgment because the results of the market as determined by the guideline companies must serve as a reasonable guide in assessing the target. The less similar the guidelines are to the target, the less reliable the results will tend to be.

If the initial search based on industry parameters identifies an adequate population of potential guidelines, further selection criteria must be employed to determine which guidelines are most similar to the target. Many different criteria can be used but the following are commonly recognized:

- *Size.* Usually based on sales volume.
- *Products or services.* When the guidelines have multiple product or service lines, these and the sales volumes of each must be compared with those of the target for similarity.
- *Markets served.* The markets of many industries are divided into segments determined by geographic considerations, customers, products or services, or technology, each of which could affect the suitability of a company to serve as a guideline.
- *Financial performance.* Differences here often reflect distinctions in product lines, quality, or markets served, all of which should be considered in comparing the target to the guidelines.

With these criteria in mind, larger well-known public companies, particularly conglomerates, are seldom appropriate guidelines. Their size, breadth of products, extensive markets, and financial strength usually make them a poor basis for comparison with a middle-market company. Once such comparisons are made, be particularly sensitive to the resulting multiples and the weight that comparison is given in the overall determination of value.

Just as the target company's financial statements may require adjustment for nonoperating or nonrecurring items, the financial statements of guidelines may need to be adjusted. The objective in either case is to produce financial statements that provide the most accurate indication of the true economic performance of the entity. Adjustments also may be necessary if one or more of the guidelines employ accounting methods that are different than the target. One of the most common of these adjustments is in the methods of accounting for inventory, most commonly FIFO (first in, first out) versus LIFO (last in, first out), if a guideline uses a different method from the target.

Once guidelines have been selected and operating multiples for them have been chosen and computed, an appropriate multiple to apply to the target must be determined. Begin this process by reviewing those competitive factors that most influence risk and value in that industry. With these factors in mind, look at the range of multiples of the guidelines used in your analysis. Assume, for example, that the multiple you have chosen is the well-known price to earnings (P/E) ratio. Look at the range of the P/E ratios of the guideline companies. In assessing this range, consider the performance of each of the guidelines and the strengths and weaknesses each possesses. From this analysis, identify what characteristics and performance the market is rewarding with high multiples and what factors contribute to lower multiples. In the process, also begin to relate the target's operating performance, products, and other characteristics more closely with certain of the guideline companies than others. That is, identify those guidelines with which the target is most similar. Next, compute and analyze the mean and median guideline multiples, the upper and lower quartiles, and the range from lowest to highest. Look further at the statistical dispersion of the guideline multiples, noting in particular their coefficient of variation, which should provide an indication of the consistency or reliability of the data.

Next, return to those value drivers and risk drivers that appear to be most influential in the industry and compare the target to each of the guidelines with respect to those factors. Then compare the target to the guidelines in terms of significant measures of financial performance, such as profit margin, asset utilization, return on assets, and liquidity. With these qualitative and quantitative factors in mind, rank the target compared to the guidelines in terms of each of these characteristics and overall.

Based on this comparison, judgmentally assess whether the target is as strong as the average—the mean or median—of the guideline companies. If it is not, which is usually the case with smaller or middle-market-size companies compared to public guidelines, then the mean or median multiple of the guidelines is probably too high for the target. After all, a selection of the mean or median guideline multiple implies that the target possesses the approximate level of strength of the average of the guidelines against which it is being compared.

If the guidelines appear on average to be stronger than the target, next compare the target to the one or two guideline companies that have the lowest multiples. It is not unusual for all of the guidelines to be stronger than the target, in which case the multiple chosen for the target would be outside of, or below, the range for the guidelines. Such a result does not invalidate the use of the guideline method; on the contrary, it suggests that an investor who is considering a variety of investments, including the guidelines and the target and their respective levels of risk, would pay a lower multiple of earnings to own the target than the guidelines that are stronger.

Growth tends to be a factor that drives higher market multiples. Therefore, look carefully at both historical and forecasted growth in both revenues and earnings. More important, study carefully those factors that are causing growth to occur in the guideline companies, and carefully assess their future growth prospects. Then apply this same analysis to the target both on a stand-alone basis and operating as a segment of the buyer.

Armed with this analysis, select an appropriate multiple for the target. It should reflect the competitive conditions that are driving risk and value in the industry and the strengths and weaknesses of the target relative to the guideline companies and their respective multiples. The multiples selected for the target also should make sense when compared to the mean, median, and range of multiples of the guidelines.

One of the biggest benefits of using the guideline public company method is the opportunity it provides to thoroughly analyze companies operating in that industry to determine what drives their value. In the process of performing this analysis, usually one develops a much better insight into those strategies that have created strength and success in companies, as well as those characteristics that hamper companies and create problems or weaknesses. These conclusions should reconcile with the analysis of the industry and those competitive factors that most influence value in the industry. Armed with this insight, much of the mystery that sometimes surrounds the market approach is eliminated and value is much easier to understand and quantify.

SELECTION OF VALUATION MULTIPLES

Many different market multiples are used. Some are quite popular and have been widely accepted in a specific industry, while some practitioners use the same one or two multiples in every appraisal that they do.

We suggest care in this selection because multiples of different levels of operating performance or financial position may disclose different information about the target company. Market data and company performance may allow use of only certain multiples. For example, in technology or emerging industries, where many guideline companies are in the development stage or relatively new, revenues may be the only operating measure for which a multiple can be determined because many of the companies do not generate profits. However, so much of a company's ultimate performance is determined by what happens "below" the revenue line with expenses that revenue may not provide an accurate picture of performance or value.

As Chapter 6 explains, in merger and acquisition analysts are considering an acquisition of a controlling interest in the target, and they most commonly do not want the analysis to include distortions that could be caused by the target's current capital structure. The same concerns apply when employing the market approach, so an invested capital model is generally preferred over directly valuing equity. Therefore, the numerator in the multiple should be the market value of invested capital (MVIC) rather than stock price. Correspondingly, when the numerator indicates a value of debt and equity, the denominator must also. (This will be explained in the next section, "Market Multiples Commonly Used.")

The time periods for which the multiples or ratios apply also must be considered carefully. The objective should be for the time period of the guideline company multiples to be approximately the same as that of the target. Typical time periods include the latest fiscal year, most recent 12 months, forecasted future 12 months, or an average of some number of historical years. If the ratio involves a balance sheet measure such as equity or assets, it is often of the latest available balance sheet date.

Because guideline companies have different fiscal year ends, variations in the timing of this data are common. It is wise, however, to consider carefully the effect, if any, of these variations, particularly when operating in cyclical or, to a lesser extent, seasonal industries. In certain cases, variations in dates by as little as one quarter can create material differences.

Also be sensitive to general fluctuations in market levels, particularly in volatile industries or in periods of volatile market activity. Stock prices and their resulting multiples can change dramatically in a short period of time. This fact again suggests a need for careful assessment of overall market trends and changes in the guideline company stock prices and multiples over time.

MARKET MULTIPLES COMMONLY USED

Although a variety of market multiples appear in financial literature, only a few receive wide recognition and application. While there may be variation in the application of those that follow, these are the multiples that are most commonly used to determine value for M&A.

P/E   Price/earnings, is certainly the best known, if not the most popular multiple. The price of common stock is the numerator, and income after taxes is the denominator. This multiple is appropriate for most profitable companies with a stable capital structure that is consistent with the capital structure of the selected guideline companies. This equity multiple will produce an equity value directly.

P/R   Price/revenues, another popular multiple, assumes a homogenous industry where the revenues can reasonably be expected to produce a consistent quantity of earnings or cash flow. This multiple produces confusing results because the numerator is a measure of equity while the denominator is a return to debt and equity. A more appropriate application is market value of invested capital (MVIC) to revenues, which produces an invested capital value.

MVIC/EBIT or MVIC/EBITDA   Market value of invested capital/EBIT (earnings before interest and taxes) or EBITDA (earnings before interest, taxes, depreciation, and amortization) are widely used in the M&A community. These returns include the interest expense return to the debt holder, so the numerator must be the aggregate market price of the equity and debt. Multiples of EBIT or EBITDA frequently are quoted without substantiation, particularly by sellers or their intermediaries. For this reason, these multiples should always be challenged to identify their source, if any, and how they were derived. While the source commonly is based on little more than rumor or speculation about unsubstantiated prices paid in an industry, the multiples sometimes are based on a single, strategic transaction that may reflect unique synergies to that buyer, synergies that may not be relevant in any other transaction. When developed correctly, these multiples can provide substantial insight into both investment value and fair market value. The key is to ensure that they are supported by proper calculations of transactions that are appropriate for comparison.

P/CF   Price/cash flow, where cash flow is most commonly gross cash flow, is net income plus depreciation and amortization (and depletion in some industries), not net cash flow. Net cash flow is not selected because it may be difficult to estimate the net cash flow for each of the public guideline companies. (Remember, net cash flow components should be shown in amounts necessary to fund anticipated operational needs, not simply those that historically occurred.)

P/BV Price/book value, where book value equals stock-holders' equity on the balance sheet (which is not a measure of value). This multiple used to be popular in M&A valuation in the banking industry. Although commonly quoted, it is seldom a reliable measure of performance or value because it does not involve an accurate measure of the company's performance or financial position.

While other multiples may be computed, the ones just listed are seen most often. Some multiples have become particularly popular in certain industries. When these are encountered, they should be evaluated carefully to determine if they do provide an accurate indication of value. Exhibits 10-2, 10-3, and 10-4 provide illustrations of how various multiples of five public companies in the furniture manufacturing industry can be computed and displayed for analysis.

In reviewing the data in the exhibits, consider the points made in the previous discussion about how to select an appropriate multiple for the target from the guideline company data. Consider first which multiple or multiples would provide the best indication of value for the target, including whether multiples of stock price (equity) or invested capital should be used. Look at the range of the multiples and the resulting mean and median multiples. Each of the guideline companies presented should have been evaluated carefully for similarity to the target in terms of size, products, markets served, operations, and financial attributes. The multiples of those companies that appear to be most similar to the target then should be reviewed relative to the overall range of multiples and the mean and median. The strengths and weaknesses of the target also should be compared with the guideline companies in assessing a multiple that would be appropriate for the target.

In selecting the multiple for the target, the goal is to choose a number that accurately positions the target relative to these alternative investment choices. If the target is approximately equivalent to the average of these choices, then a multiple near the mean or

Exhibit 10-2   Equity Basis

Price/Earnings Ratios of Guideline Companies for Most Recent Fiscal Year

Guideline Company	Year-End Stock Share Price		Latest Fiscal Year Earnings Per Share		Stock Price/ Earnings Multiple
Chromcraft	$10.50	/	$1.25	=	8.40
Pulaski	$17.00	/	$2.77	=	6.14
Rowe	$ 8.00	/	$0.91	=	8.79
Stanley	$10.88	/	$2.70	=	4.03
Winsloew	$9.75	/	$2.26	=	4.31
Mean					6.33
Median					6.14

Price/Earnings Ratios of Guideline Companies for a Simple Average of Most Recent Five Years

Guideline Company	Year-End Stock Share Price		5-Year Average Earnings Per Share		Stock Price/ Earnings Multiple
Chromcraft	$10.50	/	$1.33	=	7.89
Pulaski	$17.00	/	$1.39	=	12.23
Rowe	$ 8.00	/	$0.74	=	10.81
Stanley	$10.88	/	$2.05	=	5.31
Winsloew	$ 9.75	/	$1.91	=	5.10
Mean					8.27
Median					7.89

median would be appropriate. Conversely, if the target is weaker than all of the choices, the multiple chosen for it should reflect this.

Remember that the multiples generated by the guideline method reflect prices paid by minority owners for marketable securities. If the multiples derived from this data are then used to determine the value of a controlling interest in a closely held company, which is usually the case, adjustments may be necessary to reflect differences, if any, in the degree of control and marketability of the interest in the target being acquired. When the multiple is applied to a control return for the target, a control, marketable value results.

Exhibit 10-3   Invested Capital Basis

MVIC/EBIT Ratios of Guideline Companies
for Most Recent Fiscal Year

Guideline Company	Year-End MVIC Share Price		Latest Fiscal Year EBIT Per Share		MVIC/EBIT Multiple
Chromcraft	$13.06	/	$2.17	=	6.03
Pulaski	$38.95	/	$4.24	=	9.19
Rowe	$10.97	/	$1.53	=	7.14
Stanley	$16.28	/	$4.77	=	3.42
Winsloew	$37.44	/	$5.04	=	7.43
Mean					6.64
Median					7.14

MVIC/EBITDA Ratios of Guideline Companies
for Most Recent Fiscal Years

Guideline Company	Year-End MVIC Share Price		Latest Fiscal Year EBITDA Per Share		MVIC/EBITDA Multiple
Chromcraft	$13.06	/	$2.64	=	4.95
Pulaski	$38.95	/	$6.35	=	6.13
Rowe	$10.97	/	$1.84	=	5.95
Stanley	$16.28	/	$10.83	=	1.50
Winsloew	$37.44	/	$5.70	=	6.56
Mean					5.02
Median					5.95

This chapter began with a caution that the market approach produces multiples that often are applied incorrectly in estimating the value of a business. Caution is necessary because many times this data is misinterpreted. The market approach can, however, provide substantial information about prices and trends within an industry as of the appraisal date. The transaction method, which most likely generates a control, marketable value to a strategic buyer, often reveals prices that well-informed buyers are willing to pay for targets in their industry. The guideline method can reveal fair market value on a control or minority, marketable basis, reflecting the price paid by financial buyers. Successful use of both methods requires that adequate transactions in companies suffi-

Exhibit 10-4   Equity and Invested Capital Basis

Price/Equity Ratios of Guideline Companies for Most Recent Fiscal Year

Guideline Company	Year-End Stock Share Price		Latest Fiscal Year Equity Per Share		Stock Price/ Equity Multiple
Chromcraft	$10.50	/	$9.55	=	1.10
Pulaski	$17.00	/	$22.35	=	0.76
Rowe	$8.00	/	$3.69	=	2.17
Stanley	$10.88	/	$11.19	=	0.97
Winsloew	$9.75	/	$11.20	=	0.87
Mean					1.17
Median					0.97

MVIC/Revenue Ratios of Guideline Companies for Most Recent Fiscal Years

Guideline Company	Year-End MVIC Share Price		Latest Fiscal Year Revenue Per Share		MVIC/Revenue Multiple
Chromcraft	$13.06	/	$23.49	=	0.56
Pulaski	$38.95	/	$69.26	=	0.56
Rowe	$10.97	/	$15.77	=	0.70
Stanley	$16.28	/	$37.21	=	0.44
Winsloew	$37.44	/	$22.23	=	1.68
Mean					0.79
Median					0.56

ciently similar to the target are available to constitute a market and that adequate data about those transactions can be obtained to permit a thorough analysis. In the process of gathering and analyzing this information, much useful information can be learned about what drives risk and value in that industry and in those companies. This information can be very helpful in assessing the target. The review of the market data should complement the competitive analysis of the target that has already been completed in the valuation process. Although the market approach must be used carefully to generate accurate estimates of value, it can be most illuminating and its use is strongly encouraged.

11

Asset Approach

So far, discussion has heavily emphasized the value that can be created through strategic acquisitions. As a result of the synergies created by the combination of two companies, revenues may be enhanced, expenses reduced, and the companies can take advantage of other benefits that working together allows. The advantage is quantified by comparing the present value of the combined returns to those on a stand-alone basis, recognizing how risk changes in the process.

Not all targets are evaluated this way, however. Buyers sometimes make acquisitions primarily to achieve control of the assets owned by the target. Asset value also may be important in capital-intensive industries, or in acquisitions where valuable nonoperating assets can be sold after the purchase of the company to recover some of the acquisition cost. Some targets are underperforming and generate little or no return. This absence of a return on a stand-alone basis means that the company's operations are generating no net cash flow and, therefore, no general intangible value. In the absence of general intangible value, the company's value on a stand-alone basis is derived from a hypothetical sale of its assets.

Thus, the primary circumstances where the asset approach (sometimes referred to as the "cost approach") would be used to value a business for merger and acquisition are when the buyer's primary goal is to acquire specific tangible or intangible assets or the target's value is limited to the total of specific tangible assets because its operations fail to generate adequate intangible value.

The asset approach often is applied by opportunistic buyers who look for owners who must sell under adverse circumstances. One classic example of this is the family business that is heavily reliant on a key individual—often the founder—who has become incapacitated or left the company and cannot be replaced. This unfortunate circumstance does not always occur in a quick or unexpected fashion. Owners may wait too long to groom successors or have unrealistic expectations about their children's ability or a reluctance to replace them. As time passes and the chosen successors are unavailable or prove to be incompetent, the chief executive officer may experience declining energy or health. Without this leadership, performance may drop suddenly, customers begin to lose faith and look elsewhere, and the company's intangible value quickly diminishes or disappears altogether.

Shrewd buyers, sometimes known as "bottom fishers," look for these situations, particularly when they possess the key attributes that the target has just lost. In this case, on a stand-alone basis the target frequently possesses only tangible asset value, and the owners must sell at a relatively low price.

This same result—little or no general intangible value—may occur in industries that are rapidly consolidating or those where excess capacity exists. The consolidation often is driven by economies of scale, new technologies, or changes in selling or distribution procedures that render smaller companies uncompetitive on a stand-alone basis. In these circumstances, even when a company operates at its maximum efficiency and serves its customers well, the business may possess no general intangible value—goodwill—because changing competitive conditions have eliminated its ability to compete as a stand-alone.

These conditions are common in business, particularly when management is not proactive in adjusting to changing competitive circumstances. Wise investors routinely monitor industry and company conditions to assess their ability to compete in the long term. When competitive circumstances put them at a disadvantage, they change operations or liquidate and seek investments that provide a better return. Failure to do this commonly results in a sale price based on asset value.

BOOK VALUE VERSUS MARKET VALUE

"Book value" and "net book value" are accounting terms, which unfortunately include the word "value." Book value, however, is rarely an indication of market value because it typically reflects the net undepreciated historical cost of assets as determined by accounting procedures. There is no attempt in the depreciation process to report assets at what they are actually worth, so it is unwise to assume that specific assets are worth the amount at which they are carried on the company's books. The market value of an asset is dependent on many factors, including the market of available substitutes, technological changes, and inflation. While some assets, such as vehicles, tend to decline rapidly in market value, others, such as real estate, often appreciate. For this reason, where asset values are a material influence on the outcome of a business valuation, it is generally advisable to have appraisals on the major assets involved.

PREMISES OF VALUE

Asset or cost methods are conducted under either a *going concern* or a *liquidation* premise. The going concern premise assumes that the business will continue operating and the assets are appraised at their value "in use." Conversely, if it is assumed that the operations of the business will cease and a liquidation will occur, a liquidation premise is appropriate. Under the liquidation premise with an orderly liquidation value assumption, the assets are valued at the proceeds they can generate in a sale that includes a reasonable amount of time which allows the items to be sold piece by piece in pursuit of higher prices. Under a forced liquidation value assumption, the assets are valued under a forced sale circumstance, such as at an auction. Under either assumption, the costs involved to liquidate the business must be considered and subtracted in determining the net proceeds.

USE OF THE ASSET APPROACH TO VALUE LACK-OF-CONTROL INTERESTS

When the acquisition or sale of a lack-of-control or minority interest is considered, using the asset approach to determine value is generally inappropriate. Because this approach determines value based on the hypothetical sale of the underlying assets, implicit is the assumption that the interest being appraised possesses the authority to cause a sale of those assets. Unless a legal agreement provides to the contrary, minority ownership interests generally cannot cause assets to be sold or the cash proceeds to be paid to the owners unless the controlling owner agrees. For the same reason, do not conclude that a pro rata portion of excess cash or other nonoperating assets is available to the minority shareholder, particularly if a control shareholder is present. The control shareholder can determine, first, if the assets are sold and, second, if the proceeds are to be distributed to shareholders.

A common exception to avoidance of the asset approach to appraise a minority interest is in the valuation of holding companies. When the purpose of such an entity is to hold assets for appreciation, the return generated by the assets often is inadequate to produce an appropriate value under an income or market approach. These conditions commonly make the asset approach more appropriate because it is the assets owned by this type of business that attract the buyers in this marketplace.

ASSET APPROACH METHODOLOGY

Whether determining fair market value or liquidation value, the common procedure under an asset approach is to adjust the company's balance sheet accounts from book values based on accounting computations to market value. Doing so includes adding assets not on the balance sheet and deleting any on the balance sheet that lack market value. The adjustments to specific assets involve consideration of the following factors.

Cash

Cash generally does not require adjustment. The most common exception occurs when the cash position is either excessive or deficient.

Accounts Receivable

The relevant question to consider is whether 100% of the receivables are collectible. If not, the uncollectibles should be removed, based on the following primary considerations:

- The company's history of collections as a percentage of total receivables
- A review of the aging of receivables
- The industry's ratio of bad debts to total receivables
- The company's credit-granting policies
- The state of the economy
- The status and outlook for the company's industry
- The status and outlook for the company's dominant customers, if any
- The status and outlook for the primary industry of the company's customers
- Whether the company delays commissions or other benefits to salespeople, manufacturers' representatives, or other sales agents pending collection of the receivables from the sales; if so, that portion is an expense that will reduce the asset value of the trade receivables

Inventory

Depending on the industry—retail, wholesale, or manufacturing—the composition of a company's inventory will vary. In most instances it will be comprised of one or more of the following:

- *Raw materials.* Materials purchased for use in production of the product but that have not yet been used in the manufacturing process. It could be valued under last in, first out (LIFO), first in, first out (FIFO), or average cost and may need to be adjusted to reflect shrinkage, obsolescence, or similar factors.

- *Work in progress.* Products or services that ultimately will be sold and on which process has begun but is not yet completed. The value should be equal to the accumulated cost as of the balance sheet date for raw materials, plus direct labor and applicable overhead. If any interruption in operations is anticipated, this inventory probably has a very low sale value.

- *Finished goods.* Assuming there is no reason to question the marketability of these completed products, value should be equal to total cost of production or cost to replace, without provision for profit.

Differences in inventory cost flow methods, LIFO, FIFO, or average cost frequently cause material effects on the income statement and the balance sheet and must be adjusted. When a company uses LIFO, the notes to its financial statements provide the amount of the LIFO inventory reserve. If the company's statements do not have accompanying notes and it uses LIFO (a rare situation), the company's accountant should be able to provide the necessary information for adjusting the balance sheet to a FIFO basis. During periods of inflation, the FIFO inventory method records earlier, lower inventory costs on the income statement, which reduces cost of goods sold and increases gross profit and taxable income. This procedure leaves the more recent higher costs—those that most closely approximate current market value—in inventory on the balance sheet. Thus, the FIFO method tends to overstate income but produce a more realistic inventory. Conversely, the LIFO method charges the later, more inflated costs into cost of goods sold, which reduces gross profit and taxable income and produces a more realistic measure of income. Last in, first out leaves the earlier inventory costs—which are generally below current market value during a period of inflation—on the balance sheet, which leads to an unrealistically low inventory balance.

The magnitude of the potential distortion depends on both the level of inflation and the rate of a company's inventory turnover. It is

Exhibit 11-1   LIFO to FIFO Inventory Valuation Conversion

Line Item	LIFO Basis	LIFO Reserve	FIFO Basis
Beginning Inventory	2,000,000	335,000	2,335,000
Add: Purchases	4,000,000		4,000,000
Available for Sale	6,000,000		6,335,000
Less: Ending Inventory	−400,000	−440,000	−840,000
Cost of Goods Sold	5,600,000		5,495,000
Increase in Profit			105,000

generally not advisable to compare a target company that uses a one cost flow method for inventory to other companies before making necessary adjustments for differences created by these inventory accounting methods. Also note that adjustments to both the balance sheet and the income statement may require tax adjustments as well. Such adjustments can be accomplished either by creating a current liability, called deferred income tax, or by netting the tax against the increased value of the inventory on the balance sheet. Adjustments to the income statement should be tax affected as well.

Exhibit 11-1 illustrates a conversion from LIFO to FIFO inventory accounting when a company had a LIFO reserve of $335,000 at the beginning of the period and of $440,000 at the end of the period. The resulting increase in profit would be shown on the income statement, and both financial statements could be adjusted for the tax effects of these changes.

Prepaid Expenses

This account generally does not require adjustment as long as the buyer can acquire the benefits of the item purchased or receive a refund for the advanced payment.

Other Assets

Look at the composition for possible adjustment. Common examples of items that may require adjustment are marketable securities, other nonoperating assets, covenants not to compete or goodwill previously purchased, and notes receivable, particularly from the selling shareholders. If these items are not used in the company's operations, they should be removed from the balance sheet. Other items should be converted to market value based on the benefit that they provide to the company.

Fixed Assets

When fixed assets are written up to market value, consider recognizing the tax that would be due on the increased value. Considerations include:

- The tax, if it is applied, could be netted against the written-up value or shown as a deferred tax liability.
- Nontaxable entities, such as S corporations, face different levels of taxation.
- The level of the tax to be applied, recognizing that the well-informed seller and buyer, each realizing that trapped-in capital gains affect value, may negotiate some difference between the "no tax" and "full tax" positions.
- As an alternative, the tax on the trapped-in gain could be reflected through an increased lack of marketability discount. This reflects the likely buyer's recognition that the fixed asset with lower book value provides less tax shelter and creates greater eventual taxable gain.

Intangible Assets

The intangibles on the balance sheet often are based on the allocated portion of cost from an acquisition or the costs to create. In either event the objective is to adjust them to their market value from their unamortized book value. If specific intangibles, such as patents, copyrights, or trademarks, possess value, this value could be determined using an income, market or cost approach with the intangible then listed at that amount.

On the balance sheet, goodwill or general intangible value should be removed and replaced with its market value.

Nonrecurring or Nonoperating Assets and Liabilities

This category consists of nonrecurring activities or items not expected to recur. Nonoperating assets are assets not needed to maintain the anticipated levels of business activity. Examples could include one-time receipts or payments from litigation, gains or losses on sales of assets, cash in excess of that needed to fund anticipated operations, marketable securities, income from interest or dividends received on nonoperating cash, or investments or interest paid on nonoperating debt.

When appraising a control interest, nonoperating assets usually are added to the operating enterprise value to calculate the total enterprise value. When valuing a minority interest, this value may not be added back, recognizing that the minority interest may not have access to it.

Off Balance Sheet Assets

Capital leases should be recorded on the balance sheet. They require adjustment only if the lease terms do not reflect market conditions. Operating leases are not shown on the balance sheet but may require adjustment to the lease expense on the income statement if the lease is not carried at a market rate.

Warranty obligations are another significant type of asset (dealer) or liability (manufacturer or service provider) which will be "off balance sheet" in many companies. Discussion with management, manufacturers, and industry data sources can often assist in the quantification of these items.

Although there are usually few adjustments, the liability section of the balance sheet requires scrutiny, and common liability adjustments include:

- *Asset-related liabilities.* Liabilities related to assets that were adjusted also may require adjustment. For example, if real property was removed as an asset, any related liability(ies) also may need to be removed. If later, at the total enterprise level, the value of the real property is added to the operating value (which was developed using a market-rate rent), the related debt can be netted against that real estate value.

- *Interest-bearing debt.* If the interest charged on a note payable is a fixed rate that is materially different from the market rate on the valuation date, the debt should be adjusted. This process is similar to the adjustment to determine the market value of a bond with a fixed rate of interest when market rates of interest are significantly different.

- *Accruals.* Often accruals for vacation, sick time, and unfunded pension or profit-sharing plans and the effects of exercise of employee stock options are not on the balance sheet but are obligations at the time of the valuation and should be recorded.

- *Deferred taxes.* Based on the treatment of the deferred tax due on assets written up from book to market values, a deferred tax liability may be appropriate.

- *Off balance sheet liabilities.* Common unrecorded items, particularly in closely held companies, include guarantee or warranty obligations, pending litigation, or other disputes, such as taxes and employee claims, or environmental or other regulatory issues. These liabilities are generally assessed and quantified through discussions with management and legal counsel. It is also useful to inquire as to whether the company has made commitments to purchase quantities of raw material from specific suppliers over a future period or made guarantees or cosigned for obligations of other companies or individuals.

Generally speaking, the adjustment to the equity section is only to bring the statement into balance by netting the adjustments to the assets and liabilities sections. Most often these adjustments are made to retained earnings. Another adjustment often made is to eliminate any treasury stock so that the statement reflects only the issued and outstanding shares.

TREATMENT OF NONOPERATING ASSETS OR ASSET SURPLUSES OR SHORTAGES

When the operating value of a target is determined by an application of the income approach or market approach, adjustments for the value of specific assets owned by the target may be necessary to determine the total value of the entity being appraised. This situation occurs most frequently when a target owns assets not used in its operations, has excess operating assets such as surplus cash or fixed assets, or has an asset shortage such as a deficient level of working capital. When any of these conditions is present, the operating value determined by the income or market approach probably will not reflect the effect on value of these factors, and they must then be treated as an adjustment to the preliminary determination of operating value.

In the negotiation process, either the buyer or the seller may be unwilling to have the nonoperating assets or excess assets included in the transaction. When this happens, adjustments to value for these items must be made. Depending on the circumstances, these adjustments may reflect the specific sale terms that are negotiated and the price the buyer is willing to pay under those terms rather than the specific value.

SPECIFIC STEPS IN COMPUTING ADJUSTED BOOK VALUE

The application of the adjusted book value method under a going concern premise is most commonly referred to as the *adjusted book value method* and involves the following five steps:

1. *Beginning point.* Obtain the target's balance sheet as of the appraisal date or as recently before that date as possible. (Audited financial statements are preferable to reviewed or compiled statements, and accrual basis statements are preferable to cash basis.)
2. *Adjust line items.* Adjust each asset, liability, and equity account from book value to estimated market value.
3. *Adjust for items not on the balance sheet.* Value and add specific tangible or intangible assets and liabilities that were not listed on the balance sheet.
4. *Tax affecting.* Consider the appropriateness of tax affecting the adjustments to the balance sheet. Also consider whether any deferred taxes on the balance sheet should be eliminated.

5. *Ending point.* From the adjustments, prepare a balance sheet that reflects all items at market value. From this amount, determine the adjusted value of invested capital or equity, as appropriate.

Asset-intensive targets or companies that lack operating value because they generate inadequate returns are frequently valued by the asset or cost approach. This approach usually is appropriate only for appraisal of controlling interests that possess the authority to cause the sale that creates the cash benefit to shareholders. Whether using the adjusted book value method to determine the value of the assets "in use" or liquidation value to determine their worth under either orderly or forced liquidation conditions, this approach involves adjusting balance sheet accounts to market value. These adjustment procedures also are used to reflect the value of nonoperating assets or asset surpluses or shortages that may exist in companies whose operating value is determined by an income or market approach.

12

Adjusting Value through Premiums and Discounts

Sit back and take a deep breath before applying a premium or discount. It often has a larger effect on value than any other adjustment made, so it should receive careful consideration. These adjustments are not made automatically and should not always be at a constant percentage. Care at the beginning of this process is often rewarded with time saved and a better value estimate.

This care begins with terminology because in the application of premiums and discounts, various terms, particularly minority and control, are often misused. *Control* describes an interest, whether minority or control, that possesses a material degree of control. A control interest is not always a majority interest and a minority interest may possess control, depending on the presence or absence of rights of various ownership interests. *Minority* describes an interest, whether minority or majority, that lacks a material degree of control. Ownership of less than 50% of the outstanding shares of stock does not always constitute lack of control; this could be the case if the majority interest owned nonvoting stock. While "control" and "noncontrol" would be more accurate, "minority" and "control" are widely used in business valuation and are employed in this discussion under the definitions that have been presented.

APPLICABILITY OF PREMIUMS AND DISCOUNTS

Each valuation method or procedure may generate different characteristics of value. The merger and acquisition (M&A) method typically results in a control marketable value, while the guideline public company method may generate a control or minority marketable value. The income approach can generate a control or minority value, which probably carry different levels of marketability, and the asset approach most commonly generates a control marketable value. Consequently, premiums and discounts must be considered for each value indicated because adjustments that are appropriate for one indicated value may not apply to another. This point is emphasized because a common error in business valuation is to assume that a discount or a premium is required based on the characteristics of the company being appraised. For example, if the target company is a closely held business in which a controlling interest is being acquired, do not automatically assume that a control premium and a discount for lack of marketability must be applied to each value determined for the company.

The correct methodology is to identify the nature of the value initially computed by each appraisal method. This value is then compared to the characteristics of the subject company to determine what adjustments, if any, are required. The applicability of adjustments for control or lack of control can be determined by answering the following question for each valuation method: Was the degree of control implicit in the valuation method the same or different from the degree of control inherent in the interest being valued?

If the degrees of control are different, a premium for control or a discount for lack of control may be required. For example, the M&A method implies a degree of control approximately equivalent to the degree inherent in the acquisition of a 100% interest in a business. If this data is used to appraise a comparable ownership interest, no discount or premium is required because the method produces a value that reflects a degree of control appropriate to the interest being valued. If the characteristics of the value initially determined are different from the interest being appraised, then a premium for control or a discount for lack of control may be required to determine the appropriate value.

After the issue of control versus lack of control is determined, the degree of marketability must be considered. Although the degree of marketability is distinct from the degree of control, they are related, and marketability is influenced by control. Therefore, the adjustment, if any, for the degree of marketability should be made *after* the adjustment for control. Similar to the process just applied, determine the need for an adjustment for marketability by asking the following question: Is the degree of marketability that is implied in the method employed to compute the initial indication of value the same or different from the degree of marketability inherent in the interest being valued?

For example, if the guideline public company method generates an initial indication of value on a minority marketable basis and a minority interest in a closely held company is being appraised, a discount for lack of marketability is warranted. Conversely, if the M&A method generates a control marketable value and the interest being appraised possesses those characteristics, no adjustment for lack of marketability would be required.

In summary, to begin the process of application of premiums and discounts, identify the nature of each value initially determined in terms of its degree of control and marketability. Then compare each result to those characteristics of the ownership interest in the target company to determine if any adjustments must be made to the initial indication of value of that method.

APPLICATION OF PREMIUMS AND DISCOUNTS

As previously mentioned, although the adjustments to value for control and marketability are related, they are distinct. Therefore, whenever possible, they should be applied separately while their interrelationships are recognized and considered. The degree of control inherent in a company can affect its degree of marketability. Therefore, control premiums or lack-of-control discounts are imposed prior to adjustments for the degree of marketability. Further, these adjustments are applied in a multiplicative, rather than additive, procedure. For example, if a minority interest discount of 25% and a lack-of-marketability discount of 40% are to be applied to a control marketable value initially determined to be $10 million, these adjustments would be applied as follows:

Control, marketable value initially determined	$10,000,000
Application of minority interest discount of 25%	× (1–25%)
	$ 7,500,000
Application of lack-of-marketability discount of 40%	× (1–40%)
Minority, marketable value	$ 4,500,000

Control Premiums

A control premium is imposed to reflect the increase in value that is provided through the benefits of control when the initial indication of value does not reflect this capacity.

Control premiums are derived from studies, conducted annually in the United States, of acquisitions of controlling interests in public companies. Since the publicly traded entities involved must report the results of the transactions to the U.S. Securities and Exchange Commission, they are available for analysis and review. Each year during the 1990s, controlling interests in several hundred public companies were acquired.

From the control premium data, minority interest or lack-of-control discounts can be derived. The derivation of the discount is necessary because there is no direct source of market data to substantiate these discounts.

When these transactions occurred, the premiums offered by the acquirer over the fair market value of that public company's stock on a minority marketable basis was recorded as the control premium. The results of these studies indicate surprising consistency in the premiums and discounts during the 1990s.

The average and median premiums offered, as percentages based on the buyout price over the market price of the seller's stock five business days prior to the announcement date, each year fell within ranges of 35 to 45% and 27 and 35% respectively. The resulting average lack-of-control discount ranged from 26 to 31%, and the median from 21 to 26%.[1] From this date one could quickly conclude:

- Control is worth approximately 30 to 40% more than lack of control.
- If buyers pay a premium of approximately this amount, they are negotiating a good deal.

Such conclusions, however, are shortsighted and incorrect in some respects, and certainly can lead to poor investment decisions for buyers. It is widely recognized that most of the transactions in these studies involve acquisitions by strategic buyers. Their primary motivation for making the acquisition is to achieve synergies and related strategic benefits. Although the buyer acquires control in the transaction, the primary factor driving the above-market price paid is the *synergies* rather than *control*. For this reason, the price above market that is paid is more accurately described as an "acquisition," rather than a "control," premium. How much, if any, of this premium reflects the benefits of control is unknown. It is generally recognized that buyers will rarely pay a premium unless they perceive synergies from the transaction. Therefore, it is likely that little, if any, of the premium is paid for control. To be clear, while the acquirer most likely would not be interested in the acquisition without control, it is the perceived synergy, not the control per se, that drives the premium. Therefore, to conclude that a controlling interest in a company is worth about 40% more proportionately than a lack-of-control interest cannot be substantiated based on this data.

Buyers can make an even more dangerous interpretation of this data if they conclude from it that it is always economically justifiable to pay premiums of about 30 to 40% for acquisitions. As Chapter 1 discusses, the value of a target to an acquirer can vary substantially, depending on the synergies and other integration benefits that vary with each buyer. So investment value and the size of the premium that could be paid must be assessed on a case-by-case basis depending on the synergies.

---

[1] *Mergerstat® Review 2001* (Los Angeles: Mergerstat®, 2001).

It also should be emphasized that although the control premium studies indicate that premiums have consistently been in the range of about 30 to 40%, one should not conclude that these acquisitions always have been value-creating investments for the buyers. On the contrary, studies of acquisitions consistently indicate that well over half have not produced adequate returns on investment for the buyers. Thus, if anything, one should conclude from these studies that in a majority of these transactions, the premiums paid have resulted in poor investments for the buyers.

It is important to emphasize that the control premium seldom indicates the target's maximum investment value to the acquirer. As Chapter 1 explains, investment value reflects the *maximum* value of all synergies. The buyer who pays a premium of this amount creates no value; instead, this value is transferred to the seller in the form of the premium paid. Thus, every prudent buyer must first recognize that because the target is likely to be worth a different investment value to each potential buyer, the premium each can afford to pay will vary depending on each buyer's circumstances. These buyers also must recognize that every dollar of premium they pay above fair market value reduces the total synergistic value that can be created by the acquisition.

Conversely, some buyers have paid premiums well above the 30 to 40% range and achieved very successful investments. This fact reinforces the point that the investment value of a company varies with each buyer depending on synergies that are unique to each transaction.

Lack-of-Control Discounts

Also known as minority interest discounts, these discounts reflect the diminution in value caused by the lack of control. This discount can be applied either to a minority interest or to a majority interest that lacks some degree of control. This discount is applied when the initial indication of value reflects control but the ownership interest being appraised lacks control.

Lack-of-control discounts are derived from market studies, and averaged about 24% during the 1990's. They result from the control premium studies and probably should be interpreted with an even greater degree of caution than the control premium results. No source of data from the public security markets enables direct computation of a lack-of-control discount. To overcome this shortcoming and provide some indication of the distinction in value between a lack-of-control and control equity interest, the discounts are indirectly computed from the control premium studies.

This computation can be explained most easily through an illustration. Assume that a public company is currently trading for fair market value of $60 per share. When it is acquired in a strategic transaction for $84 per share, the control premium of 40% is computed by dividing the $24 per share premium ($84 − $60) by the $60-per-share fair market value. From this data we can further conclude that this transaction implies a minority interest discount of 29%, which is computed by dividing the $24-per-share premium by the $84-per-share control price. Thus, the minority interest discount percentages frequently quoted do not result from acquisitions of minority interests but are derived from the premiums paid in control transactions. The nature of this data should give strong reason for caution in applying these adjustments and in the degree of reliability placed on them. The implied minority interest discount can be computed from the control premium by using the following formula:

$$MID = 1 - \frac{1}{1 + CP}$$

where:

MID = Minority interest discount

CP = Median control premium

Applying the numbers from the previous example confirms the accuracy of the formula:

$$.29 = 1 - \frac{1}{1 + .40}$$

Lack of Marketability Discounts

This discount reflects the diminution in value resulting from the inability to promptly convert an ownership interest into cash.

The lack-of-marketability discount (LOMD) also results from market data, much of which is considered to provide a more accurate indication of this value adjustment than the market data used to suggest the control premiums. The first source of LOMD percentages results from restricted stock studies. Restricted stock, which is also known as letter stock, is stock issued by a corporation that is either not registered with the Securities and Exchange Commission (SEC), which prevents it from being sold into the public market, or is SEC-registered stock that is restricted from being sold into the public market. This type of stock is most commonly sold in an initial public offering, a follow-up offering of stock, or when stock is issued related to an acquisition. The restriction is typically placed on this stock to prevent dilution in the stock price that could occur if a large number of shares of stock are sold at one time. These studies, which have been conducted by various organizations over the last 30 years, have analyzed the prices paid for securities of publicly traded companies that are otherwise marketable except for a restriction that prevents their sale for a limited period of time. The restrictions prevent the securities from being traded in transactions on the open market but allow them to be sold in private transactions. The buyer in these transactions, however, is still subject to the restriction, and therefore is willing to pay only a discounted price to acquire a security that cannot be immediately converted into cash. The holding period of the restriction varies by transaction, but before 1997 typically did not exceed 24 months. Beginning in 1997, the holding period for certain restricted securities was reduced to 12 months. Initial studies of this reduced restriction period indicate that the discounts for lack of marketability have declined with the shorter required holding period and increased market activity in these shares. The results of the restricted stock studies indicate a typical discount of approximately 35% during the 1990s. Thus, minority ownership interests in shares of stock of publicly traded corporations, which were only temporarily restricted from being sold on the open market for a fixed period, suffered a reduction in value of about one-third due to this lack of marketability. This fact indicates the market's strong demand for liquidity and the substantial reduction in value that occurs as liquidity declines.

The second source of data about the LOMD results from pre-initial public offering (IPO) studies, which have also been conducted over many years. These studies were prepared by two organizations, one of which looked at stock prices during the 36-month period preceding an IPO and the other during the five-month period preceding the IPO. In each case, the study compared the price paid for the stock in transactions while the company was privately owned to the price for which the stock initially traded in the IPO. Because these companies went public, they were required as part of their registration to go public to list transactions that occurred in the stock while it was privately held during these prior periods. The transaction data came from these sources. Like the restricted stock studies, the results of these studies were surprisingly consistent with the mean and median discounts at approximately 44%. Note that the research for both of these categories of studies are of investments in *minority* interests. Since most transactions for merger and acquisition purposes involve controlling interests, discounts of this magnitude seldom would be appropriate.

The controlling shareholder, particularly the owner of 100% of the shares, through control can decide to immediately place the company on the market for sale. With the authority that accompanies control, this shareholder also can initiate whatever steps are necessary to prepare the company for the sale and present it in the best possible light. This shareholder also controls the company's net cash flow and any discretionary expense items that the company makes on behalf of shareholders. Minority shareholders typically lack the ability to influence these items, which contributes to an investor's heightened concern when the marketability of the interest is also impaired.

The controlling shareholder frequently faces significant transaction costs in selling the business, and the sale process may consume a considerable period of time. During this period economic or industry conditions may change, which may have either a positive or a negative effect on the company's stock price. Depending on industry conditions and buying patterns, shareholders also may face market conditions where acquisitions are made with payments in the form of stock or notes that are less attractive than cash. Each of these factors may contribute to the difficulty in selling a controlling interest and is typically considered in determining the discount for lack of marketability.

Although specific market data on controlling interests is not available, many in the professional business appraisal community conclude that discounts are influenced by the nature of the industry and the size of anticipated transaction costs. Industries that are better organized with more transactions occurring tend to have lower transaction costs as sales generally occur more quickly. Industries that are fragmented, or less well organized with less merger and acquisition activity, make it harder for buyers and sellers to make contact to conduct business. In these circumstances, sales typically take longer with higher transaction costs suggesting higher discounts for lack of marketability. With these factors in mind, discounts for lack of marketability for controlling interests tend to fall in the range of 5 to 15%, with market conditions and transaction costs being the primary factors influencing the discount size.

APPLY DISCRETION IN THE SIZE OF THE ADJUSTMENT

While there is a natural inclination to view the market data presented as absolutes, premiums and discounts should not be applied on an on-or-off basis as if one was turning a light on or off. Instead, these adjustments should be applied like a dimmer switch that allows the light to be gradually raised or lowered depending on the circumstances. Discounts or premiums must be applied in recognition of the specific facts and circumstances, which could cause the adjustment to be smaller or larger. For example, a 40% shareholder in a company where the remaining 60% of the shares are owned by one other shareholder possesses less control and influence than would be the case if that same 40% interest shared ownership with many shareholders, none of whom owns greater than a 1% interest. Both circumstances featured a 40% ownership interest, yet the relative degree of control of these interests would be vastly different.

Furthermore, consider the influence possessed by the 2% shareholder when the other 98% of the stock is owned by a single shareholder. Then consider the influence of the 2% shareholder when the remaining 98% is held equally in two 49% ownership blocks. In this case, the 2% shareholder becomes the "swing vote,"

Exhibit 12-1   Specific Company Factors that Can Affect the Size of Adjustments

Factors that Affect the Degree of Control

- Effect of stock ownership structure on ability of minority owners to approve certain corporate actions
- Effect of stock ownership structure on ability of minority owners to influence selection of members of the board of directors
- Effect of stock ownership pattern that provides "swing vote" influence
- Level of legal protection to minority shareholders in that jurisdiction
- Stock that lacks voting rights
- History of consideration of minority shareholder interest

Factors that Affect the Degree of Marketability

- Presence of restrictions on the transferability of shares of stock
- Presence of buy/sell agreement that hampers transferability of shares
- Degree of attractiveness of the block of stock
- History and intent of dividend payments that are relatively small or large
- Presence of a reasonably organized market for sales of companies in that industry
- Presence of consolidation or pressures to consolidate in that industry
- Likely population of buyers of that size interest in that industry

which in spite of its very small ownership can wield substantial influence. These examples reinforce the need to consider the specific factors, which are listed in Exhibit 12-1, that could affect the size of the premium or discount. Once again, appropriate application of these adjustments are judgments that require experience and an understanding of the underlying market data for proper application.

CONTROL VERSUS LACK OF CONTROL IN INCOME-DRIVEN METHODS

In Chapter 6, adjustments to income were discussed, including those made for payments of above-market compensation to shareholders. Known as control adjustments, generally speaking these should be made *only* when the ownership interest possesses

Exhibit 12-2   Computation of Control and Lack-of-Control Values through Adjustment to the Return

	Lower Excess Compensation	*Higher Excess Compensation*
	In millions	
Net Income Before Excess Compensation (control return)	$5	$5
Less: Excess Compensation[a]	−1	−3
Net Income After Excess Compensation	$4	$2
Computation of Control Value[b]	$\dfrac{\$5}{20\%} = \$25$	$\dfrac{\$5}{20\%} = \$25$
Computation of Lack of Control Value[b]	$\dfrac{\$4}{20\%} = \$20$	$\dfrac{\$2}{20\%} = \$10$
Resulting Implied Lack of Control Discount	$\dfrac{\$25 - \$20}{\$25} = 20\%$	$\dfrac{\$25 - \$10}{\$25} = 60\%$

[a] Excess compensation includes many types of control adjustments including salary, bonuses, fringe benefits, payments to favored parties, and other forms exercised by the control shareholder.
[b] Assumes use of single-period capitalization method and 20% capitalization rate.

the legal authority to implement these control adjustments. These control-type adjustments may be less significant in larger transactions because the adjustment is not material to the company's resulting income or cash flow. For smaller companies, however, control adjustments can have a substantial effect on value. It is generally inappropriate to reflect control or noncontrol adjustments to value through application of a premium or discount. Instead, the difference in value on a control versus lack-of-control basis should be reflected through adjustments to the return—income or cash flow—rather than through application of a premium or discount. This is illustrated in Exhibit 12-2, where a company had net income before excess compensation of $5 million. In choosing to pay excess compensation of $1 million to control shareholders or their beneficiaries, an implied lack-of-control discount of 20% resulted. If, however, the company had chosen to pay excess compensation of $3 million, the reduction from control value would have been 60%. Thus, the magnitude of the discount is determined by the relative size of the excess compensation. When this compensation constitutes a significant portion of the company's income before compensation, major differences between the control versus lack-of-control value can result.

Because market data on control premiums and implied lack-of-control discounts cannot accurately reflect these variations caused by the different levels of excess compensation, in income-driven methods the differences in control versus lack of control should be computed by adjusting the return, as shown in Exhibit 12-2, rather than through imposition of a control premium to a lack-of-control value or lack-of-control discount to a control value.

OTHER PREMIUMS AND DISCOUNTS

Adjustments to value other than those to reflect the degree of control or marketability are seldom encountered in business valuation. The following is a brief description of those that are occasionally employed.

- *Discount for nonvoting shares.* This discount may be applied to nonvoting shares to reflect the reduction in their value compared to voting shares. Limited market studies generally conclude that this discount is less than 10%. While this may be surprising, the small discount occurs because these shares are typically minority interests that already reflect the low value caused by their lack of control status.

- *Key person discount.* The purpose of this discount is to recognize the diminution in value that occurs from excessive reliance on a person who is critical to the success of the business. Although this may apply in appraisals made for estate tax purposes, where the key person has died without insurance proceeds or other provisions to accommodate the loss, application of this discount is most often inappropriate. Reliance on one person or a limited management is a risk driver that is more appropriately reflected in the discount rate or value multiple derived for the company.

- *Portfolio discount.* This adjustment may apply in circumstances where a company owns an unattractive portfolio of operating divisions or combination of assets that may be worth more when considered separately than as part of a combined business. Costs to remedy the ownership structure should be considered in assessing the magnitude of this discount.

- *Blockage discount.* This discount may be imposed to reflect the negative effect on share price when a large block of a company's stock is offered for sale at one time. More applicable to public companies, this discount reflects the market being "swamped" with sell orders when insufficient demand is available to meet the supply. This discount is also applicable when a private company holds as an investment a large block of shares in a single publicly traded company.

- *Discount for trapped-in gains.* This discount applies to the sale of the stock of companies that own assets possessing a low tax basis. Upon a sale of the assets in the corporation, the low asset tax basis would trigger a large tax on the built-in gains on these assets, which renders the corporation's stock less attractive to a potential buyer.

- *Discount caused by double counting factors.* Rather than a separately identified adjustment, this point is a reminder that adjustment factors can easily and erroneously be counted twice. In recognizing these adjustments, be careful not to reflect them in the computation of the return, rate of return, or growth rate of the company and then also apply a discount or premium that reflects their effect on value a second time.

FAIR MARKET VALUE VERSUS INVESTMENT VALUE

Some of these discounts that may apply when determining the target's stand-alone fair market value may not be applicable when determining the investment value relevant to a specific acquirer. For example, the LOMD, which is appropriate for the stand-alone value of a private target, may be inappropriate for investment value when the acquirer is a public company.

Premiums and discounts frequently constitute the largest adjustment to value made in a business valuation. While these adjustments tend to be less prominent in valuations for merger and acquisition than they are for estate and gift tax purposes, they still require careful consideration. This process begins by identifying the nature of the value initially determined by each valuation method to assess whether application of a premium or a discount is appropriate. Determination of the appropriate size of the adjustment requires an understanding of the market data from which the premium and discount benchmarks are derived. These benchmarks do not constitute definitive percentage adjustments; rather, the facts and circumstances of the interest being appraised must be evaluated to determine the size of the adjustment. Ultimately, this is a professional judgment, but with background and experience, analysts can make defendable adjustments.

13

Reconciling Initial Value Estimates and Determining Value Conclusion

Once an appraiser has applied one or more valuation approaches and reached an initial conclusion of value, the inevitable question is "Is it correct?" That is, is the value that has been determined for the ownership interest reasonable and defendable based on conditions as of the appraisal date and the quality and quantity of information available?

Because there are many qualitative assessments and quantitative steps leading to the initial indications of value, the review and reconciliation process should be both thorough and methodical. Business valuation involves many computations, and most of the calculations made later in the process are dependent on the accuracy of previous numbers. So accuracy is essential and sound work habits include review of all computations.

Reaching the final value conclusion by accepting the initial estimate or by averaging the different results of several methods does not assure a defendable conclusion. The key to a sound result is a comprehensive review that challenges the underlying assumptions, methods, information, and calculations of each process employed.

ESSENTIAL NEED FOR BROAD PERSPECTIVE

Begin with the basics. Review the appraisal assignment by answering the following questions:

- What property or ownership interest is being appraised?
- Was it specific assets, an equity interest, or invested capital?
- What specific legal rights or limits are attached to this property?
- Do other ownership interests exist that possess preferential claims on this property or its returns?
- Does this ownership interest reflect control or lack of control?
- What is the degree of marketability of the ownership interest?
- What is the date of the appraisal, and did the analysis include only information about the company and its external environment that was known or knowable as of that date?
- Was the standard of value fair market value on a stand-alone basis to a financial buyer without consideration of synergies, or investment value to a strategic buyer inclusive of synergies, or both? Or was it some other standard of value?

Whenever possible, all three valuation approaches—income, market, and asset—should be employed to determine an estimate of value. One or more of these approaches may be inappropriate or less appropriate because of the nature of the assignment or the quality or quantity of information that is available. Each approach computes value based on different criteria. The income approach bases value on future returns, which are discounted or capitalized at a rate of return that reflects a relative level of risk. The guideline public company and merger and acquisition methods of the market approach base value on prices paid for similar companies in public markets. The asset approach derives value from the underlying assets owned by the business considering a hypothetical sale. Thus, each of the approaches takes a different view of the target with each view providing a unique perspective on what drives value. Analysts should attempt to use each approach or be prepared to provide an explanation of why any approach is rejected.

Once initial values are determined, often it is helpful to step away from the details of the assignment and then return to take a fresh look at the conclusions. In reviewing the work, ask whether a reasonable, unbiased individual would reach the same conclusions of value. Examine to be sure the conclusions are not influenced by a desire for a high or low value. Consider whether the value recognizes the company's history; its competitive environment, including industry and economic conditions; its internal strengths and weaknesses; and likely future conditions. If synergies are considered, be sure they are recognized only when computing investment value, not fair market value. Evaluate whether the estimate of value considers appropriate buyer and seller knowledge of market considerations and motivations in the transactions. Ask whether both the *buyer* and the *seller*, in possession of the relevant facts, would accept the assumptions as reasonable.

In making this assessment, consider further the general applicability of each appraisal approach to this assignment. Use the summaries in Exhibit 13-1 to assess whether an approach is appropriate.

Consider the applicability of each approach in light of the competitive assessment of the company. Pay particular attention to what drives risk and value in that company and in that industry and how each approach considers these key variables. Identify any risk or value drivers that may have been overlooked or not given appropriate consideration by an approach and the resulting effect of this on any of the values determined.

When the value conclusion clashes with the rule of thumb for that industry, determine why. Doing so will provide guidance as to whether the value opinion needs to change (less likely) or why the rule of thumb does not work for this specific appraisal (more likely). Also consider whether rules of thumb are commonly employed in that industry and whether they have been considered. Because rules of thumb are often simplistic generalizations that fail to adequately address factors unique to a company, they should not be used as the sole method of estimating value. If, however, they are widely recognized in that industry, they should at

Exhibit 13-1   Summary of Applicability of Business Valuation Approaches

Income Approach	*Market Approach*[a]	*Asset Approach*
The company derives significant value from its operations.	An adequate number of companies are reasonably similar to the subject company.	The company owns a significant amount of tangible assets.
The company generates a positive income or cash flow.	Merger and acquisition transactions involve acquirer circumstances and targets that are reasonably similar.	The company creates little value from its operations.
The company possesses significant intangible value.	There is adequate data available about the companies used for comparative purposes.	The company's balance sheet includes most of its tangible assets.
The company's risk can be quantified accurately through a rate of return.	The companies generate multiples that provide a reasonable indication of market conditions and prices as of the appraisal date.	It is possible to obtain accurate appraisals of the value of the company's assets.
The company's future performance can be estimated accurately through a forecast.	The subject company is large enough to be compared to the companies used in the market approach.	The ownership interest being appraised possesses control or access to the underlying asset value.

[a] This discussion of the market approach refers only to applications of the guideline public company and merger and acquisition methods.

least be computed as a reasonableness check against the primary approaches to value. Industry participants frequently refer to these metrics, so it is wise for the appraisal to consider and discuss their applicability and reasonableness.

In application of the income or market approaches, evaluate any adjustments made to the return employed and whether these adjustments were reasonable and appropriate. In doing so, again recognize that synergies should be considered only in computing investment value. Further, recognize that the income and market approaches, which determine value based on a measure of the company's performance, are heavily dependent on the reasonableness of that performance estimate. So the performance should be reviewed once again in light of the company's competitive environment. To achieve a rigorous review of the work, employ the following critiques—income, market, and asset approach reviews—to the results of each approach, considering the matters in an unbiased manner.

INCOME APPROACH REVIEW

The income approach is used most often in business valuation for merger and acquisition because of its theoretical strengths and flexibility. Investors recognize the theoretical soundness of basing value on future returns discounted at a rate that reflects their relative level of risk. In addition to being grounded in sound theory, the income approach easily accommodates computation of fair market value or investment value, using an equity or invested capital model on a control or lack-of-control basis with consideration of the appropriate degree of marketability. It can employ historical or forecasted returns and can measure the return as various amounts of income or cash flow.

For the income approach to be appropriate, the company's value should be heavily influenced by the company's income or cash flow. This is usually the case for profitable operating businesses, and this approach may not be appropriate for companies that generate low returns. As such, the review should focus on the two key variables used to compute value, which are the return and the rate of return.

For a comprehensive review of the value determined by the income approach, *objectively* assess the following:

Fair market value versus investment value:

- The return and rate of return chosen to compute the company's fair market value should reflect the company's operating performance and risk profile as a stand-alone company.
- The investment value should consider the effects of synergies on return. The rate of return should reflect the acquiring

company's risk profile and resulting cost of capital, adjusted for the risk profile of the target company.

Invested capital versus equity:

- Consider that valuation for merger and acquisition usually employs the invested capital model to prevent financing considerations from influencing operating value. Proper application requires appropriate and consistent use of invested capital returns and rates of return.

- In use of the invested capital model, look for potential distortions to the company's weighted average cost of capital (WACC) caused by extremes in the company's degree of financial leverage. Consider whether market conditions would permit that capital structure and what debt and equity costs would be appropriate for that degree of leverage.

- Recognize that the debt and equity weights in the WACC computation should be made based on market values rather than book values, which may require use of the iterative process or the shortcut formula in the computation of the WACC.

Measurement of return:

- Consider the appropriateness of the return stream chosen for the assignment. Net cash flow to invested capital generally provides the most precise measure of cash return to capital providers, and it is the return for which the most reliable rates of return are available. Other measures of return are generally less accurate, are more susceptible to manipulation, and usually must rely on less defendable rates of return.

- Consider the company's past operating performance and *why* it generated that performance in assessing the likelihood of it achieving its forecasted future performance.

- Consider the likelihood of achieving the forecast, given economic and industry conditions and the company's competitive position in light of its strategic advantages and disadvantages.

- Review any normalization adjustments made for nonoperating and nonrecurring items of income and expense, recognizing that the objective in making the adjustments is to present the most accurate possible portrayal of the company's future operating performance. Also review any adjustments to income for above- or below-market compensation paid in any form to owners or their beneficiaries. Generally speaking, these adjustments are usually appropriate only when appraising a controlling ownership interest that possesses the authority to change this compensation.
- In reviewing the company's forecasted volume, consider pricing and unit volumes, by products and product lines, given economic and industry conditions.
- Given forecasted economic and industry conditions, consider the reasonableness of forecasted expenses and resulting profit margins.
- Review the company's tax attributes as of the appraisal date and the reasonableness of estimated future tax rates, given its legal and tax status and the tax jurisdictions in which it operates.
- Review for reasonableness the forecasted level of change in working capital and investment in fixed assets. Where possible, review forecasted turnover ratios of accounts receivable, accounts payable, inventory, and fixed assets as part of this assessment, and compare this to both historical performance and industry standards.
- In choosing the long-term growth rate for use in the single-period capitalization or the terminal value in the multiple period discounting, consider the following:
  — The long-term economic and industry outlook
  — The company's current competitive condition and the likely duration of its competitive advantages and disadvantages
  — The company's profits, management capabilities, and sources of financing to fund that pace of growth

  Remember that choice of a growth rate above the forecasted industry growth rate implies that the company will be able to gain market share indefinitely.

- If the multiple-period discounting is employed, assess the reasonableness of the length of the forecast period, which should be long enough to reflect all anticipated material changes in cash flows, and should achieve a stabilized return in the final forecast year that is considered to be sustainable in the long term.
- When the potential exists for substantial variation in the company's future return, consider the use of probability analysis or real option analysis (see Chapter 6) to reflect the effect of this variation on value.

Choice of rate of return:

- Check for the compatibility of the rate with the return used to measure performance. Common areas where the return or the rate of return are misapplied include:
  — Equity versus invested capital elements
  — Pre tax versus after-tax returns
  — Net cash flow versus net income
- Consider the appropriateness of the methodology in arriving at the equity discount rate:
  — The capital asset pricing model (CAPM) is seldom appropriate in the appraisal of a closely held company because its underlying assumptions seldom apply to such companies.
  — The modified capital asset pricing model (MCAPM) overcomes many of these limitations when a beta for the target company can be derived from an appropriate list of guideline companies. So when the guideline public company method is used within the market approach, MCAPM may work in the income approach.
  — The buildup method, with its assumption of a beta of 1, is generally most appropriate to appraise a closely held company, particularly businesses where the guideline public company method was rejected.
- Consider whether the size premium recognized is appropriate for the subject company.

- Consider whether the discount rate accurately reflects risk within the industry, either through choice of the beta or the specific company risk premium.
- Consider whether the discount rate reflects specific company risk factors recognized in the competitive analysis. This rate also should reflect the primary risk drivers and value drivers influencing the company's performance and the company's relative level of strategic advantages and disadvantages.

Single-period capitalization method:

- Consider that for this method to be appropriate, the single-period return chosen should accurately represent the company's long-term annual performance.
- Consider also that this method assumes that that return will grow at a constant rate to infinity and that this long-term growth rate must be reasonable given the company's competitive position and long-term economic and industry conditions.

Control versus lack-of-control value:

- Consider that in an income approach, the major factor that determines the difference in value on a control versus lack-of-control basis is the choice of the return stream.
- Generally speaking, normalization adjustments for above-market compensation in any form paid to owner employees or their beneficiaries should not be made when valuing interests that lack the authority to institute these changes.
- The distinction between control and lack-of-control value may be less clear when above-market compensation is not paid and the return to the controlling and minority shareholders is approximately the same. However, this is likely to be reflected in the application of any appropriate premiums or discounts.
- Recognize the limitations in the accuracy and appropriateness of employing control premiums or minority interest discounts. Also recognize the theoretical limitations of data from which these adjustments are derived.

Degree of marketability:

- Recognize that controlling ownership interests generally possess substantially more marketability than minority interests, and that discounts for lack of marketability for controlling interests are typically in the range of 5 to 15%. This range often reflects the time and transaction costs required for the buyer to resell that controlling interest.

- Recognize that minority interests in closely held companies are highly unmarketable and subject to discounts that are typically at least 35 to 50%.

- Recognize that the degree of control or marketability can be influenced by numerous factors unique to the subject company and that the resulting discounts or premiums will vary in size depending on these factors.

Other adjustments to value:

- Consider that nonoperating items of value excluded in the computation of the company's operating value may have to be added to operating enterprise value to compute the total value of the enterprise.

- Consider that the value of nonoperating assets frequently is not added back in the computation of the value of a lack-of-control interest that lacks the authority to liquidate these assets. Conversely, the presence of substantial liquid nonoperating assets could improve the liquidity and safety of a lack-of-control interest; when that occurs, the discount rate should reflect this financial characteristic.

MARKET APPROACH REVIEW

Although the market approach is less widely employed in M&A valuations than the income approach, values determined by it also require careful review. Because the market approach primarily determines value as a multiple of some measure of operating performance or financial position, these two variables—the performance measure and the multiple—require close scrutiny in assessing the accuracy of the results of this method.

In reviewing the accuracy and reasonableness of the market approach and the multiples chosen for the target, review the following:

- Consider how similar the guideline public companies are to the subject company in terms of the following factors:
  — Size
  — Products or services, and their breadth
  — Markets and customers
  — Competition
  — Management depth
  — Financial performance
  — Financial leverage and liquidity
  — Access to capital
  — Customer concentration
  — Vendor or supplier reliance
  — Technology and research and development capability
  — Quality and capacity of physical plant
  — Accuracy of financial information and internal controls
- Review whether the multiples for the guideline companies in the current year are consistent with longer-term trends, or if the market appears to be abnormally high or low as of the appraisal date.
- Consider whether the anticipated future conditions are similar to the past, and what the likelihood is that any differences are reflected accurately in the multiples of the guideline companies for the current period.
- Consider how the target company compares to the guideline companies in terms of major performance characteristics, including:
  — Growth
  — Profitability
  — Efficiency in asset utilization
  — Financial leverage and coverage
  — Liquidity

- Consider the range, mean, and median multiples of the guideline companies, to which of the guidelines the target is most and least similar, and whether the target company is stronger or weaker than all of the guidelines, and why.

ASSET APPROACH REVIEW

Because the asset approach does not adequately recognize the profitability of a business, it is frequently inappropriate in the appraisal of profitable companies. This method is used most often in the appraisal of asset-intensive companies or underperforming businesses that do not generate an adequate return on capital employed.

In assessing the results of the asset approach, review the following:

- Consider whether the value determined is under a going-concern premise or a premise of liquidation. The liquidation premise assumes the company will cease operations, which generally renders use of the income or the market approach to be unreasonable.
- Consider whether the interest being appraised possesses the legal authority to execute a sale of assets. Because noncontrol interests typically lack this capacity, the asset approach is seldom appropriate to appraise a minority interest of an operating company.
- Consider whether the company's value is derived primarily from ownership of its assets rather than from the results of its operations. This condition would support use of the asset approach.
- Consider the quality and reliability of the asset appraisals or other means under which the net asset value was determined. Although an asset approach may be an appropriate choice, its reliability is dependent on accurate asset valuations.
- Consider whether any of the target company's assets are carried on its balance sheet at a low tax basis, which could subject a buyer to a potential built-in gains tax on a subsequent sale.

Some Quick Checks to Make When Values from the Income Approach and the Market Approach Disagree

The market approach generally should produce a value that supports the results from the income approach. When they disagree, consider the following:

- If appraising a control interest, as is most common in valuations for merger and acquisition, check to see that the results of both methods reflect this. Do the approaches use substantially different measures of return on a control basis? If one of the approaches computes value based on a minority return and applies a control premium, while the other reflects control through the use of a control return, what differences or distortions do these techniques cause?

- While the income approach generally uses a forecast, the market approach typically computes value as a multiple of a historical return. If the historical and forecasted returns are substantially different, determine why this difference occurs and which more accurately portrays the company's potential as of the appraisal date. The other computation may require further adjustment.

- The market approach most commonly employs a multiple of the operating performance of a single period, such as earnings per share. Because this multiple is the reciprocal of a capitalization rate that is applied to the return of a single period, convert the multiple to a capitalization rate and add back the estimated long-term growth rate to compute the implied discount rate. Compare this rate to that used in the income approach after allowing for differences in the return used (e.g., income versus cash flow, pretax versus after-tax income, etc.). Where differences occur, consider adjustments to the multiple or rate that appears to be less reasonable or is based on less reliable data.

- The M&A method, depending on the character of the transaction, typically generates investment value on a control basis. In assessing this, first review whether the strategic transaction(s) provides a realistic indication of the market for the subject company. Also compare this to the investment value on a control basis computed through the income approach, looking to see which computation provides a greater degree of confidence and why their results differ. *(continued)*

- When the guideline public company method is used, look at the range of multiples as well as the mean and median multiples of the guidelines. Again allowing for differences in the return stream used, compute the implied capitalization rate and discount rate generated by these multiples. Next, consider the reasonableness of these rates compared against the discount rates and long-term growth rates employed in the income approach. This comparison should highlight the implied short-term growth rate included in the market multiples.

- Look at the multiple chosen for the target company and its resulting equivalent discount rate and growth rate for that return stream. Assess the reasonableness of these rates in light of the conclusion from the income approach. When inconsistencies occur, one may need to reassess the selection of a multiple for the target company.

VALUE RECONCILIATION AND CONCLUSION

After the results of each procedure have been thoroughly reviewed, the final estimate of value must be determined. When more than one approach has been employed, the results can be averaged, but this is not recommended. Computing a simple average implies that each method was equally appropriate to the assignment or that each produced an equally reliable result. Although this could happen, it is more likely that one of the procedures more accurately portrays and quantifies the key risk and value drivers present and generates a more defendable estimate of value. When this occurs, the methods may be weighted, which can be determined mathematically or subjectively. The reconciliation form presented in Exhibit 13-2 provides a convenient way to present results for review and consideration. Ultimately, the choice of mathematical or subjective weightings, the amount of the weightings, and the final opinion of value is a professional judgment. If this were not the case, software programs could be employed and business valuation would be greatly simplified. The process, however, is simply too complex to be reduced to a formula or program.

Exhibit 13-2 illustrates the reconciliation process when initial values were determined by the multiple period discounting, guideline public company, and merger and acquisition methods. In reviewing each of the methods to determine a final opinion of fair market value, the appraiser concluded that the multiple period discounting method generated a value on which a high degree of confidence could be placed. The forecasted return appeared to be achievable based on the company's historical experience, competitive strengths and weaknesses, and industry conditions. The net cash flow to invested capital return, adjusted to reflect control through the add back of above-market compensation paid to owners, appeared to provide an accurate indication of the company's earning capacity. The rate of return was developed using sound methodology and was able to accurately reflect the major risk drivers and value drivers present in the company.

The guideline public company method used a return to minority shareholders without consideration of excess compensation and employed a 30% control premium to convert from a minority to control estimate of fair market value. The appraiser had a reasonable level of confidence that the guideline companies provided an accurate indication of market prices from which to determine an appropriate multiple for the target company. Due to the lack of confidence in the 30% control premium, the results of this method were given only a 20% weighting in the final computation of value. (If above market compensation is paid, normally it would be added back to income to generate a control return from which control value could be computed directly through use of the guideline public company method, thus avoiding the need for application and defense of a control premium.)

The M&A method looked at several strategic transactions that the appraiser concluded represented investment value to a specific buyer. These transactions did, however, provide an indication of what well-informed buyers in that industry were willing to pay for controlling interests in strategic transactions, and therefore they were recognized but given very little weight.

CANDIDLY ASSESS VALUATION CAPABILITIES

This chapter has presented a summary of risk and value drivers and the resulting reconciliation of methodologies and computations required to produce a defendable opinion of value. In

Exhibit 13-2 Reconciliation of Indicated Values and Application of Discounts or Premiums Appropriate to the Final Opinion of Value

Valuation Method	Interest Being Valued	Indicated by Method (Preadjustments)		Adjustments for Differences in Degree of		Adjusted		Weight	Weighted Component Value
		Value	Basis	Control	Marketability	Value	Basis		
Multiple Period Discounting Method	100%	$36,000,000	Control, as if freely traded	none	10% discount	$32,400,000	Control marketable	70%	$22,680,000
Guideline Public Company	100%	$35,000,000	Minority, as if freely traded	30% premium	10% discount	$40,950,000	Control marketable	20%	$8,190,000
Merger and Acquisition	100%	$44,000,000	Control, as if freely traded	None	10% discount	$39,600,000	Control marketable	10%	$3,960,000

Fair Market Value of a 100% Closely Held Interest on an Operating Control, Marketable Basis	$34,830,000
Plus: Nonoperating Assets	$1,500,000
Fair Market Value of a 100% Closely Held Interest on a Control, Marketable Basis	$36,330,000
Divided by: 2,000,000 Issued and Outstanding Shares	÷ 2,000,000
Per Share: Fair Market Value of a Closely Held Share on a Control, Marketable Basis	$18.17

considering these issues and computations, it is time for appraisers to take a cold hard look at their appraisal knowledge and skills in assessing a potential sale or acquisition. Valuations should routinely analyze the many points reviewed in this chapter. The points summarized here should make sense, and appraisers should be comfortable with the underlying theory and computations.

Where there are gaps in knowledge or experience, candidly consider the consequences of a lack of expertise in these issues. Merger and acquisition usually involves large amounts of money and long-term commitments. If appraisers are not suitably comfortable with business valuation theory and techniques as it is summarized in this chapter, they probably should be seeking professional assistance before making large decisions that carry such substantial consequences. The cost of professional assistance is generally small relative to the potential benefits: an accurate valuation followed either by completion of a successful transaction or, more importantly, rejection of one that should be avoided.

14

Art of the Deal

The preceding chapters have emphasized the essential need for managers and shareholders to understand value to successfully operate a company and to make sound estimates of value. In the merger and acquisition (M&A) world, however, much of the real action takes place *after* stand-alone fair market value and investment value have been determined. Structuring and negotiating a transaction—"doing a deal"—is the next step in the M&A process. This chapter describes the process of negotiating a deal from both the buyer's and the seller's viewpoint. While every transaction is different and each may present unique demands, needs, or circumstances, the concepts and principles presented here provide excellent guidelines to help buyers and sellers reach their ultimate goal: successfully negotiate and close the transaction.

UNIQUE NEGOTIATION CHALLENGES

A broad range of knowledge and skills are required to accomplish this task. Negotiators in M&A should be skillful communicators— in listening, speaking, and writing—must understand value, and

The authors gratefully acknowledge the contributions to this chapter made by Michael J. Eggers, ASA, CBA, CPA, ABV, of American Business Appraisers, San Francisco, California; email: mjeaba@pacbell.com.

should possess a reasonable knowledge of the tax code and accounting principles. As discussed in Chapter 4, the M&A team
should include legal, tax, and valuation specialists, one of whom
also may serve as the negotiator. Buyers and sellers who fail to recognize the need for this breadth of knowledge frequently negotiate the wrong price or terms of sale.

In considering these transaction issues, it may be helpful to
review the discussion in Chapter 4 in the sections "Sales Strategy
and Process" and "Acquisition Strategy and Process."

Sellers sometimes feel that as the owner or chief executive officer (CEO) of their company, they understand the business better than anyone else and, as a result, are best qualified to negotiate the sale. Similarly, CEOs or controlling shareholders of the
buying company may conclude that their authority best equips
them to negotiate the ideal price and terms of sale. While sellers
and buyers may possess extensive knowledge and the authority to
approve or reject the deal, they must recognize that a negotiation
is a process in which they have a role. The key is to understand the
role that each member of the negotiating team should play and
then have each member stick to that function.

Interpersonal and communication skills are emphasized because the deal-making process frequently plunges buyers and sellers into intense negotiations that will determine the course of a
company's operations for a long time. The negotiations may affect
numerous careers, where people will work and what they will do,
and people's personal fortunes are often hanging in the balance.
And with so much at stake, the key negotiators are usually
strangers to each other and often are relying on M&A team members whom they hardly know.

With these circumstances in mind, avoid the urge to rush into
discussions of price. *Price is not value.* Price can be affected dramatically by the deal terms, including:

- The amount of cash exchanged at closing
- Deal structure—stock sale/purchase versus asset
  sale/purchase
- Terms of sale—cash versus stock versus some combination
- Presence of a covenant not to compete

- Employment or consulting contract for seller
- Seller financing and/or presence of collateral and security agreements

In the early negotiation stages, seek agreement on other essential but less confrontational issues, such as plans for the future of the business and the role of the seller or other key people after the sale. In this preliminary stage of negotiation, the seller's non-financial or personal concerns also can be identified and assessed by both sides. In the process, the operational capability of the new venture can be evaluated. In resolving these initial issues, buyers and sellers are simultaneously developing a level of trust and negotiating process that will assist both with the more difficult issue of price. At a later stage, differences in price may appear to be smaller and both sides will have built momentum toward resolving the inevitable gap that will exist.

When it is time to discuss price, remember the dictum "Seller's price, buyer's terms." Given the array of techniques available to structure transactions, buyers often can develop an offer that both "fits the budget" and makes the seller want to sell. Typically, if the buyer can meet or approach the seller's price, the seller often will be flexible as to how consideration is paid.

DEAL STRUCTURE: STOCK VERSUS ASSETS

Sellers are wise to recognize that when experienced buyers evaluate a potential acquisition, they carefully assess its *risk*. One of the first and most important risk assessments is the consideration of whether to purchase the stock of the target from the shareholders or all or selected corporate assets from the corporation.

While most of the well-publicized acquisitions of public companies are stock transactions, in the middle market, both stock and asset sales are common. Buyers and sellers should be aware of the advantages that each structure provides. Too often, parties on one side of a transaction will insist on only one possible structure without considering creative ways to close the deal with a different structure. Generally, the advantages that a given structure provides to one side create corresponding disadvantages for the other side. Therefore, both sides are wise to recognize the consequences that the structure creates as they form their negotiating strategy. In general, sellers prefer stock sales, which provide the advantage of having taxation occur only at one level. Conversely, buyers typically prefer an asset acquisition, where they receive a stepped-up tax basis in the assets acquired and reduce their risk by acquiring only identified assets and liabilities. Because the circumstances of each transaction vary, each side should seriously evaluate both transaction structures to identify and quantify the pros and cons involved, particularly the risk and net after-tax cash flow consequences, to ultimately negotiate the best possible deal. The following is an overview of the advantages and disadvantages when the transaction is structured as a stock sale and as an asset sale.

Stock Transaction

Generally speaking, in a stock transaction, all of the tangible and intangible assets and all of the liabilities, including unknown and contingent liabilities from current or prior acts of the seller and its agents, are acquired by the buyer. These include the unknown "skeletons in the closet" that buyers fear so much.

Seller's Viewpoint

Sellers in general strongly prefer a stock sale because as long as the stock was held for more than one year, shareholders only pay tax *once,* at the personal level on the difference between the sale price and their cost basis in the stock. This tax is computed at long-term capital gains tax rates, which are generally more favorable than ordinary income tax rates. In negotiations, sellers may attempt to allocate as much of the proceeds as possible to the stock sale and the least amount possible to consulting contracts or covenants not to compete because they are taxed as ordinary income versus the lower capital gains tax rate on the stock sale.

Because the seller receives this tax advantage and this structure creates tax and other disadvantages for the buyer, the seller typically must accept a lower sale price in a stock deal. In addition, a stock deal causes buyers to accept all known, unknown and contingent liabilities of the company, which can substantially increase their risk. As a result, buyers frequently demand extensive representation and warranties to be part of the sale agreement to protect them from unknown potential liabilities that may accompany any acquisition of stock.

Thus, sellers should identify and, wherever possible, make any necessary changes to minimize the risks to which the buyer may be exposed in acquiring the seller's company. By taking these steps, the seller may make a stock deal sufficiently less risky to a potential buyer that the transaction can be structured as a stock purchase.

Because stock deals are so unattractive to buyers, sellers frequently find far fewer buyers willing to purchase stock. Where minority shareholders exist, sellers usually must obtain their approval, which may require separate negotiations with them.

Risk Management through Insurance

Insurance is often a practical tool to assist in risk reduction. Liability insurance known as tail coverage usually can be acquired at a reasonable marginal cost to the buyer, structured as an additional rider on the buyer's existing policy. If the buyer requires that the seller purchase this insurance, the premium likely will be much higher as a separate new policy. This is a good example of something the buyer can provide to the transaction at a lower cost than the seller for the same benefit. Deal price can be affected and benefit provided to both buyer and seller.

Buyer's Viewpoint

A major disadvantage in a stock acquisition for the buyer is assumption of the target company's fixed assets at their existing tax basis, which is often after substantial depreciation already has been deducted. Thus, the buyer is able to write off far less of the acquisition cost, although some special tax elections may be available to avoid this consequence.

To reduce the charge against earnings, some public company acquirers may prefer that more of the cost be classified as general intangible value subject to amortization rather than shorter-term depreciation. This reflects the fact that public companies are frequently more focused on earnings, while private company buyers generally aim to minimize taxes.

In addition to the unfavorable tax consequences to a buyer of a stock purchase, this structure also creates added potential risks for the buyer. With the stock purchase, the buyer acquires all of the target company's liabilities. The buyer's principal concerns are contingent liabilities, underfunded retirement plans, and potential product liability claims from current or prior acts of the seller or its agents. The potential for loss from these liabilities often creates a more extensive due diligence process for the buyer, who must search much more carefully for these liabilities. The buyer also may be constrained by the seller's unwillingness or inability to provide warranties and representations that the buyer desires.

In a stock acquisition where less than 100% of the stock is acquired, buyers must contend with minority shareholders who may file dissenting shareholder actions. Because of all of these negative consequences for buyers, they can typically negotiate a much better price and sale terms with a stock transaction.

Stock transactions provide some benefits to the buyer, although they carry substantial disadvantages. Because the corporate structure has not changed, the corporation's contracts, credit agreements, and labor agreements tend to remain in place unless they are specifically voided or subject to approval as if assigned when there is a material change of shareholders. Having these agreements in place may ease the acquisition and integration process for the buyer. The buyer also acquires any favorable tax attributes of the seller, such as ordinary or capital loss carryforwards. Buyers may be able to elect IRS §338 provisions, which allow for a stepped-up basis in the stock, which they can offset with tax attributes acquired or through payment of a tax. As part of the negotiation process, buyers may attempt to allocate as much of the sale price as possible to consulting contracts or covenants not to compete because these are generally tax deductible to the buyer.

Collars and Packaging Adjustments

When a buyer purchases stock, he or she acquires the company's "current position." That is, the seller's working capital, defined as current assets less current liabilities, is part of the value of the company. When the price is negotiated to be effective as of a future closing date, the current position is often "guaranteed" by the seller to be within a range, say 10%, of the agreed value at the closing date.

For example, Sellco has had an average working capital balance of $10 million for the last two years. This normalized working capital amount is an agreed part of the value exchanged in a purchase of all of the outstanding common shares of SellCo. As part of the definitive agreement, a 10% "collar" is negotiated that states that if the working capital is less than $9 million, a dollar-for-dollar reduction in the purchase price will result. Similarly, if working capital is more than $11 million, a dollar-for-dollar additional consideration will be paid.

Asset Transaction

In a transaction structured as the sale and purchase of assets, only those tangible and intangible assets and liabilities specifically listed in the purchase agreement are transferred. While buyers tend to favor this structure because they can specifically exclude assumption of all or selected liabilities, it typically works to the disadvantage of the seller.

Generally, sellers retain cash, receivables, and payables in an asset transaction. Any of a seller's debt assumed by the buyer amounts to an increase in the purchase price for the buyer and represents additional consideration paid to the seller. Early in the negotiating process, both parties should identify any assets that are not intended to be part of the transaction so that these may be excluded from those assets listed in the definitive agreement. When elements of working capital are excluded from the transaction, buyers must consider the short and intermediate cash flow and financing needs of the new operation when it starts without the seller's cash, receivables, and payables.

Seller's Viewpoint

The major disadvantage to the seller of an asset sale is that the *proceeds are taxed twice,* first at the corporate level on the asset sale and second at the individual shareholder level when the corporation is liquidated and the proceeds are distributed to the shareholders.

The seller may face additional onerous tax consequences in the form of recapture of depreciation deductions, which must be classified as ordinary income to the corporation at the time of sale. The corporation also must immediately recognize any amount paid for goodwill as a capital gain. This double taxation of asset sale proceeds can dramatically reduce what the seller actually receives after all taxes are paid in an asset deal. On the plus side, because buyers strongly favor an asset purchase, they are generally more willing to pay a higher price for this type of deal.

Because an asset sale involves only the transfer of specifically identified assets and liabilities, this form of transaction leaves the seller responsible for any remaining liabilities that were not part of the sale. These liabilities commonly include contingent liabilities, accrued retirement fund contributions, accrued employee benefits, lease obligations, and ongoing litigation costs. The seller also may face one-time fees and taxes associated with the transfer of the assets, such as real estate transfer taxes. In an asset sale where the sellers intend to continue to operate the business that remains, the sale of the assets may temporarily disrupt operations as the assets are removed and the business adjusts to their absence.

Sellers usually face fewer representations and warranties with an asset sale because buyers are able to identify more accurately exactly what is involved in the transaction. When all or only specific assets are being purchased, the buyer has no need to extend due diligence to a review of the sellers' by-laws, corporate minutes, financial statements, credit agreements, and so on. Sellers should resist such attempts, which are appropriate only in a stock sale. Where minority shareholders exist, asset transactions also generally reduce legal actions from dissenting shareholders that could take place in a stock sale.

Buyer's Viewpoint

With an asset acquisition, the buyer achieves the major tax advantage of being able to carry the assets purchased at their current fair market value. This stepped-up basis allows the buyer to depreciate much of the acquisition cost. In addition, any amount of the purchase price in excess of the fair market value of the tangible assets that was paid for specific intangible assets, such as patents or copyrights and general goodwill, generally may be written off for income tax purposes.

Buyers also benefit in an asset acquisition by acquiring only those liabilities that are specifically identified as part of the sale. Thus, they avoid contingent and unknown liabilities.

In an asset sale, buyers also can avoid acquiring risky assets. Most commonly risky assets include real estate that may carry environmental hazards and uncollectable receivables or unsalable inventory. Buyers also can determine the entity that acquires and owns the assets, which may create tax planning and risk management opportunities.

In return for these benefits, buyers usually must pay a substantially higher price to purchase assets than if stock were purchased. The higher price recognizes both the benefits provided to the buyer and the substantial tax disadvantages created for the seller. Asset acquisitions frequently create problems for buyers, although these are usually offset by the benefits that have been described. In acquiring assets rather than the stock, technically speaking the buyer fails to acquire the target's employees, customers, or contracts. While the buyer may have preferred to avoid certain employees or contracts, he or she may have difficulty negotiating with other employees, labor unions, and customers. The company's relations with suppliers, including credit arrangements and its relations with banks and lessors, also must be established. In addition, buyers may be unable to use some of the target's licenses or permits that provided it with certain advantages. However, with an asset transaction, the buyer can selectively rehire desired employees and may have the opportunity to selectively continue the most advantageous contracts.

By buying assets, the buyer also cannot carry over any favorable tax attributes owned by the seller and typically loses the seller's unemployment compensation and worker's compensation insurance ratings.

Allocation of the Purchase Price

If the transaction is structured as an asset sale and purchase, one of the very first things both buyer and seller should do is prepare a Preliminary Purchase Price Allocation, even if the purchase price is not yet fully developed or determined. The purpose of the draft allocation is to encourage both sides to consider the concepts and taxation of the planned transaction. Form 8594, which is required by the U.S. Internal Revenue Service, is an excellent tool to start these discussions. Too frequently, parties reach agreement on price, terms, financing, and even discuss the concept of purchase price allocation without confronting the related tax consequences. Misunderstanding of the purchase price allocation often has been the source of a failed transaction and hard feelings at the end of deal negotiations. Therefore, Form 8594 should be completed on a tentative and preliminary basis on acceptance of the letter of intent. It will help to ensure that both sides appreciate the tax consequences of each asset allocation decision and how each ultimately affects the buyer's net after-tax cash cost and the seller's net after-tax proceeds from the sale.

Transaction structure is complicated. Those provisions that benefit one side tend to work to the disadvantage of the other side. Therefore, both sides constantly must focus on the risks that each transaction structure provides and avoids. Equally important, each side must constantly focus on both the buyer's net after-tax cost and the seller's net after-tax proceeds from the deal. The final terms of a stock transaction may involve a significantly lower price but increased proceeds to the seller and/or reduced risk to the buyer. Creativity in the deal structure is essential to work out the most mutually advantageous transaction. When both parties are aware of the tax consequences to the other of the terms of sale, they can negotiate a transaction that minimizes the overall tax consequences and works to their mutual benefit.

TERMS OF SALE: CASH VERSUS STOCK

In large acquisitions by public companies, the buyer frequently pays for the target with stock rather than cash. These terms of sale can have a substantial effect on both the risk and the return of the parties to the transaction. While cash sales tend to be rather simple and straightforward, transactions paid for in the buyer's stock of either a publicly or a privately held company may be more complex and require careful examination.

When cash is paid, the buyer's shareholders bear the entire risk of the transaction. Sellers' risk in a cash transaction is straightforward: All they must determine is if they are getting the highest possible price and whether they can generate a higher return by continuing to hold the stock.

When the seller receives payment in the form of stock, he or she must recognize that this currency carries far more risk and volatility than cash. Also, in a sale for stock, the seller shares in the buyer's risk of success in the transaction. When the buyer is a public company, this risk begins with the immediate threat that the market will react negatively to the announcement, causing the stock price—the seller's proceeds—to diminish in value. Furthermore, public company shares received as consideration probably will be restricted from subsequent sale for a fixed period under U.S. Securities and Exchange Commission Rule 144.

As a result, when payment in stock is offered, sellers must carefully assess the quality and marketability of the currency they are receiving to determine the attractiveness of the offer; that is, sellers must exercise careful due diligence on the buyer's stock. At a minimum, sellers should obtain answers to the following questions about the acquirer's stock:

- What is the condition and growth potential of the acquirer's industry?
- What is the acquirer's historical performance and future prospects?
- How is the acquirer's stock priced relative to these prospects, and how is it expected to change in the next year?
- What restrictions, if any, prevent or delay sale of any shares of the stock received?
- What is the typical trading activity in the acquirer's stock, and does it provide an adequate market for the new shareholders should they wish to sell their shares?

Since the selling shareholders will lack control of the acquirer's stock, the most influence they typically exert on the buyer's postacquisition policies and performance is through their votes if they hold a minority seat on the buyer's board of directors.

Buyers sometimes can negotiate this position, but they must recognize that their minority seat may provide little more satisfaction than the ability to dissent in votes on policies approved by the majority of the buyer's board.

Because the seller knows so much about the company the acquirer wants to buy, the seller should make use of this knowledge. When paid in the acquirer's stock, the seller assumes the same risk as the buyer for the success of the acquisition. Thus, if the seller suspects that the buyer has been too optimistic in forecasts of revenue or expense synergies or the timing to achieve them, the seller will share with the buyer any failure to create this value.

Transactions structured as stock sales often receive the benefit of favorable tax treatment under certain circumstances. Under U.S. tax laws in effect as of the date of this publication, when sellers exchange their stock for stock in the acquirer and receive less than 20% of the sale proceeds in cash, the "exchange" portion is not currently taxed. The seller's basis in existing shares carries over to the exchanged shares, and the deferred tax does not have to be paid until the exchanged shares are eventually sold for cash.

The seller also must examine whether the offer includes a *fixed stock price* or a *fixed stock exchange ratio*. With a fixed stock price, the seller receives a quantity of shares based on the market value of the buyer's stock on a certain date divided by that established price. If there is a fixed exchange ratio, the seller will receive a fixed number of the buyer's shares for each of the seller's shares. With a fixed exchange ratio, the seller loses value if the buyer's stock price declines and benefits if the seller's stock value increases. Floors and ceilings, called collars, may be imposed to limit the parties' loss or gain. For example, if at the date of close, the price of the shares is "out of the money," that is, lower than a previously agreed price, then buyer or seller (probably both) can terminate the transaction. The stock price collar goes both ways (a price less than agreed and a price more than agreed) for fairness reasons to both buyer and seller. In the long run, temporary changes in the market value should have little effect on the transaction.

A seller also must carefully examine the rights that accompany any shares received. In addition to transfer restrictions and similar limitations, sellers should look for *bring-along rights,* which are similar to *change-in-control provisions*. These rights typically provide sellers with the opportunity to have the shares they have received be "brought along" with the acquirer's shares in a subsequent transaction that creates further gains on the sale of the acquirer's stock. These provisions provide sellers with the opportunity to profit a second time if the acquirer's stock is bought in a subsequent transaction.

The discussion thus far has assumed that the buyer is paying for the acquisition with publicly traded stock. Should the transaction currency be stock of a privately held company, the risks to the seller are even greater. With the value of the stock unknown and probably highly volatile, and the stock most likely less marketable, particularly for a minority interest, the value of a stock offer should be sharply discounted from its cash equivalent. Sellers may wish to negotiate legal provisions that provide a market for their shares. These could include a *put,* which allows them to tender their shares, either for an established price or one set through a valuation process, where the corporation must acquire the shares in accordance with the terms of the agreement. Buy/sell agreements and formal exit strategies are also options because without a mutually agreeable contracted time period within which to market the now-combined company, the sellers risk never realizing liquid or spendable cash value from the sale of their shares. Selling or exchanging private company stock for other private company stock is not a common practice and should be considered carefully before execution. Control premiums, lack-of-control discounts, and discounts for lack of marketability that relate to this topic are discussed in Chapter 12.

Sellers who are offered stock in the acquirer's company in exchange for their shares should recognize that they are taking substantial risks over the alternative of receiving an equivalent payment in cash. If the acquirer is a public company, the seller faces the immediate risk of a decline in stock value if the market reacts negatively to the acquisition. In addition, the seller is assuming all of the buyer's risk that the synergies from the acquisition can be achieved. Therefore, sellers who are offered stock by the buyer must evaluate carefully whether the buyer's stock is properly valued as of the acquisition date, the likely success of the acquisition, and the underlying marketability of the shares they receive. Unless all of these issues can be resolved favorably, sales paid for in the acquirer's stock should be avoided or should carry a substantially higher price.

BRIDGING THE GAP

What can be done when the buyer and seller respectfully disagree about value? First, each side should reassess the pros and cons of doing the deal, including the likely effects on their shareholder value and competitive position. This analysis will help each side to focus on price and the price range over which they can negotiate a successful transaction. Next, each should look to the deal structure and the net after-tax cash cost to the buyer and net after-tax proceeds to the seller. Each should consider different possible transaction structures that may be more tax efficient to each side to help bridge the gap that separates them. For example, consider different cost allocations that may offer the seller capital gain versus ordinary income tax treatment or a structure that provides the seller with a single level of taxation versus double taxation. By concentrating on the buyer's net after-tax cost and the seller's net after-tax proceeds rather than the actual purchase price, there is usually a smaller gap to bridge. Doing this also focuses both sides on their true net cost and return.

When the transaction structure is not sufficient to close the deal, an *earnout* should be considered. Usually defined as a percentage of some performance measure, the earnout provides an opportunity for the seller to create more value than the buyer sees in the current transaction and share in it. Earnouts usually favor buyers who do not have to pay for benefits until they are realized. Thus, earnouts require sellers to share in the transaction risk and not be rewarded unless specific goals are achieved. The calculation of the earnout itself is often difficult, subject to interpretation, and may lead to disputes. Some examples of earnout terms are:

- Percentage of revenues in excess of a base amount
- Percentage of earnings before interest, taxes, depreciation, and amortization (EBITDA) when gross cash flow is most important

- Percentage of buyer net income and percentage of seller net income when competition for future capital and resources is an issue

There are numerous possible performance measures, but most important to any earnout agreement is the definition of terms. Consider the following definitional issues that could cause disagreements or confusion in an earnout:

- What does "profit" mean?
- Is profit before or after income taxes, year-end bonuses, corporate donations, and similar deductions?
- Is profit after actual salaries and other forms of compensation, or after agreed-on or industry standard compensation levels?
- Should policies be established to limit the amount of central office overhead or other corporate charges allocated to that business unit?
- Should separate accounting for the acquired business continue to allow for comparison and earnout calculation, or should the earnout be based on some combination of the combined business units?
- Should the effect of a covenant not to compete or goodwill amortization from the acquisition price affect the earnout?

Any earnout calculation should have a detailed example in the exhibits to the definitive agreement and should include specific, verifiable definitions of terms.

Another tool used to bridge the gap or transfer value from buyers to sellers are *employment agreements*. They provide a vehicle through which a buyer can make tax-deductible payments to the seller, which are taxed as ordinary income to the seller when received. Although employment agreements should reflect true market value for services rendered, they are sometimes "disguised" purchase price proceeds paid on a tax-advantageous deductible basis. Both sides should evaluate cautiously what a market-based level of compensation should be to ensure that these payments are not challenged by tax authorities.

Employment agreements offer many benefits to sellers. First and foremost, they keep the seller "on the payroll" with this compensation, often including lucrative employee benefits, such as use of vehicles, club memberships, vacation pay, and participation in retirement programs or stock option plans. The formal employment agreement also provides a form of "guarantee" to the seller of continued employment and a degree of "protection" to the seller from unwanted termination. This type of employment agreement typically includes an established number of years and specifies that the seller cannot be terminated except for specific reasons. The agreement also often includes a provision for payment in full of a predetermined amount if both parties agree to terminate the agreement.

Employment agreements for the seller may also include an *evergreen* provision, which perpetually renews unless the buyer provides specific notice to the seller. Another possible provision in an employment agreement is an *effective termination clause,* which includes the seller's job description at the postacquisition company, including job title and identification of the supervisory position to which the seller reports. Should the buyer wish to change this reporting relationship, the buyer "effectively terminates" the seller and all of the negotiated benefits for the seller immediately vest and become due and payable. The purpose of this provision is to provide sellers with a higher degree of certainty of their exact duties at the new company and the flexibility to leave under favorable terms should the circumstances change. These conditions are often important to entrepreneurs or individuals who are used to working as the senior executive in an operation and want to avoid close supervision or more regimented reporting requirements.

Events Subsequent to the Planned Transaction

As important as it is for sellers to focus on the pending transaction, the prudent seller also should consider future sale possibilities. If the buyer experiences a subsequent change in control, that is, the buyer is acquired or merged within a period—most commonly established as within 24 to 36 months from the acquisition date—additional provisions favorable to the seller may be triggered. The most common is for the seller who is receiving deferred payments to have the entire purchase price consideration be immediately due and payable on a change in control. The change-in-control provision also may provide for the original seller to share in any gain achieved by the buyer in the subsequent transaction over the seller's proceeds from the original deal.

SEE THE DEAL FROM THE OTHER SIDE

Buyer and sellers should recognize that in a transaction where both sides are represented by reasonably experienced advisors, neither should be able to take substantial advantage of the other side unless adverse circumstances or extreme potential exist. In smaller and middle-market transactions, however, many participants or their advisors lack adequate training and experience, and buyer and seller circumstances can be exploited. As a result, there are frequent examples of great deals negotiated by one side or the other, although most are not well publicized.

More commonly, buyers and sellers should recognize their shared goal to structure a mutually beneficial transaction. When value is reasonably well understood and options regarding transaction structure and terms have been thoroughly explored and analyzed, the agreement that is ultimately negotiated is generally one that recognizes the mutual needs of both parties. These needs include the buyer's need to pay a price that will allow a reasonable return on investment, recognizing the risks involved, while funding the acquisition with available resources. It also will recognize the seller's desire to transfer ownership, accomplish certain personal objectives, receive fair after-tax consideration for what is sold, obtain liquidity and adequate certainty of receipt of deferred payments, and receive adequate protection should future employment be part of the transaction. Buyers and sellers must also recognize that the government's participation in the transaction in the form of tax revenues affects both parties and must be negotiated to their mutual benefit. Both sides should recognize further that businesses are usually complex operations that carry substantial uncertainties which must be identified and, within reason, provided for in the sale/purchase agreement.

With these factors in mind, both sides are strongly encouraged to consider the other's needs. While sellers will want selected nonfinancial considerations to be recognized and their financial objectives met, they must correspondingly acknowledge the buyer's risk sensitivity, competitive challenges, capital constraints, and cash flow needs.

While all of this may appear to be reasonable as it is written, objectivity is much more difficult in the heat of a negotiation. Once again, this fact emphasizes the benefits to buyers and sellers of establishing a relationship in advance of the transaction to build trust and understanding. It further emphasizes the need for sellers to begin the succession planning process years in advance of the anticipated transaction date. By doing so, the seller can better understand and provide for the buyer's needs. More important, the seller can begin to cultivate a reasonable number of likely buyers to minimize reliance on a single suitor and maximize negotiating position and return on the sale.

The planning and search process should be a continuous one for buyers as well. The best deals are frequently companies that are not formally on the market, and identification of these opportunities is greatly enhanced by building relationships with acquisition prospects. Buyers who rely exclusively on transactions brought to them by intermediaries may experience a steady diet of overpriced targets that are being heavily promoted to many other prospective buyers as well. The complexity of the M&A process prevents most purchase or sale opportunities from luckily happening at the best possible time. Understanding value and what drives it and the mechanics of the deal process provides a much safer path to success in M&A for both buyers and sellers.

15

Measuring and Managing Value in High-Tech Start-Ups

Few investors have emerged unscathed from the Internet roller coaster. Yet the ride can be even scarier for shareholders and managers in nonpublic high-tech start-ups, where the stock price is unknown. For this reason, progressive owners make business valuation the centerpiece of rigorous annual strategic planning. At a minimum, an independent appraisal is a useful tool for obtaining financing. Most start-ups must obtain capital to fund ongoing growth. Potential investors will likely give more credence to a company seeking financing with an independent valuation in hand.

Given a start-up's early-stage position, often requiring capital, it may seem counterintuitive to think about gifting shares. However, this early stage may be the best time to do so in conjunction with the owner's estate planning. The confident entrepreneur will give strong consideration to gifting shares at a start-up phase in anticipation that value will increase in later years. A valuation in connection with the gifting of shares is required by the IRS, and the

The authors gratefully acknowledge the contributions to this chapter made by Chris M. Mellen, ASA, MCBA of Delphi Valuation Advisors, Inc., American Business Appraisers, Boston, Massachusetts; *www.delphivaluation.com.*

gifting of shares at a start-up phase is likely to have the least amount of tax consequences.

Perhaps the most typical trigger for a valuation is in conjunction with employee stock options as a form of incentive compensation. A start-up company may lack adequate capital to pay competitive wages to potential employees. Stock options are often the most effective tool used to attract qualified and skilled personnel, who may be drawn to the company in hopes of an initial public offering at some point in the future. A valuation of the start-up company's stock is fundamental to properly estimating the fair market value of the options as of the date of issue and to preparing for possible future review by the U.S. Securities and Exchange Commission (SEC). In addition, in anticipation of going public, a valuation of warrants may be prudent for financial reporting purposes.

Like any company, a start-up may become involved in litigation issues, such as shareholder disputes, marital dissolution of one of its principals, infringements of intellectual property, and contract disputes. The start-up also may seek advice from an appraiser in connection with the formation of a buy-sell agreement or the purchase of key person life insurance.

While all of the foregoing are solid reasons to value a start-up, the most compelling is the benefit the process provides toward achieving the company's primary financial goal: maximizing shareholder value. Only through annual strategic planning with a focus on value can shareholders and management chart the optimum direction for the company. With valuation as the focus of the plan, management continually can assess the company's strategic position and value as a stand-alone business versus increased value through a sale or merger.

The purpose of this chapter is to explain the unique challenges of measuring and managing value in high-tech start-ups to maximize shareholder value.

KEY DIFFERENCES IN HIGH-TECH START-UPS

Development-stage companies typically have a limited track record, little or no revenues, and no operating profits. High-tech start-ups share these characteristics but often possess a higher level of uncertainty because they are operating in new or emerging markets or in industries where there is no traditional model of business operations and performance for benchmarks. That uncertainty is heightened by the fact that the company also may be in the process of developing new products, which are experimental or completely unknown to their potential customer base.

Because the start-up's success is so closely tied to the time and cost involved in product development, production, and marketing issues, forecasts must be accurate and detailed. Reluctance to rigorously address key forecast parameters, including prices, volume, costs, capital investments, and the timing of each, is frequently the first step toward miscalculating the company's true performance and ultimately its value.

Continual technological changes and short product life cycles challenge accurate forecasting and contribute to the volatility of value. As will be discussed, these issues necessitate careful attention to competitive factors to identify the company's strategic advantages and disadvantages, which ultimately determine the rates of return or multiples that are chosen to compute value.

Tangible assets and the size of the company's asset base are less important in a technology company. When technology is the primary asset, most or all of the value in the company is tied to intangibles, including people. Such fragile assets, more so than property, plant, and equipment, can diminish in value quickly. Thus, the business must have ongoing internal controls to identify newly formed intellectual property and obtain adequate legal protection for it.

Particularly for medical or biotech companies, regulatory barriers frequently are major obstacles. When approvals must be obtained from agencies such as the U.S. Food and Drug Administration (FDA), the company must possess the expertise and capital required to secure adequate licenses, permits, and permissions. Established companies frequently have a strategic advantage over start-ups in this area.

Adequate capital is a common constraint because initial funding, whether from entrepreneurs, angel investors, or venture capitalists, generally is made to move the company from one development stage to the next within a certain period of time and at a certain cost. This cash "burn rate" emphasizes the necessity to stay within forecasted cost and time deadlines, because high-tech companies generally possess little or no borrowing capacity. Lack of a proven product or service, customer base, and few tangible assets allow only limited debt funding, which usually carries high rates and imposes tight constraints on management.

The mere fact that a company is a dot-com is certainly no assurance of success. While the Internet has created huge new markets and distribution channels, only a few Internet companies have sustained high value, and all have experienced substantial volatility. Furthermore, many of the publicly traded Internet stocks are trading below their initial public offering price. The markets have shown that investors are questioning the business models of many high-tech and Internet companies, especially those that have continued to reflect losses.

VALUE MANAGEMENT BEGINS WITH COMPETITIVE ANALYSIS

These same key valuation metrics, net cash flow and risk, apply to high-tech companies, including Internet businesses. Although managers may focus on industry-specific metrics, such as sales dollars per customer or visits to a Web site per advertising dollar; in a fast-paced market, the focus must be more on the company's ability to create new or improved products or services and to sustain its competitive position—and cash flow.

External Analysis

For start-ups, this analysis begins with the external or industry analysis, which is often difficult because competitors are frequently small divisions of large corporations or are relatively unknown. As a new technology emerges, there is often substantial uncertainty about its application—in what markets, for what products, and when. For example, numerous software companies lurch from one application of their technology to another as competing or collateral applications emerge and their target market changes in the process. Customers emerge and disappear rapidly as distribution channels redefine the end user of the technology.

Sales growth prospects can change rapidly as the technology develops and its associated products and customers are identified.

Value fluctuates accordingly. This uncertainty causes the high-return demands of venture capitalists during the early funding rounds of a new technology. Without more reliable information about a company's potential products, customers, and competitors, the resulting higher risk must be compensated by a higher required rate of return.

Customer concentrations frequently occur in emerging markets, where lack of information or inadequate marketing or distribution capabilities prevents start-ups from having full access to all potential customers. The typical start-up, particularly in the early stages, lacks one or more core competencies in production, marketing, sales and distribution, or finance that prevent the company from capitalizing on the value of its technology. Those companies that recognize these limitations and acquire the needed competencies can change their value dramatically as they move their technology from concept, to products, to customers, to cash flow.

This progression also emphasizes the potential distinction between a start-up's stand-alone fair market value, which could be very low or even zero, and its potentially much higher value to strategic buyers. Such buyers often can move a technology to generation of cash flows much more quickly and successfully than a start-up. Thus, management continually must identify those missing capabilities that stand as barriers to success. Barriers include routine revisions in the time and cost to bring a product to market, which can cause major swings in value as the company's technology develops or fails to develop. Setbacks or delays may leave a company particularly vulnerable on a stand-alone basis when its burn rate and borrowing limitations threaten its viability. Therefore, exit strategies, including positioning the company for merger partners or strategic buyers, also must be part of the ongoing planning.

Internal Analysis

Most important in the internal analysis is continual examination of how the technology will lead to products or services, markets, customers, and ultimately cash flows. This analysis begins with a review of the business plan and forecast, particularly an examination of costs required to complete and perfect the product. The competitive advantages that support the forecasted volume, pricing, and margins must be scrutinized carefully. Uncertainties may require adjustments to the forecast—either in dollar amounts or timing—or through application of probability analysis to quantify possible outcomes.

In assessing the company's capabilities, there is a constant need for comparison with competitors even though little strategic intelligence may be available. Lack of information ranges from knowledge of who competitors are, to how well they are financed or networked with other players in the industry, to uncertainty about their technological progress in the product development. Ultimately, these uncertainties must be quantified through probabilities and rates of return or multiples.

Because key people are usually essential in a development stage business, pay particular attention to both management and technical personnel. Executives are often scientists or research technicians with little management expertise or experience, and gaps may exist in sales and marketing, production, or finance. While competence in these functional areas may be less critical in earlier stages, it is required to advance the company to growth and maturity.

When computer scientists, engineers, or research scientists are essential, investigate their loyalty as well as the company's ability to operate in their absence or to replace them, particularly in tight labor markets. Also examine legal protection of research results and advances in product development, and assess nondisclosure and noncompete agreements.

When start-ups are developing product prototypes but possess little or no capacity to produce products at a reasonable cost in quantities required for profitability, the business plan must address the need for production expertise and the cost and time for development of a physical plant. The plan also must provide for early product warranties or guarantees and determine whether potential contingent liabilities exist from them. Gaps in capabilities do not doom a company. They do, however, create limits and frequently signal the need for exit strategies that position the business for its next growth stage.

Bringing a new concept or product to market requires different capabilities from product development. In assessing marketing and sales capabilities, be particularly sensitive to the company's ability to obtain adequate prices and volumes for profitability, and determine whether the anticipated distribution channels are realistic. For example, a market leader in surgical products recently found that its narrow product line forced excessive reliance on distributors who lacked the technical knowledge to sell their products. Unable to reach customers effectively as a stand-alone, the company sold to a market leader whose broad product line and sales network provided immediate market coverage.

Early-stage companies may not have fully complied with all legal requirements for incorporation, bylaws, and so on, and the company's legal status may hamper a transfer of ownership, particularly under favorable tax circumstances. The presence of several classes of securities sold at various prices, some of which may have been determined arbitrarily, may hamper acceptance of new stock values.

Most start-ups offer stock options to attract and keep key people, and these options can have a big effect on value per share. The cost of these options does not appear as an expense on the income statement but can be deducted on the corporate tax return. The resulting tax savings have been major sources of cash from operations for several well-known public companies.

The company must then either buy back the options or experience the dilution in stock value that they create. Because the options typically vest over three to five years and may be exercised up to 10 years, their effect on share value is not immediate.

Management should, however, recognize the effect on share value, and both employees and management should assess carefully how stock option value is computed for nonpublic shares of stock. The well-known Black-Scholes model may overstate the value of private company stock options due to their lack of liquidity, so alternative valuation procedures should be employed to value them.

Emphasis on Planning

While many established businesses survive and even thrive with little formal strategic planning, the start-up has a much greater need for the discipline that this process creates. A comprehensive strategic plan—including assessment of strengths, weaknesses, opportunities, and threats—focuses management on relentless attention to markets and customers and the products needed to serve them.

Lack of a plan or gaps in one usually suggest weaknesses, needs, or lack of expertise in key functional areas. Logical outgrowths of these inadequacies include the absence of realistic forecasts of the capabilities, costs, and time needed to move the company out of the development stage and to maturation. The result: uncertain goals, lack of clear direction, and little or no focus on future cash flows increase risk and decrease value.

When continual planning is executed effectively, the company's strategic strengths and weaknesses are regularly identified and assessed, and with that comes evaluation of the company's ability to continue to operate on a stand-alone basis. Where strategic disadvantages exist or essential capabilities cannot be acquired, the plan logically moves the company toward alternative strategies, including sale to a strategic buyer, merger, or even liquidation to minimize losses.

QUANTIFYING THE VALUE OF A START-UP COMPANY

As emphasized in Chapter 2, to focus on value investors must be able to measure it; so valuation should be an integral part of strategic planning. The valuation quantifies the risk and return consequences—the change in value—of each external and internal competitive factor. This process creates the roadmap for management to increase cash flows while minimizing risk to maximize shareholder value. In valuing a start-up, the income and market approaches are typically used, but there are often some variations to the traditional methodologies used.

Two widely used valuation methodologies, price-to-earnings (P/E) multiples and the single-period capitalization, are seldom appropriate in the appraisal of start-up companies, particularly high-tech businesses. The development-stage company's income or cash flow, if any, is hardly ever representative of long-term potential, and successful start-ups experience very rapid growth, after which increased competition or new technology slows growth to a more normal rate. Neither the earnings multiple nor the capitalization process is able to accurately portray these anticipated changes in the growth. Thus, there is usually good reason for investors to doubt high-tech multiples of 100 times earnings. The earnings are probably unrealistically low in comparison with the company's future earnings potential, and short-term versus long-term growth expectations are very different. The results are multiples that seldom make sense.

Investors must be equally wary of employing multiples that have been derived from strategic transactions. If the transaction involved is a start-up business, distortions from the two factors just described may be present. Second, multiples from strategic transactions often reflect synergies that only a specific strategic buyer could achieve. Similar distortions occur when multiples are derived from industry leaders. To value a start-up business based on multiples the market has established for Amazon or Yahoo! is to attribute to that start-up the size, growth, customer base, and brand recognition of these highly successful businesses when the start-up possesses few, if any, of these strengths.

Preferred Valuation Procedures

With these cautions in mind, are there any procedures available to compute reliable and defendable values for start-ups? One clear choice is a multiple-period discounting method (MPDM) that includes a forecast that can reflect the variations in the company's return as it moves through development stage. It also conveniently accommodates sensitivity and probability analysis. Because market multiples, such as multiples of revenues or various levels of earnings, are so widely quoted, they also can be employed, but with appropriate precautions. Given certain limitations inherent in the traditional methodologies within the income and market approaches, option pricing methodologies also may be used in valuing start-ups. Essentially, each of these methodologies should be considered in deriving a defendable value for a company in its infancy.

Market multiples often are used in valuing start-up companies because they are relatively simple to understand, market-based, easy to apply, and therefore commonly used in industry. The problem with using multiples in general for start-ups is that they are a static application to a very volatile situation. As explained in Chapter 10, market multiples can be obtained either from guideline public companies (i.e., a market multiple methodology) or from acquired companies (i.e., an acquisition multiple methodology). Generally speaking, the results from the former are marketable, minority indications of value, since the source is multiples of liquid, noncontrolling interests in public companies. The results from the latter are typically either marketable or nonmarketable controlling indications of value, since the source generally reflects multiples of entire companies that were acquired. As discussed earlier, the traditional P/E multiples are rarely applicable in valuing start-ups. While not to the same extent, even earnings before interest and taxes (EBIT) and earnings before interest, taxes, depreciation, and amortization (EBITDA) multiples are rarely applicable. Instead, multiples of revenue are commonly seen, largely because the start-up often has no earnings to which a multiple could be applied. However, given the basic fact that so much can happen in a company below the revenue line, a multiple of some level of earnings is preferable as a supplement to a revenue multiple. One such multiple is earnings before interest, taxes, research and development, and depreciation and amortization (EBITRAD), since certain start-ups incur high levels of research and development (R&D) expenses. There also may be some very industry-specific multiples. For example, a multiple of the number of subscribers enrolled by an Internet company may be a good indicator of value. As emphasized in Chapter 10, when analyzing public company multiples in general, it is important to note that there can be a significant disparity between public companies and closely held businesses. Those companies that attract public investment typically enjoy above-average revenue growth, both current and projected, and far greater access to capital. Start-ups are unlikely to be as advanced in the development of their particular product or service as compared to a company that has been able to go public.

Illustration of a Start-Up Valuation

Let us look at a fictitious company created by the authors that recently has completed its first full year of operations. Delphiwebhost.com (Delphi) provides Web design and hosting services as well as high-speed Internet access for commercial and residential markets. The company hopes to go public within the next 18 to 24 months and needs an independent valuation for financial reporting purposes. Despite these aspirations it expects to incur operating losses for the next four years. A summary of key historic and forecasted financial data is presented in Exhibit 15-1.

As far as current financial indicators are concerned, only a revenue multiple can be used. We have conducted research on public

Exhibit 15-1   Delphi, Inc.: Summary of Historic and Forecasted
Financial Data (millions)

	Historic	Forecasted					
	Year 1	Year 2	Year 3	Year 4	Year 5	Year 6	Year 7
Revenues	$1.12	$3.28	$8.44	$13.69	$17.22	$31.76	$52.53
Less: Operating Expenses	3.05	3.52	4.80	6.81	9.90	15.15	19.37
Equals: EBITRAD	(1.93)	(0.24)	3.64	6.88	7.32	16.61	33.16
Less: R&D Expenses	3.65	3.00	8.81	12.62	9.12	7.34	10.75
Equals: EBITDA	(5.58)	(3.24)	(5.17)	(5.74)	(1.80)	9.27	22.41
Less: Dep. and Amort.	0.10	0.14	0.25	0.33	0.42	0.54	0.64
Equals: EBIT	(5.68)	(3.38)	(5.42)	(6.07)	(2.22)	8.73	21.77
Less: Interest Expense	2.18	0.13	0.24	0.30	0.39	0.43	0.43
Equals: Pretax Income	(7.86)	(3.51)	(5.66)	(6.37)	(2.61)	8.30	21.34
Less: Taxes	—	—	—	—	—	0.17	4.70
Equals: Net Income	(7.86)	(3.51)	(5.66)	(6.37)	(2.61)	8.13	16.64

companies that can be used as guidelines to Delphi and on acquisitions of similar companies. We identified the six guideline public companies and seven acquired companies with revenues under $40 million, shown in Exhibit 15-2. An analysis of each individual company's relevance to Delphi and their results in the aggregate is necessary to determine an appropriate multiple. The selected multiple (in this case, of revenues) is applied to the revenues of the subject to determine one indication of value. The most common place to start is with the median of the sample. The median revenue multiple was 10.0 for the six guideline public companies and 7.0 for the seven acquired companies. On closer analysis, one can see that most of the acquired companies are smaller than the sample of public companies, not as established in their individual life cycle, and are not publicly traded. Caution should be exercised when considering medians since the use of a median presumes that the company being valued is as good as the typical guideline company. This is rarely the case for a closely held start-up.

Although Delphi expects to incur operating losses for the first four years of the forecast period, it expects to attain positive EBITRAD in the second. As such, we have considered a future

Exhibit 15-2   Delphi, Inc.: Market Approach Analysis

I. Guideline Public Company Multiples:

	Revenues ($millions)	Price to Revenues	Price to Earnings	MVIC to EBITDA	MVIC to EBITRAD
Company A	$35.2	15.5	nm	nm	27.4
Company B	$24.5	12.5	17.1	15.2	14.5
Company C	$4.8	8.7	45.3	20.9	16.3
Company D	$39.8	10.7	35.0	19.3	15.4
Company E	$24.1	7.3	nm	nm	10.1
Company F	$10.4	9.3	nm	nm	11.2
Median		10.0	35.0	19.3	15.0

II. Acquisition Company Multiples:

	Revenues ($millions)	Price to Revenues	Price to Earnings	MVIC to EBITDA	MVIC to EBITRAD
Company A	$1.5	7.0	nm	na	na
Company B	$5.1	18.8	27.1	na	na
Company C	$38.1	2.1	na	na	na
Company D	$2.2	8.9	na	na	na
Company E	$14.3	2.9	nm	na	na
Company F	$4.5	12.0	76.2	na	na
Median		7.0	nm		

MVIC = Market Value of Invested Capital (i.e., interest-bearing debt plus equity capital)
EBITDA = Earnings Before Interest, Taxes, Depreciation, and Amortization
EBITRAD = Earnings Before Interest, Taxes, Research and Development, Amortization, and Depreciation
nm = not meaningful
na = not applicable

EBITRAD multiple in our analysis. This information is typically not available in acquisition data due to the fact that many of the acquired companies are smaller and may not be publicly traded (and therefore not subject to SEC disclosure rules). In our analysis, adequate information was available on only one of the seven acquisitions to determine EBITRAD. With regard to our market multiple analysis, while three of our six guideline companies reflect operating losses, all six reflect positive EBITRAD. The median EBITRAD multiple is 15, but the standard deviation of the sample is very high, meaning that careful analysis of individual EBITRAD multiples is even more crucial.

When using future revenue or EBITRAD multiples, remember to factor in any equity infusion that would be necessary to generate the future revenues and earnings. It also may be necessary to discount the indication of value resulting from those future multiples back to present value, since we are using a future indication of value to determine value today. Forecasted cash shortfalls and discount rates determined within the analysis conducted in the income approach, using multiple period discounting, will be necessary in determining indications of value using multiples of future revenues and/or earnings, due partly to the fact that the results will need to be discounted to a present value.

Values estimated using multiple-period discounting are typically less subject than market multiples to variations that can occur in the public markets. Multiple-period discounting involves discounting future cash flows or some other level of earnings back to present value, using the traditional two-stage or three-stage model. In a two-stage model, value is calculated based on the sum of the present value of forecasted earnings over several discretely forecasted years and the present value of the residual value. The residual value often is determined based on either a multiple of some level of earnings or cash flows. In a three-stage model, there is an interim step. Since the start-up is unlikely to reach a steady state of growth after the forecast period, an interim level of growth is estimated for the appropriate number of years, after which the residual value is computed.

As seen in Exhibit 15-1, Delphi management forecasts the company will enjoy substantial growth for six years (years 2 through 7). Then revenue growth will stabilize at 15% for each of the following four years, with margins held constant at Year 7 levels. After the tenth year, growth is expected to stabilize at a rate slightly above inflation due to competition, maturity in the industry, and general economic cyclicality. As such, we have conducted a three-stage multiple-period discounting model. Using a discount rate of 30%, based on a buildup of market and company-specific risk factors, the results of our MPDM model yield an indication of equity value for Delphi of $10.7 million, as shown in Exhibit 15-3.

Net cash flow to invested capital is clearly the preferred measure of return in a multiple-period discounting model because it most

Exhibit 15-3   Delphi, Inc.: Multiple-Period Discounting Analysis
               (millions)

	Forecasted					
	Year 2	Year 3	Year 4	Year 5	Year 6	Year 7
Net Income (from Exhibit 15-1)	$(3.51)	$(5.66)	$(6.37)	$(2.61)	$8.13	$16.64
Plus: Dep. and Amort.	0.14	0.25	0.33	0.42	0.54	0.64
Equals: Gross Cash Flow	(3.37)	(5.41)	(6.04)	(2.19)	8.67	17.28
Less: Capital Expenditures	0.90	0.79	1.00	0.85	1.80	0.60
Less: Increases in Working Cap	0.80	1.26	1.26	1.28	3.42	4.62
Less: Principal Repayments	0.13	0.39	0.66	0.93	1.33	1.56
Plus: New Debt Incurred	0.90	0.79	1.00	0.85	1.80	0.60
Equals: Net Cash Flow to Equity	(4.30)	(7.06)	(7.96)	(4.40)	3.92	11.10
Times: Discount Factor	0.8771	0.6747	0.5190	0.3992	0.3071	0.2362
Present Value of Cash Flows	(3.77)	(4.76)	(4.13)	(1.76)	1.20	2.62

Present Value of Forecasted Cash Flows	(10.60)
Present Value of Interim Cash Flows for 4 years following 2005	7.79
Present Value of Residual Period	13.49
Indicated Fair Market Value of Equity (rounded)	10.70

accurately portrays value-creating performance. While traditional companies generate earnings and cash outflows for capital expenditures and working capital, high-tech start-ups more often create losses and, particularly Internet companies, cash inflows from working capital. Customer advance payments, for example, fueled much of Amazon.com's phenomenal growth. Accounting principles do not treat long-term expenditures consistently. While plant and equipment costs are capitalized, those that build product quality and market share—R&D and advertising—are expensed. The financing choices of initial investors, and the company's resulting debt-to-equity balance, also could create distortions due to financial leverage. To prevent this, the invested capital model is used to portray performance before financing considerations. This model reflects the net cash flows to the company's equity and interest-bearing debt.

In the forecast, major attention must be paid to volume, prices, margins, and capital reinvestments necessary to achieve the company's projected revenues. The strategic analysis performed on the company's competitive position should provide insight and justification for the price and margin targets. The future rather than the past is the key, so a history of losses or weak current performance should not distort future prospects. For example, less emphasis should be placed on existing products. With short product life cycles and continual technological change, the keys to value rest with the company's capabilities to produce products, that is, its ability to achieve sustainable competitive advantages. Thus, the forecast should reflect the company's strategic plan and its associated competitive analysis, with a continuing effort to resolve uncertainties as they arise.

NEED FOR ADDITIONAL RISK MANAGEMENT TECHNIQUES

For a start-up with little history, particularly in an emerging industry full of uncertainty, the thoughtful investor or manager must deal next with the likelihood of the forecast being achieved. The company's success in assessing and managing this uncertainty will determine much of its future performance and therein its value today based on that anticipated performance. For this reason, sensitivity must be introduced into the analysis and estimation of value. As the company progresses, management continually should review and challenge forecast scenarios. Valuing a start-up is typically an ongoing and time-consuming process.

Traditional probability analysis calls for management to identify likely outcomes (e.g., optimistic, most likely, and pessimistic) and then weigh the likelihood that each will occur. These outcomes, of course, depend on the company's ability to achieve key metrics, most commonly targeted revenues, operating margins, and capital reinvestments and ultimately net cash flow to invested capital. Therefore, each of these key metrics can be included in the analysis as a variable to create a grid or spreadsheet of potential outcomes. As an illustration, assume that Delphi has successfully developed software (Software A) that is reflected in the forecasted revenues of the company. A second software (Software B), not reflected in the forecasts, is in the process of being developed. Software B takes the input data from Software A and applies it to a new form of Web design being developed but not yet sold by other companies. For strategic planning purposes, the company has requested a separate valuation be conducted to determine the impact Software B would have on its value. In conducting this analysis, management has determined that there are three possible scenarios:

1. A pessimistic scenario that B is not developed successfully and the company is forced to abandon this project after two years, resulting in zero incremental value.
2. A most likely scenario in which B is developed successfully after two years and revenue growth ranges from 10 to 60% in the foreseeable future, resulting in incremental value of $10 million.
3. An optimistic scenario in which B is developed successfully after one year and revenue growth is between 40 and 90% in the next five years, resulting in incremental value of $30 million.

The probability of scenarios 1, 2, and 3 occurring are 20%, 50%, and 30%, respectively. The projected cash flows in each scenario are discounted to the present and weighted by the probability of occurrence estimated by management as shown in Exhibit 15-4 to yield an incremental value estimate of $14 million. Corresponding to this spreadsheet or quantitative analysis is the even more essential strategic analysis that aims to identify those competitive and operating factors most likely to influence each quantitative outcome. This returns us to our competitive analysis of the industry and market to identify a company's core advantages and disadvantages relative to other major players in its industry. These can range from the cost to attract new customers, to customer turnover, to gross profit percentages, to the time and cost to bring new products to market.

The process of ongoing competitive analysis feeds into the start-up company's continually evolving business plan and produces the regular updates to the spreadsheets and the sensitivity analysis of the key parameters and related probabilities. Three months after the initial valuation was completed, our company was progressing positively in the development of Software B. However, a competitor had begun to develop a similar application that could undermine the forecasted growth of Delphi. The probability that Software B is developed successfully after one year has increased, but the revenue growth projections must be reduced to allow for the increased competitive threats. Nonetheless, the incremental

Exhibit 15-4   Delphi, Inc.: Probability Analysis

Scenario	Probability	Incremental Value	Calculation
Pessimistic	20%	$0	$0
Most Likely	50%	$10,000,000	$5,000,000
Optimistic	30%	$30,000,000	$9,000,000
Incremental Value Estimate			$14,000,000

value estimate has increased to $16 million, which is computed using a Monte Carlo simulation (MCS). Traditional scenario analysis just described results in one value from a range of "best guesses" within a given scenario. A Monte Carlo, or probabilistic, simulation considers all possible combinations of input variables and generates a probability distribution describing the possible outcomes for each input variable. The result is a calculation of value that includes both a most likely outcome and a series of reasonably probable but less likely outcomes. Monte Carlo simulation, which is described in Chapter 6, provides a more thorough analysis of the possible outcomes than does a standard sensitivity analysis.

A variation to this process is the preparation of a "Required Performance Analysis" (RPA) to achieve a targeted stock price. If investors or managers believe the company now is worth a certain value, or aim to achieve a target value at a specified future time, RPA determines what performance—and ultimately cash flow— must be generated to create that value. Management is then directed toward the specific steps that must be achieved to create the required cash flows and resulting stock value. Alternatively, the strategic analysis and resulting valuation conclude that the targeted value cannot be achieved as planned.

Investors can employ another tool to manage risk in a highly uncertain environment. If the MPDM lacks the needed flexibility when investors or venture capitalists have the ability to make "follow-on" investments—for example, a right of first refusal for a later stage of financing—this right takes on similar characteristics to a call option on a company's stock. Option pricing methodologies account for the buyer's ability to wait, gather and analyze newly available competitive data, and then decide to buy equity at a later date. Since an option's value is based on the value of an underlying asset, the typical methodologies under the asset, income, and market approaches do not apply to option valuation. At expiration, a call option is worth the stock price less the exercise price. Prior to expiration, a call option is worth the stock price less the present value of the strike price after both prices are adjusted for the riskiness of the option. Each of the option pricing models is based on the volatility of the underlying stock price, the difference between the current stock price and the strike price, and the length of time until expiration. Real Option Analysis (ROA) is described in Chapter 6.

RECONCILIATION OF VALUE

As indicated in Exhibit 15-3, the results of the MPDM analysis yield a value estimate of $10.7 million for Delphi. Given the start-up nature of this company and our confidence in the data used in both the income and market approaches, it is our opinion that the company's value, as determined by the income approach (i.e., MPDM methodology), is $10.7 million. In this instance, we have determined that the best use of the results from our market approach is as a test of reasonableness of the MPDM. This value implies a revenue multiple of 9.5, which is slightly below the median of the six guideline companies of 10.0 and above the 7.0 median of the seven acquired companies. Given negative cash flows in Year 2 of $4.3 million and a discount rate of 30%, this value implies a multiple of 5.95 times Year 2's revenues. Given negative cash flows in the Year's 2 and 3 totaling $11.3 million, this value implies a multiple of 10.2 times Year 3's EBITRAD. This figure is below the median EBITRAD multiple of 15.0 from the six guideline companies. Based on an analysis of each individual guideline and acquired company, outlined in Exhibit 15-2 as they compare to Delphi, we conclude that our opinion of $10.7 million is reasonable.

High-tech start-ups can be valued with reasonable accuracy if proper techniques are employed. When adequate data exists, market multiples should be used to support the value determined by the MPCM. Successful management of these new companies is heavily dependent on continual planning, budgeting, and valuation. In the process, risk can be managed further with MCS and ROA.

16

Merger and Acquisition Valuation Case Study

The theory and procedures presented in this book are much easier to understand when they are applied in a real-world situation. This chapter presents a comprehensive case that illustrates application of many of the concepts that have been presented. The Cardinal Publishing Company Merger and Acquisition Case involves a company created by the authors based on the many companies we have appraised. Because of our obligation to client confidentiality, all of the details here, including the guideline public companies, are fictitious, but we believe they represent the typical middle-market merger and acquisition circumstances that buyers and sellers must be prepared to encounter. Any similarity between Cardinal Publishing Company or the fictitious public companies described in this case and any actual company is purely coincidental. The case is designed to present a reasonable procedure based on the facts and circumstances presented. They may not be appropriate for other valuations. In our attempt to present a realistic scenario, some factors in the case are not completely clear and some issues remain unresolved. Information is not perfect and assumptions and estimates must be made, which certainly reflect real world circumstances.

The case begins at the end of Year 5, with Cardinal facing competitive threats and the clear need for transition planning. To begin this process, Cardinal's stand-alone fair market value is determined, first using net income to invested capital as the measure of return rather than net cash flow. This is done to demonstrate the use of an income measure because this is the "language" that is frequently spoken by sellers and their intermediaries. The single-period capitalization method also is employed to demonstrate its use, although for a transaction of this size, the added detail provided by the multiple-period discounting method would be preferred. Cardinal's stand-alone fair market value is also computed by the guideline public company method, and we present brief applications of the merger and acquisition method and the adjusted book value method. The results of these various methods are reconciled into a final opinion of the fair market value on a stand-alone basis of Cardinal's invested capital and equity.

Although several potential buyers are introduced in the case, Omni Publications emerges as the strongest strategic buyer. Various synergies are estimated, and the investment value of Cardinal's invested capital and equity to Omni is computed using the multiple-period discounting method.

Throughout the case we attempt to present sufficient explanation to allow the reader to understand each step in the valuation process. Valuation at this level employs seasoned judgment based on knowledge of general economic conditions, industry circumstances, the competitive position of the target and guideline companies, and a thorough understanding of business valuation theory. In determining value, the appraiser serves as a surrogate for the hypothetical buyer and seller in the fair market value determination and for the strategic buyer in the investment value determination. Those parties typically make estimates and assumptions based on the facts and circumstances available as of the appraisal date. That is the challenge presented in valuing Cardinal. We trust you will find our value conclusions to be reasonable.

HISTORY AND COMPETITIVE CONDITIONS

Cardinal Publishing Company was founded 10 years ago by entrepreneur Lou Bertin after he had completed a successful career as an advertising executive. Cardinal, which was organized as a C corporation incorporated under the laws of the state of Illinois, has one class of common stock with 1 million shares outstanding, 80% of which is owned by Bertin with the remaining 20% owned in equal amounts by two passive investors. Over the last five years, Cardinal has paid cash dividends, although it cut the payment in the last year in response to its lower income and internal cash needs.

In Bertin's prior career, he had achieved substantial success in direct mail advertising and made use of this knowledge in marketing Cardinal. Through use of industry mailing lists and consumer research data, Bertin identified an underserved market consisting primarily of individuals from rural communities who enjoyed a simple "country" lifestyle. Beginning with a single publication that featured country cooking recipes and the pleasure of general farm living, his company has expanded to six monthly magazines aimed at this same market. Annual subscriptions are no more than $24 for any of the journals, which feature almost no advertising. All of the magazines promote the outdoors, simple homespun living, and celebration of seasonal activities in different climates and locations throughout rural America.

A workaholic, Bertin initially employed a small staff of writers, photographers, and production personnel. As the publications and sales volume grew, he added publishing, production, editorial, and financial expertise, but the company is still heavily dependent on one key person in each of these major functional areas. Because the company does little advertising, the production, features, design, and layout for all of the journals are similar, which helps to control costs. The company is best known for its high-quality photography that features the beauty of rural America. The consistent layout, high-quality photographs, and homespun stories also help to establish the company's brand awareness. Each of the journals features the company's distinctive logo, the roof line of a barn, including a cupola and a weathervane in the shape of a rooster.

As the company grew, Bertin continued to debate his advertising policy. Feedback from his customers praise the simplicity of the journals and the absence of advertisements. Lack of advertising limits the company's revenue base and, to some extent, its ability to diversify. Account executives and other promotional experts aiming at Cardinal's customer base are typically unresponsive to initial solicitations to advertise in Cardinal because of its failure to provide readers with information in alternative formats, including online, face to face, television, radio, or CD.

Production challenges also exist. Cardinal's consistent production layout for all of its journals has kept its capital costs down, but the company's growth and need for creativity are causing strains on its production capability. Through an investment in the industry's latest technology and a doubling of plant capacity, per-unit production costs could be reduced dramatically with no loss in quality. The new technology also would accommodate advertising that requires more sophisticated layout, but lack of capital prevents these improvements.

Much of Cardinal's growth has been financed with debt, due in part to Bertin's decision to pay dividends regardless of unfavorable tax consequences. The minority shareholders wanted annual cash returns for their willingness to invest in the risky start-up business, and Bertin needed the funds to pay off loans from an earlier unsuccessful business venture. Toward this goal, over the last five years he has also paid himself an annual salary and fringe benefits that totaled about $1 million per year, while the market rate for his services in the latest year was about $250,000. Bertin's uncle, Jeffrey Meier, was paid $100,000 annually as Vice President of Marketing but seldom came to work, and Cardinal suffered from his incompetence.

In the last two years, several factors were increasingly pressuring Bertin to sell the company. His family had a history of heart problems, and in recent annual physical exams his doctor has encouraged him to "slow down." He knows that his energy level and enthusiasm for the day-to-day challenges of the company are declining, and Cardinal is facing substantial increased competition from full-line "media" companies. Much of this is coming from *Better Houses & Gardens* and a series of women's journals that are being published by Hurst Publications, Inc. through their *Oprah Belfrey Magazine* division and by TimeVerner. Each competitor is bringing massive financial resources, marketing contracts, distribution outlets, creativity, and pricing power that threaten Cardinal as a stand-alone business. These media companies have moved beyond print to such platforms as the Web, the Internet, research, events, broadcast and cable TV, books, shopping clubs, and related services. Thus far Bertin has been able to withstand these challenges through Cardinal's superior knowledge of its market, customer lists, product quality, and loyalty. Innovation and consolidation throughout the publishing industry, however, lead Bertin to conclude that the major publishers could acquire this industry-specific knowledge within a few years and successfully duplicate his best ideas. He also recognizes that creating and building the business was much more enjoyable for him than the management and administrative tasks that he has assumed as the company has grown.

POTENTIAL BUYERS

Bertin was approached recently by a private equity fund that targets companies in diverse industries based on growth potential. In initial discussions, he was discouraged by their attention to profits and apparent desire to grow the company rapidly over the ensuing five years and then either take it public or sell to a major publisher. Since they had no experience in magazine publishing, he saw little potential for a sale to them.

An investment banker approached Bertin on behalf of Century Publications, a privately held company that had achieved major success with over 10 publications in the travel and leisure industry. Looking to expand into new markets, they were considering an investment either in Cardinal or in one or more technology journals. Although discussions with them had not advanced to the point of an offering price, they had disclosed that their offer would be primarily stock with payments over a period of years. From his ownership of Cardinal, Bertin recognized the lack of marketability of the stock of a privately held company, particularly a minority interest. With this in mind, he broke off discussions with Century.

Ultimately, Omni Publications, a broad-line media conglomerate traded on the New York Stock Exchange (NYSE) and ranked in the 30 to 50% "midcap" range by market capitalization of firms trading on the NYSE, approached Bertin. They also recognized the rural North American market, particularly older consumers, as underserved and had initiated several successful media services targeting this customer base. To more quickly enter the homemaker market, they saw Cardinal as a key acquisition.

Although Omni respects Cardinal, they consider it to be a "fat-and-happy dinosaur" because of its failure to use information technology to extend its relationship with its loyal customers. Omni sees Cardinal as a potential gold mine, not so much for its present products as for its underutilized and underexploited customer information. Omni intends to employ new analytical customer relationship management software to collect and analyze customer information to determine what products and services their customers want, need, and will pay for. Armed with this information, Omni, as a full-line media company, can offer extensive additional products and services to their customer base.

It appeared likely that Omni also could improve Cardinal's bottom line, without changing Bertin's salary, by approximately $1 million annually for each of the first four years through a combination of integration of the operations and implementation of these improvements. This would probably take 18 months, although the company's goal for completion was within 12 months of the acquisition date.

After Omni business development executives made the initial contact with Bertin, they turned negotiations over to their investment banking firm of Merrill Goldman. To negotiate effectively, Bertin retained an experienced team of legal, tax, and valuation advisers to determine the fair market value of Cardinal as a stand-alone business, its maximum value to Omni including synergistic benefits, and a strategy to succeed in the negotiations. That team developed the information shown in Exhibits 16-1 through 16-6, which led to the determination of Cardinal's fair market value on a stand-alone basis found in Exhibits 16-7 through 16-18 and its investment value to Omni inclusive of synergistic benefits shown in Exhibits 16-19 through 16-20.

GENERAL ECONOMIC CONDITIONS

As the negotiations were taking place, the economy appeared to be ending a long period of sustained economic growth, with most major economic indicators signaling a substantial downturn over the next 12 months. Within the publishing industry, analysts anticipated a tightening of advertising spending with failures predicted for a number of weaker publications. Interests rates were relatively high with no indication from monetary authorities that reductions were expected in the near future.

The economy grew 2.9% last year and is forecasted to increase next year by 2.1%. Forces identified to support moderate growth in the United States include low inflation, a small federal budget deficit, and stable stock prices. American consumers indicate declining confidence, but there are improving economic conditions, particularly in Europe and Asia. As foreign economies strengthen, import prices on both finished goods and raw materials are expected to increase.

The unemployment rate fell below the forecasted 4.8% last year and is expected to increase moderately, primarily due to a tight labor market in the United States. The prime interest rate is expected to decrease from last year, and the yield on 30-year Treasury Bonds is expected to average 6.5%, both increases over last year.

In summary, consumer spending is moderating, while inflation and interest rates are decreasing. Economic and employment growth have slowed but continue to be healthy. These conditions suggest a stable, moderately growing economy.

SPECIFIC INDUSTRY CONDITIONS

After a strong performance last year, magazine publishers expect softer demand and profits. Although the magazine segment commands only about 5% of total advertising expenditures, its growth has been among the highest in the publishing industry. One key reason for this has been the growing trend toward brand extensions, which occur when a journal licenses its name to a manufacturer. Continued growth in this technique is anticipated, and through improved customer research, broader product offerings also support growth.

The supply of magazine titles has ballooned over the last few years, even as newsstand sales have been declining. This additional supply, when coupled with less shelf space because of lower numbers of both convenience stores and corner newsstands, has significantly increased competitive pressures on magazine publishers.

While magazine sales volume is dominated by conglomerates, the majority of magazines are produced by independent publishers. Other competitive factors affecting independents include rising paper prices and postage costs, lack of economies of scale in production and technology, and the inability to appeal to major retailers as an attractive advertising location.

GROWTH

Bertin expects that Cardinal, if it continues as an independent company, to achieve a 4% growth rate inclusive of inflation. Given the industry conditions, this is consistent with the industry forecasts for the near to intermediate term. This rate is modest in comparison to Cardinal's 15% compound growth over the last five years. (For the sake of brevity, the case stipulates the rate of growth and certain other industry and competitive factors without providing the typical research and analysis that these drivers should require.)

COMPUTATION OF THE STAND-ALONE
FAIR MARKET VALUE

Exhibits 16-1 through 16-6 present Cardinal's historic performance and industry average financial ratios. The adjustments to normalize Cardinal's net income to invested capital are described in the following sections.

Normalization Adjustment Issues

Exhibit 16-7 shows the normalization adjustments to Cardinal's income statement to yield adjusted pretax income to invested capital, also known as earnings before interest and taxes (EBIT).

Exhibit 16-1   Cardinal Publishing Company: Statements of Income and Retained Earnings, Five Most Recent Historical Years

	Year 1	Year 2	Year 3	Year 4	Year 5
Net Sales	$42,900	$49,300	$56,700	$65,200	$75,200
Cost of Sales	24,400	28,000	32,100	37,800	44,700
Gross Margin	18,500	21,300	24,600	27,400	30,500
Operating Expenses	11,600	13,800	16,200	18,900	22,200
Net Operating Income	6,900	7,500	8,400	8,500	8,300
Net Miscellaneous Income (Expense)	250	200	200	200	200
Gain on Land Sale	0	0	0	1,500	0
EBITDA	7,150	7,700	8,600	10,200	8,500
Depreciation Expense	900	1,100	1,400	1,400	1,600
EBIT	6,250	6,600	7,200	8,800	6,900
Interest Expense	2,000	2,100	2,100	2,100	2,300
Net Income Before Taxes	4,250	4,500	5,100	6,700	4,600
Taxes	1,500	1,600	1,800	2,350	1,600
Net Income	2,750	2,900	3,300	4,350	3,000
Retained Earnings —Beginning Balance	1,650	3,900	6,200	8,500	11,200
Less: Dividends	500	600	1,000	1,650	900
Retained Earnings —Ending Balance	3,900	6,200	8,500	11,200	13,300

Exhibit 16-2   Cardinal Publishing Company: Statements of
Income and Retained Earning, Five Most Recent
Historical Years

	Year 1	Year 2	Year 3	Year 4	Year 5
Net Sales	100.0%	100.0%	100.0%	100.0%	100.0%
Cost of Sales	56.9%	56.8%	56.6%	58.0%	59.4%
Gross Margin	43.1%	43.2%	43.4%	42.0%	40.6%
Operating Expenses	27.0%	28.0%	28.6%	29.0%	29.5%
Net Operating Income	16.1%	15.2%	14.8%	13.0%	11.0%
Net Miscellaneous Income (Expense)	0.6%	0.4%	0.4%	0.3%	0.3%
Nonoperating Income	0.0%	0.0%	0.0%	2.3%	0.0%
Nonoperating Expense	0.0%	0.0%	0.0%	0.0%	0.0%
EBITDA	16.7%	15.6%	15.2%	15.6%	11.3%
Depreciation Expense	2.1%	2.2%	2.5%	2.1%	2.1%
EBIT	14.6%	13.4%	12.7%	13.5%	9.2%
Interest Expense	4.7%	4.3%	3.7%	3.6%	3.1%
Net Income Before Taxes	9.9%	9.1%	9.0%	9.9%	6.1%
Taxes	3.5%	3.2%	3.2%	2.6%	2.1%
Net Income	6.4%	5.9%	5.8%	7.3%	4.0%

Exhibit 16-3   Cardinal Publishing Company: Balance Sheet, As of
the End of Years 1 through 5

	Year 1	Year 2	Year 3	Year 4	Year 5
Assets					
Current Assets:					
Cash and Equivalents	$2,250	$2,500	$2,850	$2,100	$1,650
Trade Receivable	12,400	$13,100	$13,900	14,950	16,300
Inventory	3,200	3,400	4,700	6,000	7,650
Total Current Assets	17,850	19,000	21,450	23,050	25,600
Property, Plant, and Equipment (Net)	10,600	13,150	13,750	14,600	16,600
Other Assets:	1,500	1,400	1,400	1,700	1,400
Total Assets	$29,950	$33,550	$36,600	$39,350	$43,600
Liabilities					
Current Liabilities					
Accounts Payable	$7,800	$7,500	$8,150	$8,500	$9,100
Accrued Expenses	3,600	3,200	3,400	3,200	3,200
Current Portion of Long-Term Debt	4,500	4,750	4,800	5,200	5,600
Total Current Liabilities	15,900	15,450	16,350	16,900	17,900
Long-Term Debt	8,450	10,200	10,050	9,550	10,700
Total Liabilities	24,350	25,650	26,400	26,450	28,600
Equity					
Owners' Equity					
Common Stock	1,700	1,700	1,700	1,700	1,700
Retained Earnings	3,900	6,200	8,500	11,200	13,300
Net Owners' Equity	5,600	7,900	10,200	12,900	15,000
Total Liabilities and Equity	$29,950	$33,550	$36,600	$39,350	$43,600

Exhibit 16-4   Cardinal Publishing Company: Balance Sheet, As of the End of Years 1 through 5

	Year 1	Year 2	Year 3	Year 4	Year 5
Assets					
Current Assets:					
Cash and Equivalents	7.5%	7.5%	7.8%	5.3%	3.8%
Trade Receivable	41.4%	39.0%	38.0%	38.0%	37.4%
Inventory	10.7%	10.1%	12.8%	15.2%	17.5%
Total Current Assets	59.6%	56.6%	58.6%	58.6%	58.7%
Property, Plant, and Equipment (Net)	35.4%	39.2%	37.6%	37.1%	38.1%
Other Assets:	5.0%	4.2%	3.8%	4.3%	3.2%
Total Assets	100.0%	100.0%	100.0%	100.0%	100.0%
Liabilities					
Current Liabilities					
Accounts Payable	26.0%	22.4%	22.3%	21.6%	20.9%
Accrued Expenses	12.0%	9.5%	9.3%	8.1%	7.3%
Current Portion of Long-Term Debt	15.0%	14.2%	13.1%	13.2%	12.8%
Total Current Liabilities	53.1%	46.1%	44.7%	42.9%	41.1%
Long-term Debt	28.2%	30.4%	27.5%	24.3%	24.5%
Total Liabilities	81.3%	76.5%	72.1%	67.2%	65.6%
Equity					
Owners' Equity					
Common Stock	5.7%	5.1%	4.6%	4.3%	3.9%
Retained Earnings	13.0%	18.5%	23.2%	28.5%	30.5%
Net Owners' Equity	18.7%	23.5%	27.9%	32.8%	34.4%
Total Liabilities and Equity	100.0%	100.0%	100.0%	100.0%	100.0%

Exhibit 16-5   Cardinal Publishing Company: Five Most Recent
Historical Years

	Year 2	Year 3	Year 4	Year 5
Cash Flows from Operating Activities				
Net Income/(Loss)	$2,900	$3,300	$4,350	$3,000
Noncash Expenses, Revenues, Losses, and Gains Included in Income:				
Depreciation and Amortization	1,100	1,400	1,400	1,600
Gain on Land Sale	0	0	(1,500)	0
(Increase) Decrease in Receivables	(700)	(800)	(1,050)	(1,350)
(Increase) Decrease in Inventories	(200)	(1,300)	(1,300)	(1,650)
Increase (Decrease) in Accounts Payable	(300)	650	350	600
Increase (Decrease) in Accrued Expenses	(400)	200	(200)	0
Net Cash Flows from Operating Activities	2,400	3,450	2,050	2,200
Cash Flows from Investing Activities				
Purchase of Fixed Assets	(3,650)	(2,000)	(2,550)	(3,600)
Disposal of Fixed Assets	0	0	1,800	0
(Increase) Decrease in Other Assets	100	0	(300)	300
Net Cash Flow from Investing Activities	(3,550)	(2,000)	(1,050)	(3,300)
Cash Flows from Financing Activities				
Dividends	(600)	(1,000)	(1,650)	(900)
Increase (Decrease) in Long-Term Debt	2,000	(100)	(100)	1,550
Net Cash Flows from Financing Activities	1,400	(1,100)	(1,750)	650
Net Cash Flow Increase (Decrease)	250	350	(750)	(450)
Beginning of the Year Cash	2,250	2,500	2,850	2,100
End of the Year Cash	$2,500	$2,850	$2,100	$1,650

Exhibit 16-6 Cardinal Publishing: Financial Ratio Summary of Historical Financial Statements

	Industry Norm[a]	Year 1	Year 2	Year 3	Year 4	Year 5
Current Assets/Current Liabilities	1.3	1.1	1.2	1.3	1.4	1.4
Current Assets Less Inventory/ Current Liabilities	0.9	0.9	1.0	1.0	1.0	1.0
Sales/Receivables	6.4	3.5	3.8	4.1	4.4	4.6
Cost of Sales/Inventory	10.9	7.6	8.2	6.8	6.3	5.8
Cost of Sales/Accounts Payable	8.0	3.1	3.7	3.9	4.4	4.9
Total Debt/Total Debt and Equity	0.42	0.81	0.76	0.72	0.67	0.66
EBIT/Interest Expense	3.9	3.1	3.1	3.4	3.7	3.0
Profit Before Taxes/Total Assets	0.12	0.14	0.13	0.14	0.16	0.11
Profit Before Taxes/Total Equity	0.64	0.76	0.57	0.50	0.50	0.31
Sales/Net Fixed Assets	11.2	4.5	4.9	5.3	5.6	6.0
Sales/Total Assets	2.1	1.4	1.5	1.5	1.7	1.7
Sales to Working Capital	17.5	22.0	13.9	11.1	10.6	9.8

[a] The industry norm is averages based on a performance of the five guideline public companies presented in this case for the latest fiscal year.

Exhibit 16-7 Normalized Net Income Years 1 through 5:
Invested Capital Basis (in thousands)

	Year 1	Year 2	Year 3	Year 4	Year 5
Pretax Income to Invested Capital (aka EBIT)[a]	6,250	6,600	7,200	8,800	6,900
Adjustments[b]					
Excess Officer's Compensation	600	750	800	750	750
Gain on Sale of Land	0	0	0	−1,500	0
Total Adjustments	600	750	800	−750	750
Adjusted Pretax Income to Invested Capital[a] (aka adjusted EBIT)	6,850	7,350	8,000	8,050	7,650
Normalized Pretax Income to Invested Capital[c]					8,000
Income Taxes: Federal and State, estimated at 40%[d]					3,200
Normalized Net Income Applicable to Invested Capital					4,800

[a] Invested capital is income before the subtraction of interest expense, so it is the return to debt and equity capital providers.

[b] Adjustments: The support and research related to the normalization adjustments are described in the narrative portion of the case.

[c] This amount was judgmentally selected as representative of Cardinal's long-term operating performance as of the end of Year 5. Alternatively, the adjusted pretax income to invested capital of $7,650,000 in Year 5 could be increased by the anticipated long-term growth rate of 4%, which would have generated approximately the same amount.

[d] This tax rate was supplied by Cardinal's accounting firm. Because this computation employs the invested capital model, which is predebt, it does not consider the tax deductibility of interest expense. An alternative is to reduce the income tax by 40% of interest expense.

Source: Cardinal's Income Statements for Year 1 through 5.[b]

Lou Bertin's Compensation

Lou Bertin's compensation package exceeds the market rate. Cardinal's human resources expert's research indicated that the total cost of market-rate compensation paid to an arm's-length CEO of a publisher the size of Cardinal over the past five years would have provided the following savings, inclusive of payroll-related burdens:

Year	Savings
1	$600,000
2	$750,000
3	$800,000
4	$750,000
5	$750,000

Jeffrey Meier's Compensation

This position is required for the company's success, and the salary is appropriate for a properly qualified VP of Marketing. Thus, no adjustment is required.

Market Research

In three of the past five years, Cardinal has spent between $200,000 and $300,000 for market research to allow the company to better understand its customer base. While some would argue that this is a nonrecurring expense that should be added back to determine normalized income, it was concluded that these costs enable the company to offer the attractive products that make it uniquely appealing to its customers. This adjustment is a judgment call and is considered to be a recurring cost because it is necessary for the company to remain competitive in the long term.

Gain on Sale of Land

The company sold land in Year 4 for $1.8 million that generated a gain of $1.5 million. Since this is not part of the company's ongoing income, it is subtracted as a normalization adjustment.

Other Assets

These assets include vacant land adjacent to the company and a vacation home in St. Maarten used by Bertin exclusively for personal purposes. These assets do not generate income or expenses, so no adjustment to the income statement is required. Their market value can be added to the operating value to yield Cardinal's total equity value.

Risk and Value Drivers

The factors that should influence the development of the discount and capitalization rates appropriate to Cardinal's stand-alone fair market value are described in the following sections. Exhibits 16-8 and 16-9 are used to develop the rates.

Economic Conditions

Lower forecasted advertising expenditures are expected to hurt all magazine companies in the next 12 months as economic conditions generally decline.

Industry and Competitive Considerations

Industry sales are dominated by conglomerates, which possess stronger ties to advertisers and much stronger distribution systems. Independents face higher operating costs, such as paper costs and postage rates, and are weaker technologically. Numerous magazines are launched yearly, with more than half failing within 12 months, and of the remaining, 95% will fail within five years of introduction.

Financial Condition and Access to Capital

The company carries substantial debt and lacks capital for technology upgrades.

Management

Lou Bertin, who is approaching the typical retirement age, is the only Cardinal employee capable of providing executive

Exhibit 16-8 Rates Applicable to Net Income to Equity (As of the Appraisal Date)

Symbol	Component	Increment	Rate
	Long-Term Treasury Bond Yield[a]		6.00%
+	Equity Risk Premium $(R_m - R_f)$[b]		7.50%
=	Average Market Return for Large-Cap Stock		13.50%
+	Risk Premium for Size[c]		5.50%
=	Average Market Return Adjusted to Tenth-Decile-Size Firm		19.00%
	Specific Company Risk Premium:		
+	Industry Risk (larger, stronger competitors)	3.00	
+	Financial Risk (heavy debt)	2.00	
+	Management Risk (thin management and no succession plan)	2.00	
+	Customer Base (strong loyalty)	(1.00)	6.00
=	*Rate of Return for Net Cash Flow to Equity*[d]		25.00
+	Convert to a Rate of Return to Net Income[e]		3.00
=	*Rate of Return for Net Income to Equity*		28.00
−	Long-term Sustainable Growth Rate[f]		−4.00
=	*Capitalization Rate for Net Income to Equity*		24.00

[a] This is the 20-year U.S. Treasury Bond.

[b] The Equity Risk Premium is applied to recognize the additional risk associated with investing in large cap publicly traded common stock (equities) instead of the risk-free 20-year U.S. Bond.

[c] Risk premium for size is to recognize the additional risk associated with a company the size of the tenth decile on the New York Stock Exchange.

[d] This is a rate of return, or discount rate, directly applicable to net cash flow as it is based on the return to investors, net of income tax to their corporations.

[e] The conversion from a rate directly applicable to net cash flow to a net income rate is made by applying the appropriate ratio of the company's net income to its net cash flow on a pro forma basis.

[f] Long-term sustainable growth rate was provided in the assumptions to the case.

Note: The rate developed above is appropriate to the valuation assignment in this case. This exhibit is intended to demonstrate a process for the development of this rate, and the amounts shown are for illustration purposes only. The rate appropriate to a given valuation must consider the risks, economic and industry factors, the effective date, the size of the interest being valued, and the intended use of the appraisal.

Exhibit 16-9   Weighted Average Cost of Capital (WACC) and
Capitalization Rate Applicable to Net Income
Available to Invested Capital

Applicable Rates:	
Rate of Return applicable to Net Income (Exhibit 16-8) [a]	28.00%
Cost of Debt (Prime Rate +)	10.00%
Tax Bracket	40.00%

Capital Structure (market values)[b]:	
Debt	45.6%
Equity	54.4%

Computation of WACC and Conversion to Cap Rate

Component	Net Rate	Ratio[c]	Contribution to WACC
Debt @ Borrowing Rate $(1-t)^d$	6.00%	.456	2.74%
Equity Rate of Return	28.00%	.544	15.23%
WACC Rate of Return for Net Income to Invested Capital			17.97%
Less: Long-Term Sustainable Growth[e]			−4.00%
Capitalization Rate for Net Income to Invested Capital[f]			13.97%

[a] The rate of return applicable to net income from Exhibit 16-8 is the equity discount rate of 28.00%. The computation of the equity cap rate of 24% is shown in Exhibit 16-8 but is not used in this computation. The WACC cap rate is computed in Exhibit 16-9.

[b] The equity-debt mix is provided on a market value basis. This was achieved by employing the following formula, which is explained in Chapter 9: $E_{fmv} = NCF_{IC} - (D\,(C_D - g))/(C_E - g)$

$$\$19{,}442 = \frac{\$4{,}992 - (\$16{,}300\,(.06 - .04))}{(.28 - .04)}$$

$19,442	54.4%
+16,300	45.6%
$35,742	100.0%

In this computation, the return is net income to invested capital, rather than NCF_{IC}. To adjust for this difference, the C_E is adjusted from the 25% rate for net cash flow derived in Exhibit 16-8 to the 28% rate for net income in that exhibit.

[c] The borrowing rate of 10% is reduced to a 6% cost of debt capital as the net cost of debt is reduced by the tax subsidy provided by the deductibility of interest expense.

[d] The long-term sustainable growth rate was provided in this case's narrative. It is subtracted from the discount rate to convert it to a capitalization rate.

[e] The WACC capitalization rate is applicable to net income available to invested capital, i.e., the return to equity and debt on an income basis. This amount would be equal to the net income to equity if Cardinal were debt free. Cardinal's actual interest-bearing debt will then be subtracted from invested capital value to yield equity value.

management. Marketing management is lacking, and senior management is generally thin.

Proprietary Customer Knowledge

Cardinal's market research has revealed substantial information regarding the tastes and spending habits of what appears to be a large, underserved segment of the North American population. While larger publishers are beginning to recognize the potential spending power of this customer base and wish to exploit it, Cardinal, as a stand-alone business, lacks both the financial resources and marketing expertise to capitalize on this proprietary knowledge.

Customer Base

Cardinal possesses a base of highly loyal customers who are attracted to the company's high-quality photography, homespun image, and low subscription rates.

Single-Period Capitalization Computation of Stand-Alone Fair Market Value

Using the normalized net income to invested capital of $4,992,000, computed in Exhibit 16-10, and the weighted average cost of capital developed in Exhibit 16-9, the stand-alone fair market value of 100% of the equity of Cardinal on a control basis is computed to be $19,434,000, with invested capital totaling $35,734,000. This computation uses the single-period capitalization method because Cardinal's returns over Years 1 through 5 have been sufficiently stable to derive a reliable estimate of the company's performance by using a return for one period. Use of this method is also supported by the choice of a long-term growth rate of 4%, which appears to be appropriate for Cardinal given economic, industry, and company conditions.

The invested capital model, which is usually employed in valuations for merger and acquisition, is used with debt and equity weightings adjusted to market values rather than book values. Net income, rather than net cash flow, is chosen as the return to demonstrate its use, although net cash flow is generally preferred.

Exhibit 16-10   Single-Period Capitalization Method Invested
                  Capital Basis Converted to Equity

	Indicated Value (*in thousands*)
Normalized Historical Net Income to Invested Capital (Exhibit 16-7)	$4,800
Apply Long-Term Sustainable Growth to Historical Net Income (4%)	× 1.04
Normalized Forecasted Net Income to Invested Capital	$4,992
WACC Cap Rate to Net Income to Invested Capital (Exhibit 16-9)	13.97%
Indicated Value of Invested Capital	$35,734
Less: Interest-Bearing Debt	$16,300
Stand-Alone Fair Market Value of Equity	$19,434

The rates of return have been adjusted from net cash flow to net income to prevent distortions that occur when rates and returns are mismatched.

The invested capital value of $35,733,715 from Exhibit 16-10 is divided by the normalized EBIT and earnings before interest, taxes, depreciations, and amortization (EBITDA) amounts for Year 5 to yield the resulting implied multiples of EBIT and EBITDA shown in Exhibit 16-11.

Guideline Public Company Computation of Stand-Alone Fair Market Value

Using three normalized returns to invested capital for Year 5 and operating multiples, the guideline public company method developed the stand-alone fair market value of 100% of the invested capital and equity of Cardinal. The guideline public company method is used because the search identified a sufficient number of publicly traded companies in the printing and publishing industry that

Exhibit 16-11   Stand-Alone Fair Market Value: Implied Multiple
of Adjusted EBIT/EBITDA (in thousands)

	Year 5	Implied EBIT Multiple	Implied EBITDA Multiple
Normalized EBIT for Year 5	$7,650	4.67	
Normalized EBITDA for Year 5	$9,250		3.86

were adequately similar to Cardinal to determine value based on the price paid for alternative investments in the public markets.

The guideline public company method employs the invested capital model where returns to debt and equity include EBIT, EBITDA, and revenues. These returns are compared to the market value of invested capital (MVIC), rather than the equity price per share, because the returns are to debt and equity. Based on research and analysis of the guideline companies, considering their performance and strategic strengths and weaknesses, along with industry conditions and trends, they were compared to Cardinal based on various operational performance measures. The following ratios were computed for each of the guideline companies, including the mean and median for each ratio:

MVIC to EBIT
MVIC to EBITDA
MVIC to Revenues

To begin the search for guideline companies we selected the following criteria:

Public Guideline Companies

Industry	SIC 2841: Printing and Publishing
Size	Annual sales between $7.5 million and $750 million (within a factor of 10 times the size of Cardinal)
Time	Transactions as of the valuation date
Type	Minority interest transactions

Status	Profitable companies, financially solvent and reasonably leveraged, that are freely and actively traded
Growth	Companies whose recent historical growth rates and forecasted growth rates are reasonably similar
Domicile	U.S. corporations

The guideline companies that were selected are:

| | Guideline Companies | |
Name	Latest Fiscal Year	Latest Fiscal Year Sales
CRP Publications	12/31/Year 5	144,496,402
Night Rider, Inc.	9/30/Year 5	66,851,000
Industry Trends	6/30/Year 5	597,165,000
Hanover Media	3/31/Year 5	361,822,000
Leisure Living	12/31/Year 5	662,501,000

The following is a brief description of each company.

- CRP Publications: a diversified media company that produces nine journals that cover emerging technology industries. It also provides market research services.

- Night Rider, Inc.: operates through three subsidiaries, which publish special-interest magazines relating to the motorcycle, trucking, and tattoo industries.

- Industry Trends: publishes 21 industry-specific journals and newsletters, which it markets through affiliations with industry trade associations.

- Hanover Media: publishes, produces, and distributes Christian-oriented magazines, online services, and books, and markets a line of religious gift and stationery products.

- Leisure Living: markets resorts and time-sharing resort properties as well as three consumer magazines that cover the travel and leisure industry.

From available public sources, extensive information about the five public guideline companies was gathered, including their annual reports, U.S. Security and Exchange Commission's Forms

10-K, and information from various stock reporting services and industry analysts' reports. The operating performance, financial position, and cash flow of each company was analyzed. Their competitive advantages and disadvantages were considered in light of industry and economic conditions. From this data, the information in Exhibit 16-12, about the companies' operating performance, is summarized.

From the data in Exhibit 16-12, operating multiples that compare the market value of invested capital to EBIT, EBITDA, and revenue per share are computed and presented in Exhibit 16-13, along with the resulting mean and median multiples of each operating measure. These multiples reflect investor consensus of the value of these five companies in this industry and present a basis for selection of appropriate multiples for Cardinal based on these alternative investment choices.

Exhibit 16-12   Guideline Company Operating Performance Per Share

	MVIC/ Share	EBIT/ Share	EBITDA/ Share	Revenue/ Share
CRP	$19.85	$1.12	$1.32	$15.27
Night	$ 5.32	$1.62	$2.83	$17.73
Industry	$61.05	$9.63	$11.70	$88.48
Hanover	$13.69	$1.58	$1.93	$11.80
Leisure	$28.03	$4.92	$5.73	$63.70

Exhibit 16-13   Guideline Company Operating Multiples Per Share

	MVIC/EBIT	MVIC/EBITDA	MVIC/Revenue
CRP	17.66	15.07	1.30
Night	3.29	1.88	.30
Industry	6.34	5.22	.69
Hanover	8.67	7.10	1.16
Leisure	5.70	4.89	.44
Mean	8.33	6.83	.78
Median	6.34	5.22	.69

Cardinal's strategic position and operating performance is compared to the guideline companies considering the various risk factors previously discussed, including Cardinal's limited management, heavy debt, strong customer loyalty, and larger, stronger competitors. Comparison of Cardinal with the guidelines on specific financial measures is presented in Exhibit 16-14.

Exhibit 16-14   Comparison of Cardinal With Guideline Companies

	Discussion	*Comparison to the Guideline Companies*
Liquidity	Cardinal's current ratio and quick ratio are both just above the industry average shown in Exhibit 16-6. Cardinal's cash position has declined while its current liabilities have increased in the last year.	Slightly weaker
Asset Management	Cardinal's total assets, accounts receivable, inventory, and fixed assets are all carried at substantially higher levels relative to the company's sales than any of the guideline public companies. This reflects substantial inefficiency in the utilization of all of these assets and sharply reduces the cash flow to capital providers.	Much weaker
Financial Leverage	Cardinal's debt, though decreasing steadily over the last five years as a percentage of total assets, is higher than four of the five guideline companies.	Weaker
Profitability	Cardinal's stronger profit margins compensate somewhat for the company's weaker asset utilization to generate profits similar to the guideline companies.	Average
Growth	Cardinal's 15% annual compound growth rate over the last five years is less than three of the five guideline companies, but its projected long-term growth is similar to that of the guideline companies and the industry.	Average

Based on this comparison of Cardinal with the guideline public companies, the following value multiples shown in Exhibit 16-15 were selected as appropriate for Cardinal when compared to the guideline companies considering Cardinal's performance and risk profile.

Estimate of Equity Value of Guideline Company Method

The market value of the company's long-term debt is subtracted in Exhibit 16-16 from the previously determined value of invested capital, to obtain an equity value, which for the market approach is rounded to $21 million.

Merger and Acquisition Method Computation of Stand-Alone Fair Market Value

In the search for market data, one strategic acquisition was identified that was considered for comparative purposes. In this transaction, which occurred in the first quarter of Year 5, Granite Publishing purchased Western Media, which was a chain of six local

Exhibit 16-15   Calculation of Invested Capital Value of Cardinal Based on the Guideline Company Approach

Procedure	Normalized Operating Results for Year 5	×	Value Multiple	=	Estimated Invested Capital Value
MVIC/EBIT	7,650	×	5.00	=	38,250
MVIC/EBITDA	9,250	×	4.00	=	37,000
MVIC/Revenue	75,200	×	.50	=	37,600

Exhibit 16-16   Calculation of Equity Value of Cardinal Based on the Guideline Company Approach

Procedure	Estimated Invested Capital Value	−	Market Value of Long-Term Debt	=	Estimated Equity Value
MVIC/EBIT	38,250	−	16,300	=	21,950
MVIC/EBITDA	37,000	−	16,300	=	20,700
MVIC/Revenue	37,600	−	16,300	=	21,300

newspapers and electronic reporting services located in the southwestern United States. Western was traded on the NASDAQ stock exchange, and, in that transaction, Granite paid a 72% premium over Western's preacquisition stock price. This transaction, which was paid for in Granite's stock, reflected a multiple of nine times Western's forecasted EBITDA. Over the last 10 years, Granite has made numerous such acquisitions of local and regional newspaper chains, which is part of a long-term trend of consolidation in the newspaper industry. Further analysis of this transaction and others made by Granite led to the conclusion that the price paid and the resulting multiples from this transaction reflect synergies unique to Granite and do not provide a reliable basis for determination of Cardinal's value. In general, it is inappropriate to attempt to establish "the market" based on the results of a single transaction.

Rejection of the Adjusted Book Value Method

To consider the fair market value on a stand-alone basis of Cardinal from the perspective of the value of the assets owned by the company, an adjusted book value computation could be performed. This method, which assumes value is derived from a hypothetical sale of the specific tangible and intangible assets of the company, does not specifically recognize general intangible value that may exist as a result of the company's technology, customer base, reputation, and other general goodwill factors. While general goodwill value can be computed through a computation known as the *excess earnings method,* this is generally not done in valuations for merger and acquisition. This is a method that is applied usually only in the valuation of very small businesses, such as professional practices, so it will not be used to appraise Cardinal.

Summary and Conclusion of Stand-Alone Fair Market Value

The results of the valuation procedures employed to compute the fair market value of Cardinal's equity are summarized in Exhibit 16-17. After employing the various reconciliation methodologies explained in Chapter 13, the fair market value of equity is determined to be $20.1 million, including Cardinal's nonoperating assets.

Exhibit 16-17 Reconciliation of Indicated Stand-Alone Values and Application of Discounts/Premiums Appropriate to the Final Opinion of Value

Valuation Method	Interest Being Valued	Indicated by Method (Preadjustments)		Adjustments for Differences in Degree of		Adjusted		Weight	Weighted Component Value
		Value	Basis	Control	Marketability	Value	Basis		
Capitalization of Net Income to Invested Capital	100%	$19,434,000	As if freely traded	0%	7%[a]	$18,074,000	Control marketable	60%	$10,844,000
Guideline Public Company	100%	$21,000,000	As if freely traded	0%	7%[a]	$19,530,000	Control marketable	40%	$7,812,000

Fair Market Value of a 100% Closely Held Interest on an Operating Control, Marketable Basis	$18,656,000
Plus: Nonoperating Assets	$1,400,000
Fair Market Value of a 100% Closely Held Interest on a Control, Marketable Basis	$20,056,000
Divided by Number of Issued and Outstanding Shares	1,000,000
Per Share Fair Market Value of a Closely Held Share on a Control, Marketable Basis	$20.06

[a] The discount for this lack of marketability is estimated to be 7%, which approximates the transaction costs required to sell the company.

COMPUTATION OF INVESTMENT VALUE

This computation of investment value will use the multiple-period discounting method and will recognize the synergies that can be achieved through this acquisition.

Risk and Value Drivers

To develop the discount rate for equity and the weighted average cost of capital (WACC) to be used by Omni in its evaluation of Cardinal, adjustments, shown in Exhibit 16-18, have to be made to the rates developed previously in Exhibits 16-8 and 16-9 for Cardinal. Omni is a midcap-size publicly traded company, so the size adjustment for Omni is substantially less than for Cardinal. In addition, most of the specific company risk factors for Cardinal can be eliminated when it operates as a division of Omni. In developing the specific company risk premium for Omni, the additional risk created by the presence of competitors much larger than Cardinal is eliminated by Omni's size and market strength. However, because Omni does not possess substantial expertise or experience in the rural market served by Cardinal, it imposed a 1% risk premium to reflect its movement into a less certain market. Omni's financial strength eliminates the financial and management risk factors that exist with Cardinal as a stand-alone business.

While some doubt exists as to whether Cardinal's strong customer loyalty can be maintained when the company operates as a division of a conglomerate, Omni management is attracted to the very high untapped sales potential of this customer base. While Cardinal lacks the expertise and resources to take advantage of this sales potential, Omni sees this as a substantial synergistic advantage that reduces the riskiness of this acquisition.

The discount rate to equity of 14.5% from Exhibit 16-18 is combined with Omni's cost of debt at the prime rate of 9%, based on the market value of Omni's debt and equity shown in Exhibit 16-19 to yield the WACC discount rate of 12.23% and the WACC cap rate of 8.23%.

It should be obvious from a comparison of Omni's WACC discount of 12.23% in Exhibit 16-19 versus Cardinal's of 17.97% from

Exhibit 16-18   Rates of Return (Discount Rate) Applicable to
Net Cash Flow to Equity (As of the Appraisal Date)

Symbol	Component	Increment	Rate
	Long-Term Treasury Bond Yield[a]		6.00%
+	Equity Risk Premium $(R_m - R_f)$[b]		7.50%
=	Average Market Return for Large-Cap Stock		13.50%
+	Risk Premium for Size[c]		1.00%
=	Average Market Return Adjusted for Size to Mid Cap-Size Firm		14.50%
	Specific Company Risk Premium Adjustments[d]:		
+	Industry Risk	1.00	
+	Financial Risk	0.00	
+	Management Risk	0.00	
+	Customer Base (sales potential)	(1.00)	0.00
=	*Rate of Return for Net Cash Flow to Equity*[e]		14.50%

[a] This is the 20-year U.S. Treasury Bond.

[b] The Equity Risk Premium is applied to recognize the additional risk associated with investing in publicly traded common stock (equities) instead of the risk-free 20-year U.S. Bond.

[c] Empirical evidence indicates Omni's size will still justify a size premium of approximately 1%.

[d] Omni's lack of experience or expertise in this market raises its overall risk profile. Part of the synergy of Omni acquiring Cardinal is that the following risk drivers will be either eliminated or reduced: thin management and Cardinal's premerger heavy debt. Omni concludes that the sales potential of the underserved customer base reduces risk.

[e] This is a rate of return or discount rate directly applicable to net cash flow as it is based on the return to investors, net of income tax to their corporations.

Exhibit 16-19 Weighted Average Cost of Capital (WACC) and Capitalization Rate Applicable to Net Cash Flow to Invested Capital

Applicable Rates:	
Rate of Return Applicable to Forecasted Net Cash Flow (Exhibit 16-8) [a]	14.50%
Cost of Debt (Prime Rate)	9.00%
Tax Bracket	40.00%

Capital Structure (based on Omni's Market Value [b]):	
Debt	25%
Equity	75%

Computation of WACC and Conversion to Cap Rate

Component	Net Rate	Ratio[c]	Contribution to WACC
Debt @ Borrowing Rate $(1-t)$ [d]	5.40%	.25	1.35%
Equity	14.50%	.75	10.88%
WACC Discount Rate for Net Cash Flow to Invested Capital			12.23%
Less: Long-Term Sustainable Growth [e]			−4.00%
Capitalization Rate for Net Cash Flow to Invested Capital [f]			8.23%

[a] The discount rate applicable to forecasted net cash flow is from Exhibit 16-18.
[b] Omni's debt-equity mix is derived from Omni's market values of debt and equity.
[c] The ratio is the equity-debt split (see note *b*).
[d] Omni borrows at prime.
[e] The long-term sustainable growth rate was provided in the case narrative.
[f] The WACC capitalization rate is applicable to net cash flow to invested capital, that is, the net cash flow inclusive of the returns to debt and equity.

Exhibit 16-9 that Cardinal's operations are substantially safer when located within the size and depth of Omni than when operating as a stand-alone company. Thus, the first factor contributing to the increase in Cardinal's investment value to Omni over its stand-alone fair market value is the reduction in risk.

Normalization, Synergy, and Net Cash Flow Adjustment Issues

Exhibit 16-20 shows the normalization adjustments and computation of net cash flow to invested capital forecasted for Omni's acquisition of Cardinal.

Lou Bertin's Compensation

Bertin's estimated above-market compensation of $750,000 annually will be adjusted the same as it was in the valuation of the company on a stand-alone basis. Omni concluded that Cardinal's management was thin enough that market-level compensation for a chief executive officer was required. Omni further concluded that if possible, Bertin should be retained to make use of his specialized knowledge and to assist in the transition process. In structuring this transaction, an option would be to continue to pay Bertin the above-market compensation, with this payment being a tax-deductible expense to the buyer and compensation taxed only once at the individual level to the seller. The purchase price could be reduced by this excess compensation, although the parties should consult tax and legal counsel regarding the legality of this payment arrangement.

Jeffrey Meier's Compensation

No adjustment is required for Meier's compensation. It is anticipated that he would not continue with the company after an acquisition but a suitable replacement would be paid his salary.

Market Research

Market research information is of continuing critical importance to Omni, particularly since the acquirer believes that they can make better use of the untapped sales potential in this market. No adjustment is required.

Operating Assets

There remains no adjustment required to the company's return for these items, which Omni indicates it does not wish to purchase. Therefore, they are not considered part of the company's operating value but would be added to it in computing total enterprise value of invested capital and equity.

Director's Fees

Cardinal incurred annual administrative costs of $40,000, related to its board of directors, which will be eliminated immediately upon sale of the company.

Severance Costs

Omni management estimates that $800,000 in severance costs will be incurred in each of the first two years after the acquisition related to terminated employees.

Transaction Costs

Omni management estimates that legal, tax, and intermediary costs related to the acquisition of Cardinal will total $1.8 million and will be incurred at the time of the acquisition.

Revenue Enhancements

Taking advantage of Omni's much more advanced customer relationship management software, diversified distribution system, and superior capability to generate advertising income, Cardinal's revenue growth in Year 6 above the preacquisition forecasted annual 4% increase in pretax income to invested capital, shown on the first line of Exhibit 16-20, will raise this income $1 million per year for Years 7 through 9 and $400,000 per year thereafter. After this, Cardinal's growth should approximate the industry average annual rate of 4%.

Economies in Cost of Sales

Once capital expenditure improvements have been implemented in Year 6, cost of sales is expected to decline, as forecasted in Exhibit 16-20. Once again, in a real valuation situation, these forecasted changes would be supported by substantial detail and analysis.

Operating Expense Improvements

Omni will utilize its diversified advertising and distribution system to reduce Cardinal's operating expenses by $200,000 in Year 6, $400,000 in Years 7 through 9, and $100,000 thereafter.

Depreciation Expense

Depreciation expense will follow historical trends with increases to reflect capital expenditures made in the initial years after the acquisition.

Capital Expenditures

Omni employs the latest publishing technology and possesses excess capacity that will be partially absorbed to meet Cardinal's initial needs. Because Lou Bertin has required as part of the transaction that production remain at the company's present location, substantial capital expenditures will be incurred in Years 6 and 7 to bring Cardinal's facilities to current standards. After this, capital expenditures will grow commensurate with sales.

Working Capital

Working capital is expected to increase as forecasted in Exhibit 16-20, which is consistent with Omni's current performance. Omni management did not expect to generate significant cash flows from liquidation of excess receivable and inventory balances held by Cardinal at the transaction date. For the long-term or terminal period, working capital is forecasted to grow at the anticipated long-term growth rate of 4%.

Multiple-Period Discounting Computation of Investment Value to Omni

Using the forecasted net cash flow to invested capital that reflects the synergy and cash flow adjustments, the investment value of 100% of the invested capital and equity of Cardinal is computed to be $50,110,000 and $33,810,000, respectively, as shown in Exhibit 16-20.

Exhibit 16-20   Maximum Investment Value of Cardinal Invested Capital Basis (000)

Line Item	Year 6	Year 7	Year 8	Year 9	Terminal Year
Normalized Pretax Income to I/C increasing at 4% annually forecasted as a stand-alone business	$7,956	$8,274	$8,605	$8,949	$9,307
Synergies					
Bertin's Excess Salary	$750	$750	$750	$750	$750
Director's Fees	$40	$40	$40	$40	$40
Severance Costs	$−800	$−800	$0	$0	$0
Transaction Costs	$−1,800	$0	$0	$0	$0
Revenue Enhancements	$0	$1,000	$1,000	$1,000	$400
Economies in Cost of Sales	$0	$300	$500	$700	$300
Operating Expense Reductions	$200	$400	$400	$400	$100
Total Synergy Adjustments	$−1,610	$1,690	$2,690	$3,190	$1,590
Adjusted Pretax Income to I/C	$6,346	$9,964	$11,295	$11,839	$10,897
Tax (40% federal and state)	$−2,538	$−3,986	$−4,518	$−4,736	$−4,359
Normalized Net Income to I/C	$3,808	$5,978	$6,777	$7,103	$6,538
Adjustments for Net Cash Flow Applicable to Invested Capital					
Depreciation	$1,800	$2,400	$2,000	$2,000	$2,000
Capital Expenditures	$−6,500	$−4,500	$−4,000	$−4,000	$−2,400
Change in Working Capital	$−100	$−500	$−550	$−600	$−650
Net Cash Flow to I/C	$−992	$3,378	$4,227	$4,503	$5,488

Capitalization Rate Applicable to Terminal Value (discount rate 12.23 less long-term sustainable growth rate of 4%) Divide by 8.23%	÷ 8.23%
Capitalized Value of the Terminal Year's Net Cash Flow to Invested Capital	$66,683

12.23% Discount Factor with Midyear Convention (end of year in Year 10)	.9439	.8411	.7494	.6678	.6303
Present Value of the Forecast Years and Capitalized Terminal Value	−936	2,841	3,168	3,007	42,030

Investment Value of Invested Capital (aggregate present values)	$50,110
Less: Market Value of Interest-Bearing Debt	$−16,300
Investment Value of Equity	$33,810
Less: Market Value of Cardinal's Operating Equity Premerger (Exhibit 16-17)	$−18,656
Implied Increase in Value of Cardinal's Postmerger Operating Equity (maximum investment value)	$15,154

SUGGESTED CONSIDERATIONS TO CASE CONCLUSION

After studying this case, it is reasonable for readers to question their confidence in the reliability of the value estimate. Most readers, particularly those with more business valuation experience, may conclude that the authors underestimated or overestimated the importance of one or more competitive issues. And they may be right! While this process is accurate when performed correctly, it is not exact.

Before any readers conclude that they are prepared to negotiate the sale or purchase of Cardinal based on the information presented, we encourage them to consider the following questions:

- Have you carefully read each of Cardinal's magazines and carefully compared them to their major competitors?
- Are you confident that you understand the rapid transformation occurring in this industry as "publication" companies transform into "media" companies?
- What were your impressions as you toured Cardinal's facilities?
- What is your impression of employee competence and morale?
- How confident are you about Bertin's competence, motives, and future plans?
- How confident are you about your knowledge of Cardinal's "loyal customer base"?
- How confident are you about the accuracy, probability of achievement, and estimated timing of each of the synergies presented?
- Thinking as the seller, how comfortable are you with Omni's intentions, and how confident are you in their ability to achieve the forecasted synergies?
- What is your assessment of how effective the integration of the two companies would be?
- Based on the facts and circumstances in this case, what are the pros and cons for structuring the transaction as an asset sale versus a stock sale and for payment in cash versus payment in stock?

These questions constitute more than inconvenient details. They are the critical qualitative variables that must be quantified accurately in the valuation process to generate a defendable indication of value and provide the basis for a sound purchase or sale decision. These are the issues that make business valuation complex. These are the issues that must be resolved within a reasonable level of accuracy for the sellers, but more important the buyers, to achieve success in a transaction. The valuation, of course, requires appropriate methodology and application. Ultimately, however, these qualitative issues must be engaged, analyzed, and quantified. You should not feel confident in your value estimate until you are certain you can provide the most informed possible answers to these questions.

When this happens, as explained in the first paragraph of this book, buyers and sellers can both win in the merger and acquisition process. The key is to understand what value is, what drives it, and how to measure it accurately to build value in a business.

Index